ONLINE BANKING IN INDIA

ONLINE BANKING IN INDIA

R.K. Uppal
N.K. Jha

ANMOL PUBLICATIONS PVT. LTD.
NEW DELHI - 110 002 (INDIA)

ANMOL PUBLICATIONS PVT. LTD.
H.O.: 4374/4B, Ansari Road, Daryaganj,
New Delhi-110 002 (India)
Ph.: 23278000, 23261597
B.O.: No. 1015, Ist Main Road, BSK IIIrd Stage
IIIrd Phase, IIIrd Block,
Bangalore - 560 085 (India)
Visit us at: www.anmolpublications.com

Online Banking in India

ISBN 978-81-261-3678-0

PRINTED IN INDIA

Printed at Mehra Offset Press, Delhi.

CONTENTS

Foreword *vii*

Preface *ix*

1. Online Banking – A New Wave 1
2. Cyber Crime in Online Banking 25
3. Biometrics Technology–Its Implications in Banking Sector 52
4. Security Challenges in E-Banking–Agenda for Future 97
5. E-Banking – Problems and Prospects 118
6. Cheque Truncation 136
7. Transformation in Indian Banking Through E-Banking Services–An Empirical Study 170
8. E-Banking Services and Bankers' Perspective–An Empirical Study 190
9. Indian Banking: Moving Towards Information Technology–Emerging Challenges and Possible Solutions 208
10. Mobile Banking–A New Revolution 219
11. Retail Banking in India—Emerging Issues and Future Outlook 251

Index 261

FOREWORD

With the ongoing reforms in the financial sector started in the nineties, the world has become a globalized village where we need to think as one unit. Banking per se has no more remained localized, the age old wisdom that the banks are a commercial entity and should be run on commercial lines gained prominence without losing sight of the earlier emphasis on banking as an instrument of development of the economy. It's the new generation of banking in India. Most private and MNC banks have already setup an elaborate Internet banking infrastructure. And this exercise has provided them numerous benefits like:

- Greater reach to customers
- Quicker time to market
- Ability to introduce new products and services quickly and successfully
- Ability to understand its customers needs
- Greater customer loyalty

Multi-national and private sector banks in India have been very successful in setting up Internet banking services. This is mainly because these banks already had a robust automated banking environment on which they could build the Internet banking infrastructure. Most multi-national banks already have efficient Internet banking infrastructures running in other countries which could be emulated in India. And the private banks, which are relatively young, did not have to carry the burden of legacy systems. They merely invested in best-of-breed Internet banking solutions from the start.

The bank managers today face new dynamic challenges. Business has become more complex than what it used to be in the last decade. Rapidly changing internal and external environment, technology obsolescence, increasing competition, employees demanding improvement in quality of work life are some of the emerging issues. They need to update themselves in multidimensional fields so that they can accomplish the desired results in the competitive business environment.

The book has dealt in detail different dimensions of the latest banking in a globalised scenario with a particular emphasis on paperless banking. I feel immense pleasure to write this foreword and congratulate all the scholarly contributors and specially Dr. R.K. Uppal, Director of ICSSR, sponsored major research project and Principal investigator of UGC sponsored major research project and Dr. Nishikant Jha Co-Ordinator (Banking & Insurnace), Shri Chinai College of Commerce & Economics, Mumbai University. Who took the initiative to edit a book on this important subject. This book will be useful for the banking industry, planners, policy makers, academicians, researchers and those who are interested in banking studies.

Dr (Prof.) Sharda S.C. (SEO)
Smt. K.G. Mittal College
Mumbai University

PREFACE

The IT revolution has brought stunning changes in the business environment. Perhaps no other has been influenced by advances in technology as much as banking & finance, as a result, the banking pose a totally new look today. Electronic Funds Transfer, Electronic clearing System, Automated Teller Machine (ATM), Corporate banking terminal (CBT), Point of Sale Terminal (POST), Electronic Data Interchange (EDI), Tele-banking, Mobile banking & Net banking are widely in use. Technology has been used as a strategy to win market and customers. The interaction of technology with globalization has contributed to the expansion of financial market beyond national borders, heralding the end of geography. In the process, technology has changed the contours of three major functions of financial intermediaries: assess to liquidity, transformation of assets and monitoring of risks.

Now-a-days mobile phone has become a basic product of our daily life. Because of its popularity many businesses are beginning to use M-banking as a more efficient method of reaching the demands of their customers. The M-banking or mobile banking incorporates several inherent and advanced features that make it more viable in certain circumstances. This is the reason why several financial, tourism, marketing and media organizations are all entering into the field of mobile banking that is practically more suited to their area of operation. In coming years persons will use mobile phones as more than a status symbol that will make it a virtual necessity.

The present book attempts to analyze the role of Online banking in Indian context. The present book contains theoretical and practical aspects of IT in the banking sector.

We wish to express my profound gratitude to Dr. Gurdip Singh, Former Director, Yadwindra Engg. College, Talwandi Sabo and Dr. M.S. Bedi, Former Dean, Commerce & Business Management Faculty, Punjabi University, Patiala, for their kind co-operation. We are also thankful to Dr. (Mrs.) Bishnupriya Mishra, Professor, Finance and Accounts, Regional College of Management, Bhubaneshwar (Orrisa).

We are highly thankful to my family members who relaxed me during moments of tensions and facilitated the culmination of this book and always remain a source of inspiration, without their kind co-operation, it was not possible to complete this book.

We take this opportunity to express my sincere thanks to Sh. J.L. Kumar, Anmol Publications Pvt. Ltd., New Delhi for publishing this book very efficiently in a very short span.

Authors

1

ONLINE BANKING – A NEW WAVE

INTRODUCTION

In the last 10 years, technology has driven competitive advantage in the banking industry. The banks, over a long time, been using electronic and telecommunication networks for delivering a wide range of value added products and services. The delivery channels include direct dial–up connections, private networks, public networks, etc. and the devices include telephone, personal computers including the Automated Teller Machines, etc. With the popularity of PCs, easy access to Internet and World Wide Web (WWW), Internet is increasingly used by banks as a channel for receiving instructions and delivering their products and services to their customers. This form of banking is generally referred to as Internet banking.

With the widespread growth of the Internet, customers can use this technology anywhere in the world to access a bank's network. With an expanded market, banks may also have opportunities to expand or change their product and service offerings. For public sector banks, investment in ATMs and Online banking is the partly defensive in character: it is an attempt to avoid losing customers to move aggressive private sector rivals.

Multi-national and private sector banks in India has been very successful in setting up online banking services. This is mainly because these banks already had a robust automated banking environment on which they could build the online banking infrastructure. Most multi-national banks already have efficient online banking infrastructures running in other countries, which could be emulated in India. And the private banks, which are relatively young, did not have to carry the burden of legacy systems. They merely invested in best-of-breed online banking solutions from the start.

Origin of Online Banking

Internet is often described as "network of networks" born in 1970s. It is a number of computers interconnected. It is an open standard for digital communication used with World Wide Web technologies. When two or more computers are connected a network is created; connecting two or more networks create 'inter-network' or Internet. The advent of the Internet and the popularity of personal computers presented an opportunity and a challenge for the banking industry for the new development of Online banking.

Online banking dates back to late 1990's. Most banks used a very simple layout, which allowed users to sign in, see their accounts and statements, and make transfers from one account to the other. It is really simple: we do not have to go down to the bank because the bank is already on our computer desk waiting for us to enter. Today's online banking features which allows to do all those previous online banking activities and also arrange for a loan, set up direct debits, and pay bills online—all with just a few clicks of our mouse.

Internet banking is usually conducted through a personal computer (PC) that connects to a banking Web site via the Internet. For example, a consumer at home accesses a financial institution's Web site via a modem and phone line or other telecommunications connections. Now that its customers are connected to the Internet via personal computers, banks envision similar economic advantages by adapting those same internal electronic processes to home use.

Most people have heard a lot about online banking but probably haven't tried it. We still pay our bills by mail and deposit cheques at our bank branch. We might shop online for a loan, life insurance or a home mortgage, but when it comes time to commit, we feel more comfortable working with banker or an agent we know and trust. Online banking isn't out to change our money habits. Instead, it uses today's computer technology to give us the option of bypassing the time consuming, paper-based aspects of traditional banking in order to manage our finances more quickly and efficiently.

Banks view online banking as a powerful "value added" tool to retain and attract new customers and to eliminate costly paper handling in an increasingly competitive banking environment.

Internet Banking

"Internet bank" to mean a bank offering its customers the ability to transact business with the bank over the Internet. Internet banking refers to the use of the Internet as a remote delivery channel for banking services. Subsequently, dial-up connections, personal computers, tele-banking and automated teller machines (ATMs) became the order of the day in most of the developed countries.

Definition

A system allowing individuals to perform banking activities at home, via the internet. It is a web-based service that allows the banks authorized customers to access their account information. In the system, customers are allowed to log on the banks website with the help of identification issued by the bank and personal identification number (PIN). Banks replies the user and enables customers to access the desired services.

Some online banks are traditional banks which also offer online banking, while others are online only and have no physical presence. Online banking through traditional banks enable customers to perform all routine transactions, such as account transfers, balance inquiries, bill payments, and stop-payment requests, and some even offer online loan and credit card applications.

Account information can be accessed anytime, day or night, and can be done from anywhere. A few online banks update information in real-time, while others do it daily. Once information has been entered, it doesn't need to be re-entered for similar subsequent checks, and future payments can be scheduled to occur automatically.

Brick-to-click Banks

Today, most large national banks, many regional banks and even smaller banks and credit unions offer some form of online banking, variously known as PC banking, Home banking, Electronic banking or Internet banking. Those that do are sometimes referred to as "brick-to-click" banks, both to distinguish them from brick-and-mortar banks that have yet to offer online banking, as well as from online or "virtual" banks that have no physical branches or tellers whatsoever. The challenge for the banking industry has been to design this new service channel in such a way that its customers will readily learn to use and trust it.

Virtual Banks

If we don't mind foregoing the teller window, lobby cookie and kindly bank president, a "virtual" or e-bank may save our very real money. Virtual banks are banks without bricks; from the customer's perspective, they exist entirely on the Internet, where they offer pretty much the same range of services and adhere to the same federal regulations as our corner bank. Virtual banks pass the money they save on overhead like buildings and tellers along to our in the form of higher yield, lower fees and more generous thresholds.

The major disadvantage of virtual banks revolves around ATMs. Because they have no ATM machines, virtual banks typically charge the same surcharge that our brick-and-mortar bank would if we used another bank's automated teller. Likewise, many virtual banks won't accept deposits via ATM; we have to either deposit the check by mail or transfer money from another account.

Internet Banking: Concepts

There has been a paradigm shift in global banking after electronic banking became the mode of delivery of traditional as well as new innovative products to customers. Today technology is a key facilitator in strategic implementation and also shapes organizational structure. Many researchers expect rapid growth in customers using online banking products and services.

Evaluating a bank's data on the use of their Web sites, may help people to determine the bank's strategic objectives, how well the bank is meeting its Internet banking product plan, and whether the business is expected to be profitable. Internet banking originated when banks commenced hosting informational websites and graduated to simple and later to full transactional websites.

1. *Informational Websites*

In the initial stage, informational websites of banks contained general information about the bank and its various products or services to the customers including the customers' feedbacks / enquiries, etc. Here, minimum functionalities were provided but it did provide a medium to the bank for reaching out to its existing and potential customers.

2. *Simple and Full Transactional Websites*

The simple transactional websites which allow customers to submit their applications, instructions for different services on their account statements, account balance information, etc.

with proper authorization and authentication mechanism. They do not permit any fund-based transactions on their accounts.

3. Full Transactional Websites

Full transactional systems provide additional services like electronic funds transfer inter / intra bank along with a host of other services related to online credit card, demat, bill payment services, etc. Thus, the customers are able to operate their banking transactions online which in fact affected their banking accounts directly without paying any visit to the bank branches. The banks offer E-banking services in retail as well as wholesale sectors. Thus, all sorts of services have come under the roof of full transactional websites.

ONLINE BANKING SERVICES

The online banking sites offer these services:

Mobile Banking

Mobile phone banking takes banking one step ahead of Internet banking. One can do banking without even making a phone call. Mobile banking works through a set of text messages. Customer should first register for the facility and then can use either SMS or WAP in case he/she subscribes to any of the various carriers. Presently two types of services are available through mobile phone viz. Alert Services and Requests. This service really offers "Any time anywhere banking". However, the bank should have tie-up arrangement with the cellular service provider.

A pre-designated mobile number should be available at the bank. A user manual needs to be provided to the customer to acquaint him with Bank's specific codes and menus. In case of loss/theft of mobile, the customer is required to inform the bank immediately to deactivate or disable mobile banking service.

E-commerce and E-banking

E-commerce is the online selling. It is total delivery of products and services to the customer through Internet to satisfy business objectives. It allows two-way communications and is built around open standards. As a first step it will ensure the conversions of office business equipment/machines into one digital platform. The interaction/communication taking place digitally between producers, intermediaries and consumers are referred to as the electronic market place. The sum total of commercial transactions taking place in the electronic marketplace is called Digital Economy.

E-banking is an extension or a subset of E-commerce doing its process on personal computers because of their origin within the Internet, a network of computers. The first stage of expansion is within the installed base of computer users. The second wave will come when more people will get access to computers via lowered computer prices or cheaper devices. The third and more important expansion is predicted to be from those with non-computer access to the global network through broadcast TVs, Cable TVs, Telephone Networks and new appliances.

This widespread use of cheaper access media represents the phase of bringing E-commerce including E-banking into the living rooms of common people. It will give banks like ours a chance to give a run for their money to giant multibillion foreign banking corporations, both in India and abroad.

E Mail – Banking

The most common and basic use of Internet is the exchange of E-mail (electronic mail). It is an extremely powerful and revolutionary result of Internet, which has facilitated almost instantaneous communi-cation with people in any part of the globe. With enhancements like attachment of documents, audio, video and voice mail, this segment of Internet is fast expanding as the most used communication medium for the whole world. Many websites offer E-mail as a free facility to individuals. Many corporate have interfaced their private networks with Internet in order to make their email accessible from outside their corporate network. In E-mail security, a digital signature authenticates a transmission from a user in an un-trusted network environment. A digital signature is a sequence of bits appended to a digital document. Like a hand-written signature, its authenticity can be verified. But unlike a hand-written signature, it is unique to the document being signed.

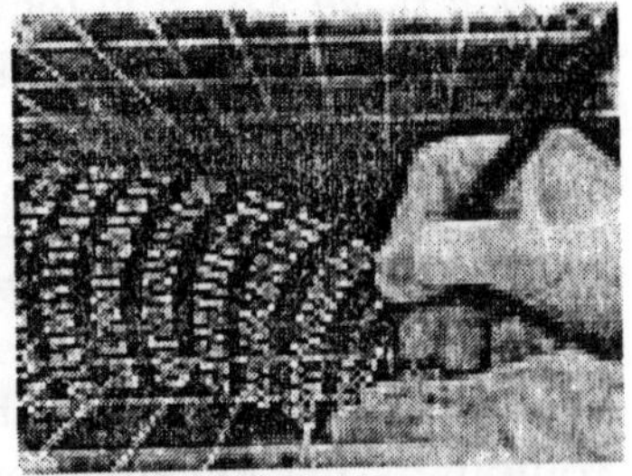

Digital signatures are a good method of securing E-mail transmissions in that the signature. Digital signatures are based on a procedure called message digesting which computes a short fixed length number called a digest for any message of any length. Several different messages may have the same digest, but it is extremely difficult to produce any of them from the digest. A message digest is 128 bit cryptographically strong one-way hash function of the message. It is very similar to a checksum in that it completely represents the message and is used to detect changes in the message. In using digital signatures for securing E-mail messages, there are two different types of encryption techniques used to ensure secured messages. Messages can be secured using a (symmetric) secret-key management system using DES or a public key (asymmetric) management using RSA.

Automated Teller Machines (ATMs)

Automated Teller Machine (ATM) is a self-service terminal system. ATM as the name indicates is a very user-friendly machine that can render 24-hour services to help the bank customer perform basic bank transactions like depositing cash or cheques and withdrawing money. It is an extension of "Anywhere, anytime" concept of banking. When an ATM is connected to an online branch network, it can additionally provide services such as balance enquiries, transfer of funds between the accounts, etc.

Electronic Data Interchange (EDI)

EDI is a transmission in a standard syntax of the unambiguous information of business for strategic significance between computers of the independent organizations. It minimizes human intervention or re-keying. The sending organization only has to send sufficient data to allow the receiving organization to perform a specific function (process a business transaction).

There is no need to send repetitive input of sender's address, operational instructions, authorized signatories which would already in the receiver's computer database. There are 3 components of EDI, a generally accepted business format called EDI standards, translation capability i.e. ensured through EDI software and a mail service called Value Added Network (VAN). The VAN acts as an electronic post office from where the messages are routed/picked up at regular intervals facilitating data inter-change between large numbers of organizations and keep the cost of network resources to the minimum.

Electronic Funds Transfer (EFT)

Electronic Funds Transfer (EFT) is the exchange is the exchange of money via telecommunications without currency actually changing hands. EFT refers to any financial transaction that transfers a sum of money from one account to another, electronically. Usually, transactions originate at a computer at one institution (location) and are transmitted to a computer at another institution (location) with the monetary amount recorded in the respective organization's accounts. Because of the potential high volume of money being exchanged, these systems may be in an extremely high-risk category. Therefore, access security and authorization of processing are important controls.

Security in an EFT environment is extremely important. Security includes the methods used by the customer to gain access to the system, the communications network and the host or application processing site. Individual consumer access to the EFT system is generally controlled by a plastic card and a personal identification number (PIN). Both items are required to initiates a transaction.

Checking Accounts

Checking accounts come in a variety of styles. Some are free, some are not. For most people, the centerpiece of their relationship with their bank is a checking account. Studies have shown that consumers overwhelmingly define "their" bank as the institution where their checking accounts are held, not the bank where they may have a mortgage or certificate of deposit. It's no wonder that banks throw a sizeable amount of money toward attracting and retaining consumer checking accounts.

Beyond the gifts:

Banks know one way to get us in the door to open a checking account is to lure with gifts. In the old days they used toasters; today's gifts are less domesticated—coolers, camping gear and beach gear are popular. What really matters is that we get a checking account that meets your needs as cheaply as possible —preferably for free. Selecting the right account isn't as simple as it may seem. Most banks carry approximately a half-dozen types of checking accounts. We can find an account that fits our needs, but if we aren't careful we could end up with one that doesn't match our banking habits and may cost us a bundle in fees.

Basic checking:

This is for people who just use a checking account to pay some bills and perhaps use a debit card to pay some daily expenses. Some basic accounts require direct deposit or a minimum balance to avoid monthly "maintenance" fees. We may be limited to a certain number of checks per month; exceed that number and we'll pay a "per item" fee for each additional check we write. We don't want to maintain a high balance in these accounts because we won't be paid interest.

Free checking:

For most people, this is the best checking account. A free checking account is "no monthly service charges or per-item fees regardless of balance or activity." In other words, write the entire checks one like and keep his balance as low as he like without worrying about paying a fee. Free checking doesn't mean he won't have to pay any fees. If, for instance, a person bounces a check, he'll pay a non sufficient funds fee.

Fees, Fees and more Fees

Fees are as common as vice presidents at banks. But if one knows what they are and when they're charged, he may be able to avoid them. Banks may charge fees for all kinds of things: credit reference, inactive account, a check deposited into account that bounced. When one opens a checking account, he can ask the bank for a printed copy of its fee schedule. It just might stun him. He'll quickly realize how costly it can be to ask the bank for a duplicate statement, a cashier's cheque, a stop payment or a host of other services he may need.

Here's a rundown of some of the more common services associated with checking accounts for which banks charge a fee. We aren't listing the actual fees because they vary from bank to bank and year to year.

Fees

Type of fee	*What it means*
Abandoned account	State laws vary, but if our account is dormant for a long time—usually three or five years—the bank hands the proceeds to the state, but not before deducting a hefty fee.

Account maintenance fee	Some accounts charge a monthly fee no matter what the balance.
Account closed early	Banks differ but, generally, if one closes an account within 90 or 180 days, you'll be charged a fee.
Account research/ reconciliation	This is usually a per-hour fee that's charged if there's a discrepancy between customer records and his record with the banks; often the bank will charge a minimum of one hour.
ATM	If one uses an ATM that doesn't belong to his bank, he'll probably be charged a fee by his bank and a surcharge by the owner of the ATM.
ATM/debit card replacement	Lose a card and people may get one new card a year for free if their bank is nice, but they will pay beyond that.
Cheque printing	Most accounts charge for cheque.
Coin counting	Some banks won't charge customers or children for this service, but most will charge non-customers.
Counter cheques	Forgot checkbook or run out of cheque? The bank may give a few for free but charge a fee beyond that.
Credit reference	If we need to rely on the bank for a credit reference, expect to pay.
Debit card	Purchases made with a debit card are deducted from checking account. Unfortu-nately, a growing number of banks are charging a fee for every purchase.

Deposited item returned (DIR)	If one deposit a check in his account and the check bounces, he'll be charged a fee.
Early-withdrawal fee for CDs	Fee Imposed when one closes a CD account before maturity.
Inactive account	This monthly or quarterly charge is assessed if we have no deposits or withdrawals over a specific period of time. Some banks charge if our account has been inactive for as few as 90 days. We may be able to avoid a fee if our balance is above a certain level. Some institutions don't start an inactivity fee until the account has been dormant for one year.
Money orders/cashier's cheque	A cashier's cheque will cost more than a money order.
Monthly service fee	Charged if a checking account balance falls below a certain amount.
Non-sufficient funds (NSF)	Bounce a check and pay one of the highest per-item fees banks charge.
Notary fees	A notary public is someone who can certify or attest to documents. If one needs something notarized, he'll pay a variety of fees depending on the document.
Overdraft	If a person overdraws his account and the bank pays the cheque or debit, it will charge him a fee. The benefit is his cheque doesn't bounce and he doesn't get charged a fee by the business that accepted his cheque.

Return of checks with statement	We used to be able to get our canceled checks returned for free; now many banks charge a monthly fee for that service.
Safe deposit box	An annual rental fee based on the size of the box.
Stop payment	Fee imposed when we use a cheque to pay for something and then change our mind.
Teller fee	Some accounts require us to do most transactions online, at the ATM or by phone. These accounts usually limit the number of times we can visit a teller each month and charge a fee for additional visits.

Ignorance is not bliss when it comes to checking accounts. We must be aware of fees if we want to avoid them. One of the best ways to avoid fees is by finding the account that's right for us. The upside is; practice good checking habits and we'll avoid many of them.

ADVANTAGES AND DISADVANTAGES OF ONLINE BANKING

Advantages

Convenience: Unlike our corner bank, Online banking sites never close; they're available 24 hours a day, seven days a week, and they're only a mouse click away. Not only this but all services that are usually available from the local bank can be found on a single website. Rather than having to ring a separate number to order a new chequebook or cancel a bankcard, or even go into the branch to do so, it is possible to do all this from our personal home page.

Ubiquity/Portability: If we are out of state or even out of the country and when a money problem arises, we can log on instantly to our online bank and take care of business, 24/7.

This is possibly the main advantage of online banking as apposed to branch based banking. Our account is extremely accesses able with an online account and all the services which we would expect to be provided by a banking service any time anywhere.

Transaction speed: Online bank sites generally execute and confirm transactions at the same rate or quicker than, ATM processing speeds. This means that if a customer withdraw or pay in money from/to his account then his balance will be updated at the same speed or often quicker than if he had done so at a branch bank ATM.

Effectiveness: Many online banking sites now offer sophisticated tools, including account aggregation, stock quotes, rate alerts and portfolio managing programs which help us to manage all our assets more effectively. Most are also compatible with money managing programs such as Quicken and Microsoft Money.

Disadvantages

Start-up may take time: In order to register for our bank's online programme, we have to provide ID and sign a form at a bank branch. If husband and wife wish to view and manage their assets together online, one of them may have to sign a durable power of attorney before the bank will display all of their holdings together.

In comparison to opening a branch account this can be done real time whereby customer goes into the branch, give them his personal details, sign some forms and once the account is activated he can use it almost straight away as the account is activated within the branch while he is there. Online accounts undergo the same form filling process but can take up to a week to be processed and validated before account can be opened and accessed.

Learning curve: Banking sites can be difficult to navigate at first. Plan to invest some time and/or read the tutorials in order to become comfortable in the virtual lobby. Time needs to be taken to understand such things as how to check the balance online or how to set up a standing order. This alone can prevent some people considering opening an online bank account even if the rates are much better than bricks and mortar banks.

Bank sites changes: The largest bank periodically upgrades their online programmes, adding new features in unfamiliar places. In some cases, one may have to re-enter account information.

The trust thing: For many people, the biggest hurdle to online banking is learning to trust it. Did my transaction go through? Did I push the transfer button once or twice? Best bet: always print the transaction receipt and keep it with bank records until it shows up on the personal site and/or bank statement.

Impersonal: Online banking lacks personal service. There is virtually no human contact involved, and some people could see this as a drawback.

The disadvantages of Internet banking can be overcome to a great extent; in the long run, the benefits outweigh the risks involved. A testimonial to the utility of online banking is the growing number of customers that are signing up for it. In one way or another, most people who require some form of banking services stand to gain from banking over the Internet.

RISK MANAGEMENT

The past few years have been characterized by rapid changes in technology and the unprecedented speed with which new technologies are being adopted. Financial institutions should have a technology risk management process to enable them to identify, measure, monitor, and control their technology risk exposure.

The risk planning process is the responsibility of the board and senior management. They need to possess the knowledge and skills to manage the bank's use of Internet banking technology and technology-related risks. Senior management should have the skills to evaluate the technology employed and risks assumed. Periodic independent evaluations of the Internet banking technology and products by auditors or consultants can help the board and senior management fulfill their responsibilities.

Implementing the technology is the responsibility of management. Management should have the skills to effectively evaluate Internet banking technologies and products, select the right mix for the bank, and see that they are installed appropriately. Measuring and monitoring risk is also the responsibility of management. Management should have the skills to effectively identify, measure, monitor, and control risks associated with Internet banking.

Internet Banking Risks

Internet is not an unmixed blessing to the banking sector. Along with reduction in cost of transactions, it has also brought about a new orientation to risks and even new forms of risks to which banks conducting Internet banking expose themselves. Risk is the potential that events, expected or unexpected, may have an adverse impact on the bank's earnings or capital and reputation as well. These risks are briefly described below:

> ***Strategic risk:*** This risk is associated with the introduction of a new product or service. It is also the current and prospective risk to earnings and capital arising from adverse business decisions or improper implementation of business decisions. For reducing such risk, banks need to conduct proper survey, consult experts from various fields, establish achievable goals and monitor performance. Also they need to analyze the availability and cost of additional resources, provision of adequate supporting staff, proper training of staff and adequate insurance coverage.
>
> ***Transaction Risk:*** Transaction risk is the current and prospective risk to earnings and capital arising from fraud, error, and the inability to deliver products or services, maintain a competitive position, and manage information. Transaction risk is evident in each product and service offered and encompasses product development and delivery, transaction processing, systems development, computing systems, complexity of products and services, and the internal control environment.
>
> A high level of transaction risk may exist with Internet banking products, because of the need to have sophisticated internal controls and constant availability. Most Internet banking

platforms are based on new platforms which use complex interfaces to link with legacy systems, thereby increasing risk of transaction errors.

Compliance Risk: Compliance risk is the risk to earnings or capital arising from violations of, or nonconformance with, laws, rules, regulations, prescribed practices, or ethical standards. Thus, the bank may face compliance and regulatory risk if it does not adhere or follow the guidelines given by the supervisor or the regulator.

Banks need to carefully understand and interpret existing laws as they apply to Internet banking and ensure consistency with other channels such as branch banking. Customers are very concerned about the privacy of their data and banks need to be seen as reliable guardians of such data. Finally, the need to consummate transactions immediately (straight-through processing) may lead to banks relaxing traditional controls, which aim to reduce compliance risk.

Reputation risk: This is the current and prospective risk to earnings and capital arising from negative public opinion. This affects the institution's ability to establish new relationships or services or continue servicing existing relationships. A bank's reputation can suffer if it fails to deliver on marketing claims or to provide accurate, timely services. A bank's reputation can be damaged by Internet banking services that are poorly executed (e.g., limited availability, buggy software, poor response).

Information security risk: This is the risk to earnings and capital arising out of lax information security processes, thus exposing the institution to malicious hacker or insider attacks, viruses, denial-of-service attacks, data theft, data destruction and fraud. The speed of change of technology and the fact that the Internet channel is accessible universally makes this risk especially critical.

Credit risk: This is the risk to earnings or capital from a customer's failure to meet his financial obligations with the bank or otherwise to perform as agreed. Credit risk arises when a counter-party fails to settle an obligation when due or any time henceforth for its full value. Credit risk is found in all activities where success depends on counterparty, issuer, or borrower performance.

Interest rate risk: This is the risk to earnings or capital arising from movements in interest rates (e.g., interest rate differentials between assets and liabilities and how these are impacted by interest rate changes). Internet banking can attract deposits, loans, and other relationships from a larger pool of possible customers than other forms of marketing. Also, given that it is easy to compare rates across banks, pressure on interest rates is higher, accentuating the need to react quickly to changing interest rates in the market.

Liquidity risk: This is the risk to earnings or capital arising from a bank's inability to meet its obligations. Internet banking can increase deposit and asset volatility, especially from customers who maintain accounts solely because they are getting a better rate. Increased monitoring of liquidity and changes in deposits and loans may be warranted depending on the volume and nature of Internet account activities. These customers tend to pull out of the relationship if they get a slightly better rate elsewhere.

Price risk: This is the risk to earnings or capital arising from changes in the value of traded portfolios or financial instruments. This risk arises from market making, dealing, and position taking in interest rate, foreign exchange, equity, and commodities markets. Appropriate management systems should be maintained to monitor, measure, and manage price risk if assets are actively traded.

Foreign exchange risk: This arises when assets in one currency are funded by liabilities in another. It is present when a loan or portfolio of loans is denominated in a foreign currency or is funded by borrowings in another currency. The consequences can be unfavorable if one of the currencies involved becomes subject to stringent exchange controls or is subject to wide exchange-rate fluctuations.

Money laundering risk: In view of the lack of personal interaction among the bank staff and the customers in the internet banking scenario, the Know Your Customers (KYC) norms may not be implemented effectively. As Internet banking transactions are conducted remotely banks may find it difficult to apply traditional method for detecting and preventing undesirable criminal activities. To avoid this, banks need to design proper customer identification and screening techniques, develop audit trails, and conduct periodic compliance reviews, frame policies and procedures to spot and report suspicious activities in Internet transactions.

Security risk: Internet is a public network of computers which facilitates flow of data/ information and to which there is unrestricted access. Banks using this medium for financial transactions must, therefore, have proper technology and systems in place to build a secured environment for such transactions.

Security risk arises on account of unauthorized access to a bank's critical information stores like accounting system, risk management system, portfolio management system, etc. For example, hackers operating via the Internet could access, retrieve and use confidential customer information and also can implant virus.

Controlling access to banks' system has become more complex in the Internet environment which is a public domain and attempts at unauthorized access could emanate from any source and from anywhere in the world with or without criminal intent. It is therefore, necessary that banks critically assess all interrelated systems and have access control measures in place in each of them.

Security Controls

Security controls need special attention because of the open nature of the ***Internet and the pace of technological change.*** Specific focus areas include:

Authentication: This means ensuring customers are verified and their identities established before conducting business over the Internet. Transactions on the Internet or any other telecommunication network must be secure to achieve a high level of public confidence. Passwords, biometric methods, challenge-response systems, public key infrastructure are some of the ways of strengthening authentication. Thus, user authentication assumes a great significance in online banking as customers log on to the system from different locations without any physical means of authentication.

Non-repudiation: It is the undeniable proof of participation by both the sender and receiver in a transaction. It is the reason public key encryption was developed, i.e., to authenticate electronic messages and prevent denial or repudiation by the sender or receiver. No customer should later claim that any particular transaction was not transacted by him / her. Thus, proper authentication and authorization mechanism using encryption, secure connection in the form of present 128 bit of Secure Socket Layer (SSL) connection and digital signature should be established.

Privacy: Privacy is a consumer issue of increasing importance. The bank should provide privacy of the data and the transaction in all circumstances except in cases when instructed by the competent legal authority or the government to divulge the same. The bank should take the primary responsibility of preventing breach of confidentiality. Thus, privacy not only covers confidentiality of the banks data but also guarantees the data level of privacy.

Availability: Availability is another component in maintaining a high level of public confidence in a network environment. All of the previous components are of little value if the network is not available and convenient to customers. Users of a network expect access to systems 24 hours per day, seven days a week. Among the considerations associated with system availability are capacity, performance monitoring, redundance, and business resumption or else the goodwill and reputation of the bank will take a beating resulting in financial loss as well as losing out loyal customers.

Trust: In the E-banking and E-commerce scenario establishment of trust among the parties is essential. This can be established through a trusted third party designated as a Certification Authority (CA). A certificate authority is a trusted third party that verifies identities in cyberspace. Digital certificates may play an important role in authenticating parties and thus establishing trust in Internet banking systems. The digital certificates issued by the CA to various entities along with at least two factor identification mechanisms can be trusted for the authentication and non-repudiation of the users and the transactions in internet banking.

The risks arising from Internet banking are not restricted to information security areas, but span across all the traditional banking areas. Risk management for Internet banking should be directed by senior management and incorporated within existing risk management disciplines in the organization. Control procedures need to keep pace with rapid changes in technology.

CONCLUSION

Banking over the Internet has attracted increasing attention from bankers and other financial services industry participants, the business press, regulators, and law makers. Among the reasons for Internet banking audience are the notion that electronic banking and payments will grow rapidly, more or less in tandem with proliferating electronic commerce; industry projections that Internet banking will cut banks' costs, increase banks' revenue growth, and make banking more convenient for customers; and some vexing public policy issues.

It also has shows two sides – advantages & disadvantages. But everyone knows that 'Impossible himself says it is possible'. Internet banking transactions carry a broad range of risks. The banks have a major responsibility to provide a risk free, safe and secure environment for banking transactions and protecting customer information and bank data. While there is no doubt that Internet banking transaction should have layered protection against security threats, the providers should also include security considerations as part of their marketing communications and their service offerings.

Internet banking, despite the uncertainties, will be an important part of transformation near future. So the challenge to all banks is to expand Internet banking into the ranks of mass customers and slowly increase the range of services customers use. How the banks fare in designing, improving, marketing and rolling out services will greatly impact the adoption trends.

The future of banking will be one in which customers can address most of their needs through self-directed means and the key differentiator will be how effective a bank is in getting its customers online and deriving measurable value from this presence. In near future, due to online banking the concept of the branch banking management will not remain and the offices will be work as a front office to the bank and customer will get anytime, anywhere banking facility.

BIBLIOGRAPHY

Authentication systems for secure networks – Rolf Oppliger, Artech House, 1996 (www.artech-house.com, rolf.oppliger@esecurity.ch).

Bankarate.com- Getting Comfortable with online Banking; *Internet Banking in India-Part I* - Dr A. K. Mishra.

Business Models for Electronic Markets–Commerce Net (www.commerce.net).

Business Standard Wednesday, Aug 30, 2006. – *Option & Analysis,* Mumbai, August 14, 2006. V. Vaidyanathan.

Customers-Case Studies Universal Banking Solution from Infosys.

Cyber Law form Internet Banking and its Challenges in India—posted by Praveen Dalal, Cyber Law Consultant and Advocate, Supreme Court of India.

e-Banking-Online Banking, Internet Banking.

E-commerce: A white Paper–Keith Hazelton University of Wisconsin-Madison, 1998.

Economic and Policy Analysis Working Paper 2000-2, Office of the Comptroller of the Currency, February.

Financial Services Solutions for Banking & Insurance.

Honest Online Banking-Online Banking–Advantages, Disadvantages, history of Online Banking.

India Mart–India Finance and Investment Guide.

Indian banks cash in on delivery channels - Banking Special - Express Computer India.

Internet Banking Comptroller's Handbook, Comptroller of the Currency October 1999.

Internet Banking: Developments and Prospects, Karen Furst, William W. Lang, and Daniel E. Nolle Economic and Policy Analysis Working Paper 2000-9 September 2000.

Internet Frontiers.html

Internet," *Quarterly Journal,* vol. 17, no. 4, Office of the Comptroller of the Currency, December.

It Security@Indian Indian Bank, Manoj Agrawal Banking frontiers JULY 2006.

MEMORANDUM SYSTEM Division of Supervision Classification Number 6370; Date May 16, 1996.

MsMoney_com - Online Banking.

Office of the Comptroller of the Currency (1999a). "Guidance to National Banks on Web Site.

Reserve Bank of India www.rbi.org.com.

Risk Management for Internet Banking, *Information Systems Control Journal,* Volume 6, 2001 By Ganesh Ramakrishnan.

Services, History, Security www.icicibank.comICICIBank.com.

Why I bank online Can Your Customers Pay By Electronic Check By David Bell.

■ ■ ■

2

CYBER CRIME IN ONLINE BANKING

WHAT IS CYBER CRIME?

You hear a lot about cyber crime, but what exactly is it? The simple answer is, "It's complicated!" Like traditional crime, cyber crime can take many shapes and can occur nearly anytime or anyplace. Criminals committing cyber crime use a number of methods, depending on their skill-set and their goal. This should not be surprising: cyber crime is, after all, simply 'crime' with some sort of 'computer' or 'cyber' aspect.

The Council of Europe's Cyber crime Treaty uses the term 'cyber crime' to refer to offenses ranging from criminal activity against data to content and copyright infringement [Krone, 2005]. However, others [Zeviar-Geese, 1997-98] suggest that the definition is broader, including activities such as fraud, unauthorized access, child pornography, and cyber stalking. The United Nations Manual on the Prevention and Control of Computer Related Crime includes fraud, forgery, and unauthorized access [United Nations, 1995] in its cyber crime definition.

As you can see from these definitions, cyber crime can cover a very wide range of attacks. Understanding this wide variation in types of cyber crime is important, as different types of cyber crime require different approaches to improving your computer safety.

Symantec draws from the many definitions of cyber crime and defines it concisely as *any crime that is committed using a computer or network, or hardware device.* The computer or device may be the agent of the crime, the facilitator of the crime, or the target of the crime. The crime may take place on the computer alone or in addition to other locations. The broad range of cyber crime can be better understood by dividing it into two overall categories, defined for the purpose of this research as Type I and Type II cyber crime.

Type I: Cyber Crime has the following characteristics:

1. It is generally a single event from the perspective of the victim. For example, the victim unknowingly downloads a Trojan horse, which installs a keystroke logger on his or her machine. Alternatively, the victim might receive an E-mail containing what claims to be a link to known entity, but in reality is a link to a hostile website.
2. Crime ware programs such as keystroke loggers, viruses, rootkits often facilitate it or Trojan horses.
3. Software flaws or vulnerabilities often provide the foothold for the attacker. For example, criminals controlling a website may take advantage of a vulnerability in a Web browser to place a Trojan horse on the victim's computer.

Examples of this type of cyber crime include but are not limited to phishing, theft or manipulation of data or services via hacking or viruses, identity theft, and bank or E-commerce fraud.

Type II: Cyber Crime

At the other end of the spectrum, includes, but is not limited to activities such as cyber stalking and harassment, child predation, extortion, blackmail, stock market manipulation, complex corporate espionage, and planning or carrying out terrorist activities. The characteristics of Type II cyber crime are:

> It is generally an on-going series of events, involving repeated interactions with the target. For example, someone who, over time, attempts to establish a relationship contacts the target in a chat room. Eventually, the criminal exploits the relationship to commit a crime or, members of a terrorist cell or criminal organization may use hidden messages to communicate in a public forum to plan activities or discuss money-laundering locations, for example.

Programmes that do not fit into under the classification crime ware generally facilitate it. For example, conversations may take place using IM (instant messaging) clients or files may be transferred using FTP.

UNITED NATIONS DEFINITION OF CYBER CRIME

Cyber crime spans not only state but national boundaries as well. Perhaps we should look to international organizations to provide a standard definition of the crime. At the Tenth United Nations Congress on the Prevention of Crime and Treatment of Offenders, in a workshop devoted to the issues of crimes related to computer networks, cyber crime was broken into two categories and defined thus:

- Cyber crime in a narrow sense (computer crime): Any illegal behavior directed by means of electronic operations that targets the security of computer systems and the data processed by them.
- Cyber crime in a broader sense (computer-related crime): Any illegal behavior committed by means of, or in relation to, a computer system or network, including such crimes as illegal possession [and] offering or distributing information by means of a computer system or network.

Of course, these definitions are complicated by the fact that an act may be illegal in one nation but not in another. There are more concrete examples, including

i) Unauthorized access

ii) Damage to computer data or programmes

iii) Computer sabotage

iv) Unauthorized interception of communications

v) Computer espionage

These definitions, although not completely definitive, do give us a good starting point—one that has some international recognition and agreement — for determining just what we mean by the term cyber crime.

HISTORY OF CYBER CRIME

How old is the phenomenon of cyber crime? It's safe to say that soon after the first computer networks were built, some people were looking for ways to exploit them for their own illegal purposes. The idea of theft is as old as the concept of privately owned property, and an element of almost all societies is dedicated to as much a possible of what isn't theirs- by whatever means they can.

As soon as it was widely recognized that computers store something of value (information), criminals saw an opportunity. But just as its more difficult to target a robbery victim who stays locked up in his home every day, the data on closed system has been difficult to steal. However, when the data began to move from one computer to another over networks, like the robbery victims who travel from one place to another, this data becomes more vulnerable.

Networks provided an advantage; an entry point. Even if the information that was of value was never sent across the wire, the coming and going of other bits of data opened up a way for intruders to sneak inside the computers, like a robber taking the advantage of a victim who leaves his house unlocked on their way out.

However, cyber crime didn't spring up like a full-blown problem over night. In the early days of computing and net working, the average criminal didn't possess either the necessary hardware or the technical expertise to seize the digital opportunity of the day. Computers were million dollar mainframe monstrosities and only a few of them were in existence.

The cyber crime problem emerged and grew as computing became easier and less expensive. Today almost everyone in industrial countries has access to computer technology; children learn to use PC's in elementary school and people who cant afford computers of their own can use PC's in public libraries or on college campuses for free or they can rent computer time at internet cafes.

THE CYBER REGULATIONS

A. Establishment of Cyber Appellate Tribunal

i) The Central Government shall, by notification, establish one or more appellate tribunals to be known as the Cyber Regulations Appellate Tribunal.

ii) The Central Government shall also specify, in the notification referred to in sub-section (1), the matters and places in relation to which the Cyber Appellate Tribunal may exercise jurisdiction.

B. Composition of Cyber Appellate Tribunal

A Cyber Appellate Tribunal shall consist of one person only (hereinafter referred to as the Residing Officer of the Cyber Appellate Tribunal) to be appointed, by notification, by the Central Government.

C. Qualifications for appointment as Presiding Officer of the Cyber Appellate Tribunal

A person shall not be qualified for appointment as the Presiding Officer of a Cyber Appellate Tribunal unless he/she

- Is or has been or is qualified to be, a Judge of a High Court; or
- Is or has been a member of the Indian Legal Service and is holding or has held a post in Grade I of that Service for at least three years.

D. Term of office

The Presiding Officer of a Cyber Appellate Tribunal shall hold office for a term of five years from the date on which he enters upon his office or until he attains the age of sixty-five years, whichever is earlier.

E. Salary, allowances and other terms and conditions of service of Presiding Officer

The salary and allowances payable to, and the other terms and conditions of service including pension, gratuity and other retirement benefits of. The Presiding Officer of a Cyber Appellate Tribunal shall be such as may be prescribed:

Provided that neither the salary and allowances nor the other terms and conditions of service of the Presiding Officer shall be varied to his disadvantage after appointment.

F. Filling up of vacancies

If, for reason other than temporary absence, any vacancy occurs in the office in the Presiding Officer of a Cyber Appellate Tribunal, then the Central Government shall appoint another person in accordance with the provisions of this Act to fill the vacancy and the proceedings may be continued before the Cyber Appellate Tribunal from the stage at which the vacancy is filled.

G. Resignation and removal

i) The Presiding Officer of a Cyber Appellate Tribunal may, by notice in writing under his hand addressed to the Central Government, resign his office:

Provided that the said Presiding Officer shall, unless he is permitted by the Central Government to relinquish his office sooner, continue to hold office until the expiry of three months from the date of receipt of such notice or until a person duly appointed as his successor enters upon his office or until the expiry of his term of office, whichever is the earliest.

ii) The Presiding Officer of a Cyber Appellate Tribunal shall not be removed from his office except by an order by the Central Government on the ground of proved misbehaviour or incapacity after an inquiry made by a Judge of the Supreme Court in which the Presiding Officer concerned has been informed of the charges against him and given a reasonable opportunity of being heard in respect of these charges.

iii) The Central Government may, by rules, regulate the procedure for the investigation of misbehaviour or incapacity of the aforesaid Presiding Officer.

H. Orders constituting Appellate Tribunal to be final and not to invalidate its proceedings

No order of the Central Government appointing any person as the Presiding Officer of a Cyber Appellate Tribunal shall be called in question in any manner and no act or proceeding before a Cyber Appellate Tribunal shall be called in question in any manner on the ground merely of any defect in the constitution of a Cyber Appellate Tribunal.

I. Staff of the Cyber Appellate Tribunal

i) The Central Government shall provide the Cyber Appellate Tribunal with such officers and employees as that Government may think fit.

ii) The officers and employees of the Cyber Appellate Tribunal shall discharge their functions under general superintendence of the Presiding Officer.

iii) The salaries, allowances and other conditions of service of the officers and employees or' the Cyber Appellate Tribunal shall be such as may be prescribed by the Central Government.

J. Appeal to Cyber Appellate Tribunal

i) Save as provided in sub-section (2), any person aggrieved by an order made by Controller or an adjudicating officer under this Act may prefer an appeal to a Cyber Appellate Tribunal having jurisdiction in the matter.

ii) No appeal shall lie to the Cyber Appellate Tribunal from an order made by an adjudicating officer with the consent of the parties.

iii) Every appeal under sub-section (1) shall be filed within a period of tony-five days from the date on which a copy of the order made by the Controller or the adjudicating officer is received by the person aggrieved and it shall be in such form and be accompanied by such fee as may be prescribed:

Provided that the Cyber Appellate Tribunal may entertain an appeal after the expiry of the said period of tony-five days if it is satisfied that there was sufficient cause tor not filing it within that period.

iv) On receipt of an appeal under sub-section (1), the Cyber Appellate Tribunal may, after giving the parties to the appeal, an opportunity of being heard, pass such orders thereon as it thinks fit, confirming, modifying or setting aside the order appealed against.

v) The Cyber Appellate Tribunal shall send a copy of every order made by it to the parties to the appeal and to the concerned Controller or adjudicating officer.

vi) The appeal filed before the Cyber Appellate Tribunal under sub-section (1) shall be dealt with by it as expeditiously as possible and endeavour shall be made by it to dispose of the appeal finally within six months from the date of receipt of the appeal.

K. Procedure and powers of the Cyber Appellate Tribunal

i) The Cyber Appellate Tribunal shall not be bound by the procedure laid down by the Code of civil Procedure, 1908 but shall be guided by the principles of natural justice and, subject to the other provisions of this Act and of any rules, the Cyber Appellate Tribunal shall have powers to regulate its own procedure including the place at which it shall have its sittings.

ii) The Cyber Appellate Tribunal shall have, for the purposes of discharging its functions under this Act, the same powers as are vested in a civil court under the Code of Civil Procedure, 1908, while trying a suit, in respect of the following matters, namely:

- Summoning and enforcing the attendance of any person and examining him on oath;
- requiring the discovery and production of documents or other electronic records;
- receiving evidence on affidavits;
- issuing commissions for the examination of witnesses or documents;
- reviewing its decisions;
- dismissing an application for default or deciding it *ex pane;*
- any other matter which may be prescribed.

iii) Every proceeding before the Cyber Appellate Tribunal shall be deemed to be a judicial proceeding within the meaning of sections 193 and 228, and for the purposes of section 196 of the Indian Penal Code and the Cyber Appellate Tribunal shall be deemed to be a civil court for the purposes of section 195 and Chapter XXVI of the Code of Criminal Procedure, 1973.

L. Right to legal representation

The appellant may either appear in person or authorize one or more legal practitioners or any of its officers to present his or its case before the Cyber Appellate Tribunal.

M. Limitation

The provisions of the Limitation Act, 1963, shall, as far as may be, apply to an appeal made to the Cyber Appellate Tribunal.

N. Civil court not to have jurisdiction

No court shall have jurisdiction to entertain any suit or proceeding in respect of any matter which an adjudicating officer appointed under this Act or the Cyber Appellate Tribunal constituted under this Act is empowered by or under this Act to determine and no injunction shall be granted by any court or other authority in respect of any action taken or to be taken in pursuance of any power conferred by or under this Act.

O. Appeal to High Court

Any person aggrieved by any decision or order of the Cyber Appellate Tribunal may file an appeal to the High Court within sixty days from the date of communication of the decision or order of the Cyber Appellate Tribunal to him on any question of fact or law arising out of such order.

Provided that the High Court may, if it is satisfied that the appellant was prevented by sufficient cause from filing the appeal within the said period, allow it to be filed within a further period not exceeding sixty days.

P. Compounding of contraventions

i) Any contravention under this Chapter may, either before or after the institution of adjudication proceedings, be compounded by the Controller or such other officer as may be specially authorised by him in this behalf or by the adjudicating officer, as the case may be, subject to such conditions as the Controller or such other officer or the adjudicating officer may specify: Provided that such sum shall not, in any case, exceed the maximum amount of the penalty, which may be imposed under this Act for the contravention so compounded.

ii) Nothing in sub-section (1) shall apply to a person who commits the same or similar contravention within a period of three years from the date on which the first contravention, committed by him, was compounded. ***Explanation:*** For the purposes of this sub-section, any second or subsequent contravention committed after the expiry of a period of three years from the date on which the contravention was previously compounded shall be deemed to be a first contravention.

iii) Where any contravention has been compounded under sub-section (1), no proceeding or further proceeding, as the case may be, shall be taken against the person guilty of such contravention in respect of the contravention so compounded.

Q. Recovery of penalty

A penalty imposed under this Act, if it is not paid, shall be recovered, as an arrear of land revenue and the license or the Digital Signature Certificate, as the case may be, shall be suspended till the penalty is paid.

INDIAN CYBER LAW

In Indian law, cyber crime has to be voluntary and willful, an act or omission that adversely affects a person or property. The IT Act provides the backbone for E-commerce and India's approach has been to look at e-governance and E-commerce primarily from the promotional aspects looking at the vast opportunities and the need to sensitize the population to the possibilities of the information age. There is the need to take in to consideration the security aspects.

In the present global situation where cyber control mechanisms are important we need to push cyber laws. Cyber Crimes are a new class of crimes to India rapidly expanding due to extensive use of Internet. Getting the right lead and making the right interpretation are very important in solving a cyber crime. The 7-stage continuum of a criminal case starts from perpetration to registration to reporting, investigation, prosecution, adjudication and execution. The system cannot be stronger than the weakest link in the chain. In India, there are 30 million policemen to train apart from 12,000 strong Judiciary. Police in India are trying to become cyber crime savvy and hiring people who are trained in the area. Each police station in Delhi will have a computer soon, which will be connected to the Head Quarter. The pace of the investigations however can be faster; judicial sensitivity and knowledge need to improve. Focus needs to be on educating the police and district judiciary. IT Institutions can also play a role in this area.

Technology nuances are important in a Spam infested environment where privacy can be compromised and individuals can be subjected to become a victim unsuspectingly. We need to sensitize our investigators and judges to the nuances of the system. Most cyber criminals have a counter part in the real world. If loss of property or persons is caused the criminal is punishable under the IPC also. Since the law enforcement agencies find it is easier to handle it under the IPC, IT Act cases are not getting reported and when reported are not necessarily dealt with under the IT Act. A lengthy and intensive process of learning is required.

A whole series of initiatives of cyber forensics were undertaken and cyber law procedures resulted out of it. This is an area where learning takes place every day, as we are all beginners in this area. We are looking for solutions faster than the problems can get invented. We need to move faster than the criminals.

The real issue is how to prevent cyber crime. For this, there is need to raise the probability of apprehension and conviction. India has a law on evidence that considers admissibility, authenticity, accuracy, and completeness to convince the judiciary. The challenge in cyber crime cases includes getting evidence that will stand scrutiny in a foreign court.

For this India needs total international cooperation with specialized agencies of different countries. Police has to ensure that they have seized exactly what was there at the scene of crime, is the same that has been analyzed and the report presented in court is based on this evidence. It has to maintain the chain of custody. The threat is not from the intelligence of criminals but from our ignorance and the will to fight it. The law is stricter now on producing evidence especially where electronic documents are concerned.

The computer is the target and the tool for the perpetration of crime. It is used for the communication of the criminal activity such as the injection of a virus/worm, which can crash entire networks. The Information Technology (IT) Act, 2000, specifies the acts, which have been made punishable. Since the primary objective of this Act is to create an enabling environment for commercial use of IT, certain omissions and commissions of criminals while using computers have not been included. With the legal recognition of Electronic Records and the amendments made in the several sections of the IPC vide the IT Act, 2000, several offences having bearing on cyber-arena are also registered under the appropriate sections of the IPC.

CYBER LAW AND INFORMATION TECHNOLOGY

By Talwant Singh Addl. Distt. & Sessions Judge, Delhi

Success in any field of human activity leads to crime that needs mechanisms to control it.

Legal provisions should provide assurance to users, empowerment to law enforcement agencies and deterrence to criminals. The law is as stringent as its enforcement. Crime is no longer limited to space, time or a group of people. Cyber space creates moral, civil and criminal wrongs. It has now given a new way to express criminal tendencies. Back in 1990, less than 100,000 people were able to log on to the Internet worldwide. Now around 500 million people are hooked up to surf the net around the globe.

Until recently, many information technology (IT) professionals lacked awareness of and interest in the cyber crime phenomenon. In many cases, law enforcement officers have lacked the tools needed to tackle the problem; old laws didn't quite fit the crimes being committed, new laws hadn't quite caught up to the reality of what was happening, and there were few court precedents to look to for guidance. Furthermore, debates over privacy issues hampered the ability of enforcement agents to gather the evidence needed to prosecute these new cases. Finally, there was a certain amount of antipathy—or at the least, distrust— between the two most important players in any effective fight against cyber crime: law enforcement agencies and computer professionals. Yet close cooperation between the two is crucial if we are to control the cyber crime problem and make the Internet a safe "place" for its users.

Law enforcement personnel understand the criminal mindset and know the basics of gathering evidence and bringing offenders to justice. IT personnel understand computers and networks, how they work, and how to track down information on them. Each has half of the key to defeating the cyber criminal.

IT professionals need good definitions of cyber crime in order to know when (and what) to report to police, but law enforcement agencies *must* have statutory definitions of specific crimes in order to charge a criminal with an offense. The first step in specifically defining individual cyber crimes is to sort all the acts that can be considered cyber crimes into organized categories. The system cannot be stronger than the weakest link in the chain. In India, there are 30 million policemen to train apart from 12,000 strong Judiciary. Police in India are trying to become cyber crime savvy and hiring people who are trained in the area. Each police station in Delhi will have a computer soon, which will be connected to the Head Quarter. The pace of the investigations however can be faster; judicial sensitivity and knowledge need to improve. Focus needs to be on educating the police and district judiciary. IT Institutions can also play a role in this area.

Technology nuances are important in a Spam infested environment where privacy can be compromised and individuals can be subjected to become a victim unsuspectingly. We need to sensitize our investigators and judges to the nuances of the system. Most cyber criminals have a counter part in the real world. If loss of property or persons is caused the criminal is punishable under the IPC also. Since the law enforcement agencies find it is easier to handle it under the IPC, IT Act cases are not getting reported and when reported are not necessarily dealt with under the IT Act. A lengthy and intensive process of learning is required.

A whole series of initiatives of cyber forensics were undertaken and cyber law procedures resulted out of it. This is an area where learning takes place every day, as we are all beginners in this area. We are looking for solutions faster than the problems can get invented. We need to move faster than the criminals.

The real issue is how to prevent cyber crime. For this, there is need to raise the probability of apprehension and conviction. India has a law on evidence that considers admissibility, authenticity, accuracy, and completeness to convince the judiciary. The challenge in cyber crime cases includes getting evidence that will stand scrutiny in a foreign court.

For this India needs total international cooperation with specialized agencies of different countries. Police has to ensure that they have seized exactly what was there at the scene of crime, is the same that has been analyzed and the report presented in court is based on this evidence. It has to maintain the chain of custody. The threat is not from the intelligence of criminals but from our ignorance and the will to fight it.

The law is stricter now on producing evidence especially where electronic documents are concerned. The computer is the target and the tool for the perpetration of crime. It is used for the communication of the criminal activity such as the injection of a virus/worm, which can crash entire networks.

The Information Technology (IT) Act, 2000, specifies the acts, which have been made punishable. Since the primary objective of this Act is to create an enabling environment for commercial use of IT, certain omissions and commissions of criminals while using computers have not been included. With the legal recognition of Electronic Records and the amendments made in the several sections of the IPC vide the IT Act, 2000, several offences having bearing on cyber-arena are also registered under the appropriate sections of the IPC.

WARNING AGAINST INCREASING CYBER CRIMES BY STANDARD BANK

We have become aware of a growing number of cyber crime incidents taking place at Internet cafés and other public places that offer Internet services. You are urged not to use computer facilities that you are not familiar with.

Our IT Security Department, working with local law enforcement agencies, has been tracking syndicates that target publicly accessible computer and Internet terminals to steal secret account information like PINs and card numbers in order to defraud customers.

Says Herman Singh, Director Technology Engineering at Standard Bank: "Syndicates are installing key logging software and hardware on unprotected computers. Customers' secret access codes and other personal information are then gleaned from the computer. We have always advised our customers to only do their banking from a secure computer, which has all the necessary anti-virus software and with a personal firewall. We have indeed provided this service free of charge to 50 000 Standard Bank Internet banking customers for over three years now as a free download from our banking website.

We remain committed to protecting the integrity of our customers' credentials. However, you also need to ensure that you have taken effective security measures when transacting over the Internet. You are also urged to adopt the following security features:

One-time password

A unique and time-sensitive password used as added security on Internet banking. The password is sent to you by email or SMS and is valid for one Internet banking session. This is a free service.

My Notification

A notification service that informs you of transactions that are being carried out on the Internet banking platform. The delivery mechanisms supported are email and SMS, while the support notifications are restricted to logons, profile amendments, new beneficiary additions, amendments to existing beneficiaries and once-off payments notification.

Payment confirmation

A notification process that informs both the payer and payee that a transfer transaction has been successfully completed.

McAfee Anti Virus Software

We are the only local bank that offers the McAfee range of security products, including anti-virus and firewall software, as a free online service to our customers.

Many of our customers have already demonstrated their willingness to adopt more secure processes with more than 190000, over a third of our Internet banking customers, already adopting one-time-password. This secure system is designed to protect you from these types of attacks. The service is mandatory for all new Internet banking customers and will become mandatory for all existing customers with effect from October 2006.

Customers should continue to play their part in this security relationship by protecting the secrecy of their PINs and passwords as they would protect their secret codes to their home alarm systems.

THREAT PERCEPTIONS

UK has the largest number of infected computers in the world followed by the US and China. Financial attacks are 16 events per 1000, the highest among all kinds of attacks. The US is the leading source country for attacks but this has declined. China is second and Germany is third. It is hard to determine where the attack came from originally.

The number of viruses and worm variants rose sharply to 7,360 that are a 64% increase over the previous reporting period and a 332% increase over the previous year. There are 17,500 variants of Win.32 viruses. Threats to confidential information are on the rise with 54% of the top 50 reporting malicious code with the potential to expose such information. Phishing messages grew to 4.5 million from 1 million between July and December 2004.

SOME INDIAN CASE STUDIES

1. Pune Citibank Mphasis Call Center Fraud

US $ 3,50,000 from accounts of four US customers were dishonestly transferred to bogus accounts. This will give a lot of ammunition to those lobbying against outsourcing in US.

Such cases happen all over the world but when it happens in India it is a serious matter and we cannot ignore it. It is a case of sourcing engineering. Some employees gained the confidence of the customer and obtained their PIN numbers to commit fraud. They got these under the guise of helping the customers out of difficult situations. Highest security prevails in the call centers in India, as they know that they will lose their business. There was not as much of breach of security but of sourcing engineering.

The call center employees are checked when they go in and out so they cannot copy down numbers and therefore they could not have noted these down. They must have remembered these numbers, gone out immediately to a cyber café and accessed the Citibank accounts of the customers.

All accounts were opened in Pune and the customers complained that the money from their accounts was transferred to Pune accounts and that's how the criminals were traced. Police has been able to prove the honesty of the call center and has frozen the accounts where the money was transferred.

There is need for a strict background check of the call center executives. However, best of background checks cannot eliminate the bad elements from coming in and breaching security. We must still ensure such checks when a person is hired. There is need for a national ID and a national database where a name can be referred. In this case preliminary investigations do not reveal that the criminals had any crime history. Customer education is very important so customers do not get taken for a ride. Most banks are guilt of not doing this.

2. The Bank NSP Case

The Bank NSP case is the one where a management trainee of the bank was engaged to be married. The couple exchanged many E-mails using the company computers. After some time the two broke up and the girl created fraudulent E-mail IDs such as "Indian bar associations" and sent emails to the boy's foreign clients. She used the banks computer to do this. The boy's company lost a large number of clients and took the bank to court. The bank was held liable for the emails sent using the bank's system.

3. Andhra Pradesh Tax Case

Dubious tactics of a prominent businessman from Andhra Pradesh was exposed after officials of the department got hold of computers used by the accused person.

The owner of a plastics firm was arrested and Rs. 22 crore cash was recovered from his house by sleuths of the Vigilance Department. They sought an explanation from him regarding the unaccounted cash within 10 days. The accused person submitted 6,000 vouchers to prove the legitimacy of trade and thought his offence would go undetected but after careful scrutiny of vouchers and contents of his computers it revealed that all of them were made after the raids were conducted.

It later revealed that the accused was running five businesses under the guise of one company and used fake and computerised vouchers to show sales records and save tax.

4. HSBC Fraud

An HSBC employee in Bangalore was arrested on Tuesday night June 28 for illegally accessing confidential information of customers and helping fraudulent in the UK to siphon of large amounts of money from their accounts.

The Corps of Detectives took 24-year-old Nadeem Hamid Kashmiri into custody, who joined HSBC Electronic Data Processing India (HDPI), Bannerghatta Road, on December 12, 2005, allegedly accessed personal information, security information and debit card information of some customers from March to May this year.

These details were passed on to the fraudsters, who diverted £233,000 from the clients' accounts, according to a complaint lodged by HDPI with the Bangalore cyber crime police. The Nadeem trail landed some of his family members and friends in custody. Nadeem is from Pillanna Garden.

The cyber crime police, probing the fraud, are contacting the UK police. The incident came to light when around 20 customers informed the bank of money being debited from their accounts without authorization.

An internal inquiry by the bank revealed Nadeem's involvement. In his complaint with the cyber crime police on June 22, HDPI vice-president Puneet Dar said ack-end system records showed Nadeem had accessed the confidential information without authorization.

To access such information for any business requirement, prior permission is needed. Nadeem went missing after he got to know about the internal probe. The bank also found out that Nadeem, who goes by several aliases, had furnished false mobile number and address at the time of employment.

He was earlier with Accenture. Nadeem passed on confidential data to the fraudsters in the UK. The gang used the information for fraudulent transactions through ATM, debit cards and telephone banking services. Nadeem's accomplices would call and clear procedural security requirements. "They requested him for the balance information and conducted the fraudulent transaction. Nadeem facilitated his accomplices to impersonate the actual customers to enable them to cheat the HDPI and HSBC customers," the complaint stated. A case has been registered under Sections 66 and 71 of the IT Act and 408, 468 and 420 of the Indian Penal Code.

AN INTERNATIONAL CASE STUDY

Yaron Bolandi, Inside the Police Jail

With his face uncovered, Israeli Yaron Bolondi, 32, is brought from the police station cell to a meeting with his Lawyer by a prison officer in Bat Yam Raziel St. 9 Israel Friday, March 18, 2005 morning. In this Police Station Israeli National Cyber Crime Unit works. Israeli police, working with British officers, arrested Bolondi Wednesday March 16, 2005 in connection with the attempt to rob money from the Sumitomo Mitsui Financial Group Inc., police in Israel said in a statement. British police foiled a high-tech attempt to steal millions of pounds from a Japanese bank's London offices by accessing its computer system and making money transfers, authorities said Thursday. Bolondi was released on bail to home arrest in March 22, 2005. Israeli and UK Cyber Crime Units in March 21, 2005 arrested an Israeli man Aharon Abu Hamra suspected of being involved in an attempt to defraud the London branch of the Japanese Sumitomo Mitsui Bank, a case British police called "one of the largest bank robbery attempts ever in the UK". Aharon Abu Hamra is a 35-year-old resident of Tel Aviv. Aharon Abu Hamra is suspected of mediating between Yaron Bolondi, and the British counterparts in the fraud. According to cyber cops, Aharon Abu Hamra offered Bolondi to serve as a straw man in Israel in order to launder approximately 20 million euro gained from the Japanese bank, from which he was supposed to receive a hefty commission. Aharon Abu Hamra was arrested for 5 days in Tel Aviv Court.

CYBER CRIME STATISTICS

During the year 2003, 60 cases were registered under IT Act as compared to 70 cases during the previous year thereby reporting a decline of 14.3 per cent in 2003 over 2002. Of the total 60 cases registered under IT Act 2000, around 33 per cent (20 cases) relate to Obscene Publication / Transmission in electronic form, normally known as cases of cyber pornography. Seventeen persons were arrested for committing such offences during 2003.

There were 21 cases of Hacking of computer systems wherein 18 persons were arrested in 2003. Of the total (21)

Hacking cases, the cases relating to Loss/Damage of computer resource/utility under Sec 66(1) of the IT Act were to the tune of 62 percent (13 cases) and that related to Hacking under Section 66(2) of IT Act were 38 per cent (8cases).

During 2003, a total of 411 cases were registered under IPC Sections as compared to 738 such cases during 2002 thereby reporting a significant decline of 44 percent in 2003 over 2002. Andhra Pradesh reported more than half of such cases (218 out of 411) (53 per cent).

Of the 411 cases registered under IPC, majority of the crimes fall under 3 categories viz. Criminal Breach of Trust or Fraud (269), Forgery (89) and Counterfeiting (53).

Though, these offences fall under the traditional IPC crimes, the cases had the cyber tones wherein computer, Internet or its related aspects were present in the crime and hence they were categorized as Cyber Crimes under IPC.

During 2003, number of cases under Cyber Crimes relating to Counterfeiting of currency/Stamps stood at 53 wherein 118 persons were arrested during 2003. Of the 47,478 cases reported under Cheating, the Cyber Forgery (89) accounted for 0.2 per cent. Of the total Criminal Breach of Trust cases (13,432), the Cyber frauds (269) accounted for 2 per cent. Of the Counterfeiting offences (2,055), Cyber Counterfeiting (53) offences accounted for 2.6 per cent.

A total of 475 persons were arrested in the country for Cyber Crimes under IPC during 2003. Of these, 53.6 percent offenders (255) were taken into custody for offences under Criminal Breach of Trust/Fraud (Cyber) and 21.4 percent (102) for offences under 'Cyber Forgery'.

The age-wise profile of the arrested persons showed that 45 per cent were in the age-group of 30-45 years, 28.5 per cent of the offenders were in the age-group of 45-60 years and 11 offenders were aged 60 years and above. Gujarat reported 2 offenders who were below 18 years of age.

Fraud/Illegal gain (120) accounted for 60 per cent of the total Cyber Crime motives reported in the country. Greed/ Money (15 cases) accounted for 7.5 per cent of the Cyber Crimes reported. Eve-teasing and Harassment (8 cases) accounted for around 4 per cent. Cyber Suspects include Neighbours / Friends / Relatives (91), Disgruntled employees (11), Business Competitors (9), Crackers Students / Professional learners (3).

Cyber crime is not on the decline. The latest statistics show that cyber crime is actually on the rise. However, it is true that in India, cyber crime is not reported too much about.

Consequently there is a false sense of complacency that cyber crime does not exist and that society is safe from cyber crime. This is not the correct picture. The fact is that people in our country do not report cyber crimes for many reasons. Many do not want to face harassment by the police. There is also the fear of bad publicity in the media, which could hurt their reputation and standing in society. Also, it becomes extremely difficult to convince the police to register any cyber crime, because of lack of orientation and awareness about cyber crimes and their registration and handling by the police.

A recent survey indicates that for every 500-cybercrime incidents that take place, only 50 are reported to the police and out of that only one is actually registered. These figures indicate how difficult it is to convince the police to register a cyber crime. The establishment of cyber crime cells in different parts of the country was expected to boost cyber crime reporting and prosecution. However, these cells haven't quite kept up with expectations.

Netizens should not be under the impression that cyber crime is vanishing and they must realize that with each passing day, cyberspace becomes a more dangerous place to be in, where criminals roam freely to execute their criminals intentions encouraged by the so called anonymity that internet provides.

The absolutely poor rate of cyber crime conviction in the country has also not helped the cause of regulating cyber crime. There have only been few cyber crime convictions in the whole country, which can be counted on fingers. We need to ensure that we have specialized procedures for prosecution of cyber crime cases so as to tackle them on a priority basis. This is necessary so as to win the faith of the people in the ability of the system to tackle cyber crime. We must ensure that our system provides for stringent punishment of cyber crimes and cyber criminals so that the same acts as a deterrent for others.

Step Safety Guide

i) Install the latest ant virus software on your computer and never ever turn it (ant virus) off, install a personal firewall and spy ware checker (all are available for free). To find them just Google using the keywords 'ant virus' & 'free'.

ii) Never download or open attachments, whose source you are not certain about. Even if the source is trusted, see if the content is relevant, if not don't open attachment.

Create another E-mail ID that you use exclusively for subscription to sites. That will prevent Spam from coming to your main ID.

Some accounts like Yahoo allow you to create topic specific E-mail IDs that you can delink.

iii) Avoid checking mail or using credit card details online in cyber cafes. It is next to impossible to be sure that this is safe. Even reputed cafes as those at international airports and 5-star hotels been have known to be key-logged.

As a matter of fact, open an additional debit card with a limit if you do want to transact online. Even in the worst-case scenario, your damages will then be limited.

iv) Do not give away your residence or cell number. Be especially careful when you are filling in contest forms, coupons, free gift vouchers, etc.

More often than not these are gimmicks to obtain your personal details. Don't believe it when they say the data will not be given to others — it most certainly will be.

Don't print these numbers on your visiting card.

v) Get into the habit of destroying documentation regarding credit cards, such as receipts, bills, invoices or any documents that contain personal details.

vi) If you are using broadband or working from home, ensure that your PC is hardened professionally. Yourself can also do this if you follow the next step.

vii) Information is a reality of modern life. Just like health or transport or communication is. The point is that you need to know something about it, even if it is just some basics.

Read about information security breaches by subscribing to some newsletters. In the case of many breaches the only defense is knowledge.

For instance, no technology could have prevented the phishing attack (wherein victims got mails seemingly from legitimate banks asking them to confirm their passwords and IDs).

viii) Use two different passwords. One for mail, work and other important access, and the other for routine purposes such as subscribing to sites, etc. But remember to switch between them when you start doing transactions after mere browsing.

ix) Create a difficult-to-guess password by taking the first alphabet from each word of a phrase. For instance a password like 1at*eomc is constructed using a phrase 'I am the star employee of my company.'

x) Educate your children about the dangers of cyber crime. Children with their unbound curiosity and unmonitored access are the single most common victims of cyber crime apart from the enterprises

CONCLUSION

The problem of cyber crime has become a key concern not only in India but also all over the world. We can conclude that it is perceived to be a critical threat and its biggest impact is in terms of revenue. Cyber crime is simply "crime" with some sort of 'computers' or 'cyber' aspect. Cyber crimes are a new class of crimes to India rapidly expanding due to extensive use of Internet. It has been noticed that the number of cyber crimes are increasing rapidly and soon there will be a time when it will exceed physical crimes.

However, it can be controlled by a number of ways and there are also several security measures given in order to prevent cyber crime.

■ ■ ■

3

BIOMETRICS TECHNOLOGY–ITS IMPLICATIONS IN BANKING SECTOR

INTRODUCTION

The fast growing security breaches around the world have forced the IT community to look for new technology to deal with such cases resulting in financial and reputational loss for the organizations. The fast conversion of paper-based records into paperless records has further heightened the need for computer access controls where most of the data have been digitized. Worldwide the losses due to access control violations are rising when compared to losses from physical security breaches. The Global Security Survey conducted by Deloitte Touche Tohmatsu in 2005 concluded that internal security breaches by employees were more than external attacks on large financial institutions. The focus of ongoing research has been to, innovate a foolproof mechanism to identify access control violations. While most of entities using computers across the globe still rely on password based access controls, some of them have realized the shortcomings of passwords and moved to dual authentication systems that generally combine password and smart card devices. The latest development in access controls is biometric systems.

Passports and documents can be falsified. Biometric–finger, face and iris–data is unique and complex, providing unprecedented protection against forgery.

BIOMETRIC ATMs FOR RURAL INDIA

ATMs with biometric devices are the latest solution in the ongoing effort to offer banking services to the rural masses. To reach the rural masses, banks are going all out in providing a user-friendly banking experience. To boost micro financing initiatives, banks are deploying biometric solutions with ATMs.

Establishing the identity of a rural depositor through biometrics makes it possible for illiterate or barely literate folks to become part of the banking user community. Establishing the identity of a rural depositor through biometrics makes it possible for illiterate or barely literate folks to become part of the banking user community. In recent years the importance of biometrics has grown tremendously with an increasing demand of security in accordance of unique identification of individuals. Its use for identification in applications other than policing is on the rise. In view of the rapidly increasing applications, the scope of biometrics is also increasing, be it identification via face, voice, retina or iris. Finger printing, however, has the advantage of being a familiar concept worldwide.

In the retail payments arena, developments in biometric technology have made their presence felt in the pervasiveness of self-service devices including Automated Teller Machines (ATMs) and Point of Service (PoS) machines. Some of the new generation PoS terminals are biometric enabled with smart card readers, allowing thumb print based authentication.

Some Indian banks have started implementing biometric applications in retail branch applications for officer authentication. Elsewhere in the world, efforts are on enabling payments through kiosks based on finger prints (non-card based). ATM enhancements with biometric support envisaged by vendors eliminate the need for PIN entry, and authenticate customer transactions by thumb-impressions. A simplified menu on ATMs coupled with possible audio guidance in local language enable easy use for rural masses. So far bank ATMs are dependent on PIN verification. The finger print authentication method is non-PIN based, and this requires enhancements to the standard Switch environment.

CONCEPT OF BIOMETRICS

Biometric authentication is an automated method whereby an individual's identity is confirmed by examining a unique physiological trait or behavioural characteristic, such as a finger print, iris, retina, or signature. Physiological traits are stable physical characteristics, such as finger prints, palm prints and iris patterns. This type of measurement is essentially unalterable. A behavioural characteristic–such as one's signature, voice, or keystroke dynamics–is influenced by both controllable actions and less controllable psychological factors. Because behavioral characteristics can change over time, the enrolled biometric reference template must be updated each time it is used. Although behaviour-based biometrics can be less expensive and less threatening to users, physiological traits tend to offer greater accuracy and security. In any case, both techniques provide a significantly higher level of identification than passwords or smart cards alone.

An identification and authentication device based on physical attributes like finger print, palm print, retina pattern, etc. is called biometric system. Continuous research and development has led to evolution of various identification and authentication devices based on physiological or behavioural attributes. Any identification methodology or technique should be accurate, time efficient and reliable, and cost as well as memory effective. Besides, it should be acceptable to users whose attributes would be captured. Signatures / thumb impression / finger prints have been an age-old mechanism of identifying individuals and well accepted by law enforcement authorities.

SECURING TRANSACTIONS WITH FINGERPRINTS

With the development of biometric solutions for the ATMs there is no need to remember PIN numbers. Software vendors are coming up with finger print solutions for the rural masses. Chennai based Financial Software and Systems (FSS) has recently launched its Biometric ATM Interface Solution (BAIS) that enables connectivity of ATMs with biometric support to Electronic Financial Transaction (EFT) switches. Elaborating on the working of the biometric solutions, G. P. Shekar, Head - Consulting Practice, Financial Software and Systems (P) Ltd. says, " Customers opting for biometric authentication can visit a nearby kiosk or ATMs or bank, where his finger print data would be scanned into a special PC with a finger-print scanner and the scanned finger print is then stored in an encrypted form in a central server. When a customer inserts (or swipes) his card in a biometric enabled ATM, he is prompted to set his finger in the finger print scanner. The transaction along with customer's biometric information is passed on to the switch. The switch verifies the finger print with the server, and if successful, requests the banking application to authorise the transaction." Based on the result, the Switch instructs the ATM to complete the transaction. FSS' BAIS solution meets this requirement, by performing requisite message translations as well as confirming authorisation.

CMC Limited, which has its presence in the biometric space for nearly two decades, has also developed solutions for banks. CMC's Fingerprint solution provides high-level authentication for accessing ATMs. Fingerprint solutions provide an interface to integrate with an ATM application.

CMC has indigenously developed FACTS (Fingerprint Analysis and Criminal Tracing System)—an advanced automated finger print identification system, using image processing and pattern recognition techniques. FACTS was initially targeted at law enforcement, but with increased concerns on security and personal identity, CMC started focusing on the banking and related sectors. B M Mehtre, DGM, R&D, CMC Ltd says, "Fingerprints of account holders are captured through the scanner in the system at the time of account opening. A template is created for each finger print by extracting features and stored in the debit card against the unique Customer ID. During verification, the finger print is captured using a finger print scanner attached to the ATM and 1:1 matching of the finger print captured is done with the templates stored in the debit card. Upon a successful match, the user is allowed to perform further transactions."

Pune based Axis technology is another Indian company which is developing biometric solutions for ATMs and kiosks in the banking sector. Says Abhay Khinvasara, CEO, Axis Technology, "Our ATMs can work with popular protocols that are being used in the financial transaction infrastructure. Axis ATMs will also work with any type of authentication required be it PIN or biometric based. The ATMs are equipped with a high quality finger print sensor ideally suited for dry, moist and rough fingers and advanced image processing and pattern recognition algorithms for finger print verification (FBI approved).There are also intelligent and dynamic security settings and other biometrics like Iris, face or even layered biometrics, which can be integrated into it.

RECENT INITATIVES

Deploying ATMs for rural masses depends largely on banks stepping forward to take the requisite initiatives. The recent directive from the government on financial inclusion ("banking for the common man") is a key driver for the growth of such solutions in India. Banks are quite aware of the untapped potential in the rural sector. The telecom industry is witnessing a blistering growth pace, and so is the Internet. The National Rural Employment Guarantee Program that guarantees employment and payment in the rural sector requires robust solutions. Using thumb print and voice guidance in ATMs reduces literacy requirements to a considerable extent. However, the technology is not restricted to rural masses.

FSS is in discussions with Andhra Bank for deploying the BAIS. Several other public sector and private sector banks have shown interest too. Says Shekar, "FSS would like to work with ATM and POS vendors to provide innovative and cost effective solutions to banks and customers." FSS is striving to modularise and 'ruggedise' the solution to perform online functions across a wide variety of delivery channels and payment systems. Apart from these banks, some other banks such as ICICI Bank are planning to introduce biometric authenticated ATMs in rural India.

CMC has been working with Institute for Development and Research in Banking Technology (IDRBT) on a pilot project in rural banking. Biometric (Fingerprints) smart cards, which consist of finger print data and financial data, will be issued to the rural banking customers for carrying out financial transactions. Elaborates Mehtre, "For building and developing various applications, CMC has a biometric technology group at its Research and Development Centre in Hyderabad.

The team evaluates the latest technologies emerging in the biometrics area. This helps CMC's solutions to be competitive and cost effective. CMC has been working with Bank of India for introducing biometric ATMs. CMC has demonstrated its Biometrics ATM solution on the eve of inauguration of mobile ATMs for the bank."

Benefits of Biometric Supported ATMs

- Provides strong authentication
- Can be used instead of a PIN
- Hidden costs of ATM card management like card personalisation, delivery, management, re-issuance, PIN generation, help-desk, and re-issuance can be avoided
- Ideal for Indian rural masses
- It is accurate
- Flexible account access allows clients to access their accounts at their convenience
- Low operational cost of the ATMs will ultimately reduce TCO No more forgotten passwords, lost cards or stolen pins. You are your own password

- Positive Identification- It identifies you and not what you have or what you carry
- Highest level of security
- Offers mobility
- Impossible to forge
- Serves as a "Key" that cannot be transferred or coerced
- Non-intrusive
- Safe and user friendly

Measurable Usefulness

Being able to accurately gauge the usefulness of a finger print authentication solution is very important. This technology saves money in password administration, user up time and user support. More importantly, finger print authentication allows you to do more with a computer. Now, remote secure network access is possible. Electronic commerce makes sense when the authentication is trusted. It is a fact that 75 per cent of all Internet users are uncomfortable transmitting their credit card information over the public network. Imagine if this was never an issue. Fingerprint authentication is an enabling technology for trusted E-commerce.

All the signs are in the market for the acceptance of finger print authentication as a simple, trusted, convenient method of personal authentication. Industry leaders are validating the technology through standards initiatives. Cost and performance breakthroughs have transformed finger print biometrics from an interesting technology to an easy to implement authentication solution. Industry trends such as electronic commerce and remote computing exacerbate the need for better authentication. Most importantly, users understand and accept the concept. Passwords and tokens are universally disliked. You cannot get much simpler than a finger print.

HOW IT WORKS.....

All biometric systems operate in a similar fashion. First, the system captures a sample of the biometric characteristic (this is known as the enrollment process). During enrollment, some biometric systems may require a number of samples in order to build a profile of the biometric characteristic. Unique features are then extracted and converted by the system into a mathematical code. This sample is then stored as the biometric template for the enrollee. The template can reside on a computer database, smart card or barcode.

In addition, the biometric system may require a trigger, or a means of matching the template to the person, for e.g., a PIN is keyed- in to access the template, or a smart card storing the template is inserted into a card reader. In either case, the end user interacts with the biometric system for a second time to have his or her identity checked. A new biometric sample is then taken and this is compared with the template. If the template and the new sample match, the end user is granted access. This is the basic premise of biometrics - that a person has a sample of their biometric data captured and the biometric system decides if it matches with another sample.

The following four-stage process illustrates the way biometric systems operate:

- **Capture-**Physical or behavioural sample is captured by the system during enrollment
- **Extraction-**Unique data is extracted from the sample and a template is created
- **Comparison-**The template is then compared with a new sample
- **Matching-**The system then decides if the features extracted from the new sample are matching or not.

The ATMs supported by biometric solutions, banks having a presence across the country are leveraging on this technology.

The ATMs are networked and connected to a centralised computer (Switch), which controls the ATMs. The use of biometrics identification is possible at an ATM. The information can be stored at a bank branch.

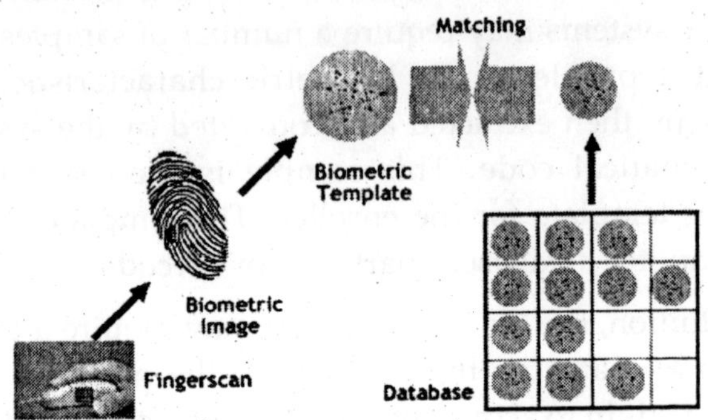

AUTHENTICATION TOOLS

 Finger Print Recognition

 Face Recognition

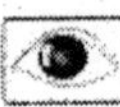 Iris Recognition

 Hand Scan

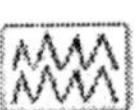 Voice Recognition

ATMs are so prevalent and you have so many people using ATMs that it becomes easy to use biometrics as a replacement for an ATM PIN. The typical ATM has two input devices (a card reader and keypad) and four output devices (display screen, cash dispenser, receipt printer, and speaker). Invisible to the client is a communications mechanism that links the ATM directly to an ATM host network. The ATM functions much like a PC, it comes with an operating system (usually OS/2) and application software for the user interface and communications.

While most ATMs use magnetic strip cards and personal identification numbers (PINs) to identify account holders, other systems may use smart cards with finger print validation. The ATM forwards information read from the client's card and the client's request to a host processor, which routes the request to the concerned financial institution. If the cardholder is requesting cash, the host processor signals for an electronic funds transfer (EFT) from the customer's bank account to the host processor's account. Once the funds have been transferred, the ATM receives an approval code authorising it to dispense cash.

This communication, verification, and authorisation can be delivered in several ways. Leased line, dial-up or wireless data links may be used to connect to a host system, depending on the cost and reliability of the infrastructure. The host systems can reside at a client's institution or be part of an EFT network. The EFT network supports the finger print authentication. Point-of-sale services that use biometric solutions are also possible.

Shekar says, "The FSS Biometric ATM Solution consists of a central server which holds a repository of customer finger prints. It also customises the Switch to enable authorisation of a customer's biometric data and interfaces with ATMs enabled with biometric devices as per FSS specifications. The central server solution is platform independent, it uses Java and can run on Unix and Oracle/ Microsoft SQL Server, customisation to BASE24 Switch (of which FSS is the distributor) is done using TAL. Biometric application and devices from Secugen are used for customer interface and application development."

Axis Technology on the other hand, has developed an innovative new product called the Biometric Retrofit Kit for ATMs. This kit converts a regular ATM to one that authenticates users based on biometrics finger print or iris. This is an affordably priced kit that has generated interest among financial institutions.

Fingerprint Biometrics

Fingerprint biometrics is probably the most common form of biometrics available today. Fingerprints, when scanned electronically, provide greater details and hence higher level of accuracy can be achieved over manual systems. The finger print's strength is its acceptance, convenience and reliability. It takes little time and effort using a finger print identification device to have his or her finger print scanned. Studies have also found that using finger prints as an identification source is the least intrusive of all biometric techniques.

Verification of finger prints is also fast and reliable. Users experience fewer errors in matching when they use finger prints as against many other biometric methods. In addition, a finger print identification device requires very little space on a desktop or in a machine. Several companies have produced capture units smaller than a deck of cards. Finger-scan technology is thus the most prominent biometric authentication technology, used by millions of people worldwide. Used for decades in forensic applications, finger-scan technology is steadily gaining acceptance in fields as varied as physical access, network security, service access, E-commerce and retail.

Face Recognition

Facial scan technology is an increasingly prominent biometric authentication technology, one well suited for a number of applications in which other biometric technologies are simply unusable. Face recognition technology involves analyzing certain facial characteristics, storing them in a database and using them to identify users accessing systems. There are various recognition methods that emphasize identification based on the areas of the face that don't change, including: upper sections of eye sockets, area surrounding the cheek bones and the sides of the mouth.

Iris Recognition

Iris biometrics is exceptionally accurate, especially in environments where the finger prints are worn out due to hard manual labor. Iris technology is relatively more expensive to use and does take-up slightly more time for the enrollment and authentication process. Iris scanners are typically multi-purpose and incorporate regular video capabilities with the scanner. Iris biometric devices are more accurate than finger print because an iris has more characteristics to identify and match than those found on the finger. These types of devices have come a long way in recent years allowing the individual to be scanned even through their glasses or contacts. The error rate for the typical iris scanner is about one in two million attempts, which further demonstrates the reliability of this technology. Two drawbacks to this device however are, that it has difficulty in reading images of people who are blind or have cataracts. These type of devices have come a long way in recent years allowing the individual to be scanned even through their glasses or contacts. The error rate for the typical iris scanner is about one in two million attempts, which further demonstrates the reliability of this technology. Two drawbacks to this device however are, that it has difficulty in reading images of people who are blind or have cataracts.There are several industries, which are interested in this type of technology, particularly banking & Finance. Banks are incorporating Iris Scanning systems into their ATMs. Some prisons are also using this technology today to identify inmates and guards.

These types of devices have come a long way in recent years allowing the individual to be scanned even through their glasses or contacts. The error rate for the typical iris scanner is about one in two million attempts, which further demonstrates the reliability of this technology. Two drawbacks to this device however are, that it has difficulty in reading images of people Who are blind or have cataracts. There are several industries, which are interested in this type of technology, particularly banking & Finance. Banks are incorporating Iris Scanning systems into their ATMs. Some prisons are also using this technology today to identify inmates and guards.

Hand Scan

Hand-scan is a relatively accurate technology, but does not draw as rich a data set as finger, face, or iris. A decent measure of the distinctiveness of a biometric technology is its ability to perform one-to-many searches - that is, the ability to identify a user without the user first claiming an identity. Hand-scan does not perform one-to-many identification, assimilarities between hands are not uncommon. The submission of the biometric is straightforward, and with proper training can be done with little misplacement. The template size of a hand scan is up to 9 bytes which is extremely small compared to most other biometric technologies. By contrast, finger scan biometric requires 250-1000 bytes and voice scan biometric commonly requires 1500-3000 bytes. This facilitates storage of a large number of templates in a standalone device. It also facilitates card-based storage, as even magstripe cards have ample room byte samples

Voice Recognition

Voice recognition is "the technology by which sounds, words or phrases spoken by humans are converted into electrical signals, and these signals are transformed into coding patterns to which meaning has been assigned." The most common approaches to voice recognition can be divided into two classes: "template matching" and "feature analysis". Template matching in voice recognition is the simplest technique and has the highest accuracy when used properly, but it also suffers from the most limitations. As with any approach to voice recognition, the first step is for the user to speak a word or phrase into a microphone, the electrical signal from the microphone is digitized by an "analog-to-digital

(A/D) converter", and is stored in memory. To determine the "meaning" of this voice input, the computer attempts to match the input with a digitized voice sample, or template that has a known meaning.

Most voice recognition systems are discrete word systems, and these are easiest to implement. For this type of system, the speaker must pause between words. This is fine for situations where the user is required to give only one word responses or commands, but is very unnatural for multiple word inputs. In a connected word voice recognition system, the user is allowed to speak in multiple word phrases, but he or she must still be careful to articulate each word and not slur at the end of one word into the beginning of the next word.

Totally natural, continuous speech includes a great deal of "co articulation", where adjacent words run together without pauses or any other apparent division between words.

A speech recognition system that handles continuous speech is the most difficult to implement. Voice recognition uses a neural net to "learn" to recognize your voice. As you speak, the voice recognition software remembers the way you say each word. This customization allows voice recognition, even though everyone speaks with varying accents and inflection.

Biometric Authentication Process

The biometric authentication process involves two stages viz. enrolment procedure, and identification or verification stage.

a) **Enrolment Procedure:** The system needs to enroll or register a biometric attribute for subsequent verification of authentic / authorized user. The system captures the data of biometric attribute like finger print, hand geometry, voice pattern, retina pattern, iris pattern, signature dynamics, keystroke pattern and the like of the authorized user. The data acquisition generally happens through digital / video camera, scanner, etc. The data acquisition process is repeated minimum 3 to 5 times except retina pattern that profiles blood vessels accurately in one attempt. The average of captured information is digitally coded and saved as a template that consumes memory varying from 9 bytes (hand geometry) to 10000 bytes (voice pattern). The storage space required for enrolment template depends on whether entire attribute or specific characteristics of an attribute are captured. The procedure is generally completed within 2 minutes. Every enrolment procedure requires keying in of personal identification number (PIN) which the user has to key in for his authentication later.

b) **Identification or Verification Stage:** User keys in PIN or swipes a card or attaches a token containing his PIN for identification and the places his finger / hand / eye / other physical attribute at the directed place or speaks into handset sensors. The PIN helps the system in verifying the template of the user from the database of stored templates of various users and thereafter it matches the stored template of the user directly with his live attribute template. This process is known as one-to-one matching process. This is also called dual factor authentication / verification.

But, when user is subjected to single factor authentication using biometrics, that is he does not have a PIN or smart card or token for his identification, the system tries to match the live attribute template with entire database of stored templates. This process is called one-to-many matching or identification process. The time taken by the system in the process of identifying or verifying a user is called system response time or transaction time. It generally ranges from about 2.5 to 14 seconds. The system response time is longer in case of voice pattern verification as some devices make the user speak as many as 10 words to properly assess air pressure. Signature verification takes longer since a user may take a little longer to sign.

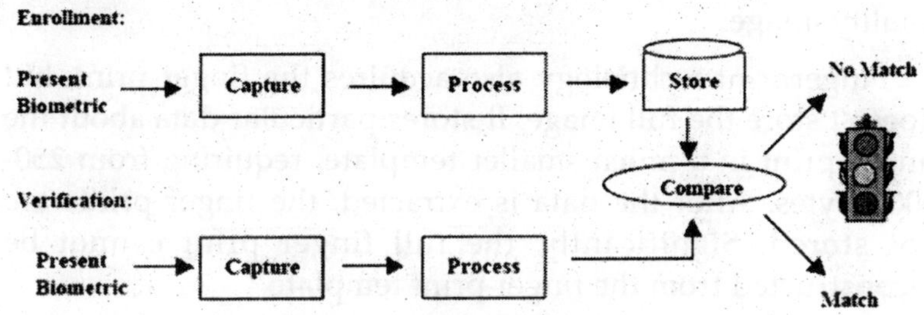

WHY BIOMETRICS?

Biometrics is an automated positive identification methodology as physical attribute of a person can not be lost like any other identification device like physical keys, passwords, token, smart cards, PIN, photo ID cards, etc. Besides, biometric does away the need of remembering several passwords, PINs, etc. It has proved a robust way of identifying especially rural/illiterate populace. The commercially available devices are generally user-friendly, with minimal and acceptable level of errors, cost effective and therefore reliable methods of authentication. Biometric technology is effective in preventing bank frauds, identity thefts, misappropriation of funds in banking sector, cooperatives, government sector. The technology can also make malice of election rigging a thing of past.

Biometric vs. Non-Biometric Finger Printing

The aura of criminality that accompanies the term "finger print" has not significantly impeded the acceptance of finger print technology, because the two authentication methods are very different. Fingerprinting, as the name suggests, is the acquisition and storage of the image of the finger print. Finger printing was for decades the common ink-and-roll procedure, used when booking suspects or conducting criminal investigations. More advanced optical or non-contact finger printing systems (known as live-scan), which normally utilize prints from several fingers, are currently the standard for forensic usage. They require 250 kb per finger for a high-quality image.

Fingerprint technology also acquires the finger print, but doesn't store the full image. It stores particular data about the finger print in a much smaller template, requiring from 250-1000 bytes. After the data is extracted, the finger prints are not stored. Significantly, the full finger print cannot be reconstructed from the finger print template.

Fingerprints are used in forensic applications: large-scale, one-to-many searches on databases of up to millions of finger prints. These searches can be done within only a few hours, a tribute to the computational power of AFIS. AFIS (Automated Fingerprint Identification Systems) - commonly referred to as "AFIS Systems" (a redundancy) - is a term applied to large-scale, one-to-many searches. Although finger print technology can be used in AFIS on 100,000 person databases, it is much more frequently used for one-to-one verification within 1-3 seconds.

Many people think of forensic finger printing as an ink and paper process. While this may still be done in some locations, most jurisdictions utilize optical scanners known as live scan systems. There are some fundamental differences between these forensic finger printing systems (used in AFIS systems) and the biometric finger print systems used to logon to a PC.

When the differences between the two technologies are explained, nearly all users are comfortable with finger print technology. The key is the template - what is stored is not a full finger print, but a small amount of data derived from the finger print's unique patterns.

Response time-AFIS systems may take hours to match a candidate, while finger print systems respond with seconds or fractions of seconds.

Cost-An AFIS capture device can range from several hundred to tens of thousands of dollars, depending on whether it is designed to capture one or multiple finger prints. A PC peripheral finger print device generally costs less than $200)

Accuracy-An AFIS system might return the top 5 candidates in a biometric comparison with the intent of locating or questioning the top suspects. Fingerprint systems are designed to return a single yes/no answer based on a single comparison.

Scale-An AFIS systems are designed to be scalable to thousands and millions of users, conducting constant 1:N searches. Fingerprint systems are almost invariably 1:1, and do not require significant processing power.

Capture-An AFIS systems are designed to use the entire finger print, rolled from nail to nail, and often capture all ten finger prints. Fingerprint systems use only the center of the finger print, capturing only a small fraction of the overall finger print data.

Storage-An AFIS systems generally store finger print images for expert comparison once a possible match has been located. Fingerprint systems, by and large, do not store images, as they are not used for comparison.

Infrastructure – An AFIS systems normally require a backend infrastructure for storage, matching, and duplicate resolution. These systems can cost hundreds of thousands of dollars. Fingerprint systems rely on a PC or a peripheral device for processing and storage.

TYPES OF BIOMETRIC DEVICES

Various types of biometric devices currently in vogue include finger print recognition, iris and retina pattern, face recognition, voice recognition, keystroke pattern, hand topography and geometry, and signature recognition. A comparison of important features of some of these devices is tabulated below:

Features	Retina Pattern	Face Reco-gnition	Fingerp rints	Signa-tures	Hand Topo-graphy & Geomet ry	Voice Recog-nition	Iris Pattern
Functioning	Captures & com-pares blood-vessel pattern inside the eyeball	Captures & com-pares facial pattern	Captures & com-pares ridges, whorls, lines, bifurcati ons, intersec-tions on finger	Captures & com-pares signature pattern, speed, direc-tion, pressure varia-tion, pen-in-air & timing	Measure s & com-pares dimen-sions of hand, fingers and side view of hand against a flat surface	Captures & com-pares throat & mouth anato-my, voice pitch & speech style	Captures & com-pares pattern of colored portion of eye around pupil
Device used	Camera	Camera	Reader plate	Sensors in Signa-ture instru-ment	Camera	Similar to standard tele-phone	CCD video camera
Enrollment Duration	< 2 minutes	<3 minutes	< 2 minutes	< 2 minutes	< 2 minutes	< 2 minutes	<2 minutes
Storage space required	96 bytes	-	500-1500 bytes	1000-1500 bytes	9 bytes	1000-10000 bytes	256 bytes
System Response Time	4-7 seconds	10 seconds	5-7 seconds	5-10 seconds	3-5 seconds	10-14 seconds	2.5-4 seconds
FRR	-	3.3%-70%	9.4%	-	<0.1%	-	0%
FAR	0%	0.3%-5%	0%-8%	-	<0.1%	-	0%
CER	1.5%	-	5%	-	0.2-2.2%	10%	<0.5%

User Acceptability Issues	Fear of eye damage, transfer of eye fluids & disease privacy issues	Privacy misuse	Hygiene concerns	Legally acceptable	Hygiene concerns	-	Fear of eye damage, privacy issues
Performance Issues	Poor eyesight, glare or reflections	Lighting, face orientation & sunglasses	Dirty, dry, worn, swelling, burns	Ned for tiny super accurate sensors; sensors do not generally withstand rough handling	Accuracy deteriorates with thousands of stored templates	Environmental noises, stress, respiratory, throat & mouth diseases	Poor eyesight, glare or reflections
Demonstrated Vulnerability	Retina pattern changes due to diabetes & heart attacks	Notebook computer with digital photographs	Artificial fingers, reactivated latent prints	Signatures change over time	None	-	High-resolution picture of iris
Variability with age	Affected by disease	Affected by aging	Stable	-	Stable	-	Stable

Commercial availability since	-	1990s	1970s	-	1970s	-	1997t>

CHOOSING A BIOMETRIC DEVICE

Choice of biometric device would depend on the physical attribute used by the device for authentication. To derive optimum results, the physical attribute must possess the following characteristics:

i) **Uniqueness:** The attribute should not be same for two persons. It is generally difficult to differentiate some physical attributes of identical twins. While a combination of hand topography and hand geometry ensures compliance with uniqueness principle, but each of these individually do not. Fingerprint should capture finer details like whorls, ridges and bifurcation pattern to accurately identify a person. Besides, system should not accept a pseudo finger or a photo image. A biometric verification system with infrared device to sense the pulse in the body minimizes acceptance of such malicious users.

ii) **Universality**: Each person should have the selected physical attribute. The system should have alternatives for authenticating say mute user if voice recognition is the selected attribute or fingerless user if finger print is the attribute of authentication.

iii) **Permanence:** The attribute should not change with passage of time. Voice, keystroke pattern, face, and signature change with time and necessitate periodical enrolment of the attribute. However, iris pattern does not vary in more than 1 year old persons.

iv) **Performance:** The attribute shall accurately authenticate the persons by minimizing aggregate of type I and II errors.

v) **Collectibility:** The process of collecting the attribute should be simple and time spent in enrolling a user should be minimal.

vi) **Acceptability:** The user should be willing to accept collection of attribute for authentication. Generally, users would oppose intrusive methods like DNA sampling. Users also resist collection of their iris / retina pattern for intrusive nature of sample collection.

vii) **Circumvention:** The attribute should not be reproducible.

ENCYRPTION AND BIOMETRICS

Encryption is a mathematical process that helps to disguise the information contained in messages that is either transmitted or stored in a database. There are three main factors that determine the security of any crypto system; the complexity of the mathematical process or algorithm, the length of the encryption key used to disguise the message and safe storage of the key known as key management.

The complexity of the algorithm is important because it directly correlates to how easy the process is to reverse engineer. One would think that this is the area of encryption that is the easiest to break, however most crypto systems are extremely well constructed and these are the least of the three factors that are vulnerable to attack. The length of the encryption key used to disguise the message is the next important part of the encryption process. The shorter the encryption key length, more vulnerable is the data to a "brute force" attack. This term refers to an individual trying to improperly access data by trying all combinations of possible passwords that would allow access to the account. For example, a key that is three characters long would be much more prone to attack than one that is ten characters long because the numbers of possible permutations that must be run to find the right key are much higher in the key that contains ten characters. Biometric encryption makes standard character encryption obsolete by replacing or supplementing the normal key characters with a personal identifier of the user for which there can only be one perfect match. Without this biometric key the information is inaccessible. Safe storage of the key is the most vulnerable area in the encryption process. What would seem to be the easiest to manage becomes the most difficult because passwords or PINs can be lost or stolen. Good encryption keys are much too long for normal individuals to remember easily so they are usually stored on paper, smart cards, or diskettes, which may make them accessible to unauthorized users. Biometric encryption systems allow the user to transport the access key around without making them vulnerable to loss or theft.

There are two broad categories of encryption systems; single key/double key (symmetric) systems and two key (asymmetric) systems. Symmetric systems utilize similar keys for both the sender and receiver for the purpose of coding and decoding data. In 1972, IBM developed DES (Data Encryption Standard) which was adopted worldwide by 1977 as the most common single key system in the banking and financial sectors. The process of transmitting this type of key over such networks as the Internet is one of the major failures of symmetric encryption. Electronic commerce requires that transactions be conducted over open networks instead of dedicated networks and symmetric key systems do not offer a high level of security for such transmissions. This is why public key systems have been developed. These two key systems use a public key to encrypt the data and a private key to decrypt the data. The asymmetric key system allows better encryption than symmetric key systems, however certification of the recipient of messages becomes an issue, which causes a hierarchy of certification to be developed resulting in a much slower processing time. Biometrics can aid in this process due to the inherent nature of using a physical trait of the desired recipient to decipher the message. It is this issue that has caused biometric techniques to be valued for electronic commerce.

DISADVANTAGES OF PIN

The self-service financial market is poised to grow manifold, both in India and the world over. Customers, by and large, are seeking increased mobility and deeper levels of services with no geographical boundaries. Anytime service is the keyword now.

ATMs have come a long way in the past thirty years. The basic functioning of the ATM system has changed very little. It always served two primary functions, a) that of establishing the identity of the user and b) that of providing the transaction services requested by the user.

Establishing the identity of the user has changed in several subtle ways initially and quite dramatically in recent times. The entire focus of establishing the identity of a person traditionally was primarily on "what you know" and partially on "what you have" and not on "what you are". The "what you know" is in the form of a personal identification number (PIN) and the "what you have" is in the form of a card or token a user carries with him/her. There are several challenges the use of the above encounters.

PIN authentication relies heavily on your PIN not being shared, unintentionally. The underlying technology used for the above is encryption technology. There is complex hardware and software working full-time in the background that generates and manages the keys required for encryption. Convoluted protocols ensure that relevant clear text is never exposed. With brute force and eavesdropping attacks becoming common, key management takes an all-new meaning. Many schemes require keys to be changed on a daily basis to stay ahead of attackers.

There have been several instances where PINs have been compromised. Users find it quite burdensome to remember the PIN. Many times the PIN is written on the back of the card that is used or the PIN is based on an event like a birthday or else the PIN is associated with the license plate of the vehicle one drives. Hence the loss of a wallet or purse can get the PIN disclosed and misused. There have been several instances where other innovative approaches have been employed to get the PIN information. Telescopes have been used to monitor the key presses on a PIN pad and even in a famous case, an out of order ATM was purposely installed at a location that collected PIN information associated with card data with a message eventually getting displayed on the ATM screen that the machine was out of cash. The so collected information was then used to withdraw money from accounts whose information had become so available.

The reliance on self-service financial terminals i.e. ATMs is increasing at a phenomenal rate. Banks across the globe have realized, mainly due to intense competition, that more and more ATMs need to be deployed for extending the business reach of the bank or for freeing-up existing employees for more value adding work or as realized in some cases, to bring more transparency to the banking process.

Fingerprint Software / Systems

Axis has a complete suite of finger print processing algorithms, which is integrated into identification system package. The software suite performs the following tasks :

Image Processing

Captured finger print images are processed through a series of image processing algorithms to obtain a clear unambiguous skeletal image of the original gray tone impression, clarifying smudged areas, removing extraneous artifacts and healing most scars, cuts and breaks.

Feature Detection for Matching

Ridge ends and bifurcations (minutiae) within the skeletal image are identified and encoded, providing critical placement, orientation and linkage information for the matcher.

WHO IS USING BIOMETRTICS AND HOW?

DIEBOLD

- In 1996, Diebold introduced the world's first live installation of biometrics on an ATM in South Africa utilizing finger print verification.
- In 1997, Diebold displayed the world's first ATM featuring facial and voice recognition to identify customers.
- In 1999, Diebold demonstrated an automated teller machine (ATM) that recognizes a customer's identity by their iris, without the need of a card or personal identification number (PIN).

Bank of America.

In Jan 1999, Bank of America rolled out a new pilot programme that uses finger print recognition to give individuals access to their online banking services. Bette Wasserman, Vice President and Manager of smart card product development for Bank of America, said the company believes that biometric technology will play an increasingly important role in security and authentication for financial services.

BANK UNITED

Bank United introduced Iris scan technology in some of their ATM's last year.

CHASE, CITIBANK AND VISA recently completed their evaluation of Biometric technologies and prepared plans to implement biometrics in a big way. Citibank is testing eye-scanning technology on some 500 employees at its development test centre. If the public accepts it and deployment makes business sense, eye scans could be incorporated into ATMs.

ING Direct-BACOB Bank

- ING Direct is providing finger-scan biometric authentication for online banking customers.
- BACOB Bank in Belgium is piloting voice verification for customer account access.

Western bank of Puerto Rico is using biometric technology to secure access to confidential information. The project includes new branch systems, integrated call center and a full virtual bank.

PRACTICAL APPLICATION OF BIOMETRICS

ICICI Bank was the first bank in India to launch biometric ATM in Andhra Pradesh (Guntur District) on pilot basis in May 2005. The bank has also entered into agreements with internet kiosks for online banking that employ biometrics for authentication. Bank of India and UTI Bank have announced their plan to install biometric ATMs employing finger print technology.

To encourage banking habits in rural illiterates, Jalagaon Peoples Cooperative bank has many ATMs embedded with finger print biometric technology. The cooperative bank has installed an indigenous biometric enabled ATM machine developed by Axis Software, Pune. The major problem in implementing biometrics in rural areas is irregular landline connectivity. ICICI Bank is employing alternative method of off-line chip embedded identification cards containing depositors thumb impression.

An iris recognition device proved robust in distributing relief to war-affected people in Afghanistan. Fujitsu has invented a contact-less palm vein authentication technology in 2005. Palm veins of a person in left hand differ from that in right hand and of course even in identical twins. The FAR of the device is < 0.00008% while FRR is just 0.01%. Bank of Tokyo Mitsubishi has installed palm vein scanner enabled ATMs in Japan. The company is also exploring the feasibility of inserting palm vein scanners in mobile phones.

The use of biometrics is expected to get a boost in India after gazette notification of Credit Information Companies (rules & Regulations). In terms of Credit Information Companies (Regulation) Act, 2005, access to credit information would be restricted to the specified users after they ink a written agreement with these companies. RBI issued draft rules and regulations under the Act in April 2006. The draft rules interalia make it obligatory on part of these companies to secure their database by using biometric access controls besides other physical & logical barriers (Draft Rule 30(2) (iii)).

Voice biometrics debuts in automated phone banking

United States–RSA Security, the security division of information management solutions provider EMC Corp., has introduced a new voice authentication product designed mainly for banks and other financial institutions. The Adaptive Authentication for Phone (AAP), which includes voice biometrics, was developed to provide a more effective automated telephone banking service and to prevent telephone banking fraud.

The AAP combines a voice biometric solution previously acquired by RSA and a voiceprint engine from speech recognition specialist, Nuance Communications. The integration of voice biometrics in automated telephone banking system is a first in the industry.

The product enables an additional layer of security for transactions that are identified as high-risk. AAP comes up with a risk score–via the voice print and other parameters such as phone number and user behaviour profile–to identify the low-risk and high-risk transactions. Transactions that generate a high-risk score are further verified, for instance, through secret questions.

AAP is set to be used in several banks in the United States and other locations in Q1 2007.

Citibank opens biometric ATMs

2006-12-02 08:23:20 Source: Moneycontrol.com

The bank has so far installed two ATMs, one each in Mumbai and Hyderabad. In the past two months, the Citibank 'Pragati' has won 700 customers and hopes to log in 50,000 customers in the next 12 months, said Ms Mona Kachhwaha, Business Manager, Microfinance, and Citibank.

Biometric ATMs have multiple language capabilities and have voice-enabled navigation facility aimed at illiterate customers.

The colour-coded buttons (yellow for deposit, green for withdrawal) guide customers through the transaction - balance enquiry, deposits and withdrawals. Citibank has tied up with MFIs such as Basix in Hyderabad and Swadhaar Finaccess in Mumbai. The ATMs are located at the offices of the MFIs or in areas where customers live or work.

Mr Jayakumar said Citibank was not looking for profits in the initial years. "For the scheme to sustain, it would have to grow in terms of scale," he said. The bank will eventually merge its no-frills accounts with the `Pragati' scheme, Mr Jayakumar said. Currently Citibank has 60,000 customers in the micro-finance segment.

EMERGING STANDARDS

IT professionals insist upon standards, multiple sources of supply and endorsement by industry leaders. It's beginning to happen, but to think that a small biometrics company can set an industry standard is ludicrous. Yet many have tried.

Any CIO or MIS manager would not bet his job or company on a proprietary solution from a small biometrics company. These people want choice and standards to provide multiple sources of supply and fair competition among vendors. The one exception to this rule is when there has been a major catastrophe, such as a significant loss of money. However, it is tough to build a sustainable business chasing disasters.

Standards need to be set by the IT industry leaders such as Intel, Microsoft, Phoenix Technologies and the top 10 computer companies. In the last year, many of these large organizations have banded together to begin the process of standardization. This is the first sign of an industry maturing.

Cost - Just as in the early days of desktop computers when a system cost more than $10,000, only a few people had systems. Now when they cost less than $1,000, everybody has one. This same "order of magnitude" cost breakthrough has recently occurred with finger print technology. What cost $1,000 two years ago is now available for less than $100. Cost alone is not the answer, but it is a necessary component of broad market acceptance of this technology.

Expected Growth

As organizations search for more secure authentication methods for user access, E-commerce, and other security applications, biometrics is gaining increasing attention. The ballooning growth in electronic transactions has resulted in greater demands for fast and accurate user identification and authentication methods. Biometric technology is now being deployed as a means of tightening security and simplifying user access in a landscape once guarded only by expensive firewalls and easily crackable passwords, subject to configuration issues, human error, and malice.

For years, the only users of biometrics were a few government and military agencies, law enforcement finger printing, and an occasional James Bond movie. For the most part, however, business and industry ignored the field and its futuristic technology because it was too obscure, too esoteric, or too expensive. All this appears to be changing. The prices of biometric products and systems are falling as demand for the technology grows and more vendors enter the market. Fraud, security breaches, and human administrative error are driving the rapid expansion of biometric technology.

Total biometric revenues, are expected to grow rapidly through 2005. Much of the growth will be attributable to PC/ Network Access and E-commerce, although large-scale public sector deployments will continue to be an essential part of the industry.

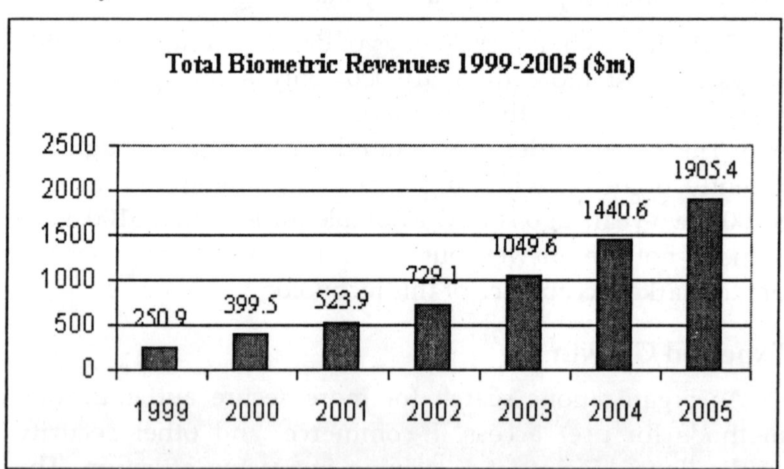

By 2004, total Emerging Sector revenue (PC/Network Access, E-commerce and Telephony, Physical Access, and Surveillance) surpassed Mature Sector revenue (Criminal Identification and Citizen Identification).

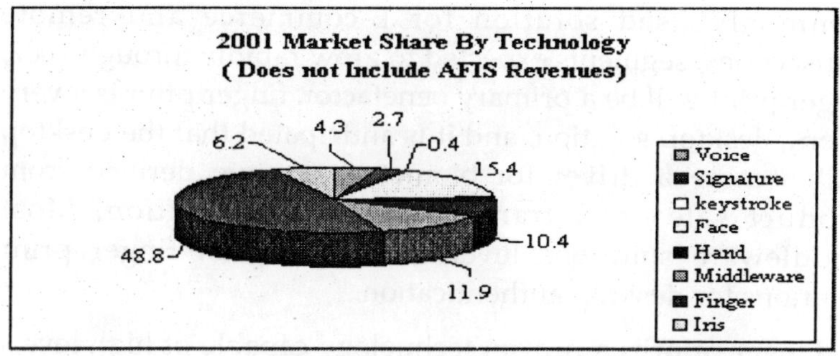

2001 estimates show that finger-scan continues to be the leading biometric technology in terms of market share, commanding nearly 50% of non-AFIS biometric revenue. Facial-scan, with 15.4% of the non-AFIS market, surpasses hand-scan, which had been second to finger-scan in terms of revenue generation.

Highlights

- Biometric revenues are expected to grow from $399.4 million in 2000 and $523.9 million in 2001 to $1.9 billion in 2006
- Large-scale public sector biometric usage, currently 70% of the biometric market, will be surpassed by private sector deployments
- Biometrics sales for PC/network access will reach $423 million in 2005
- Finger-scan and biometric middleware will emerge as two critical technologies for the desktop, together comprising approximately 40% of the biometric market by 2005
- The two industry verticals that will adopt biometrics most rapidly are financial services and health care, with revenues increasing at average annual rate of 72% and 56% respectively.

Finger Print Growth Drivers and Enablers

A number of basic factors should combine to help drive finger print revenues. If and when biometrics become a commonly used solution for E-commerce and remote transactions, segments expected to grow rapidly through 2007, finger print will be a primary benefactor. finger print is a very strong desktop solution, and it is anticipated that the desktop will become a driver for biometric revenue derived from product sales and transactional authentication. Most middleware solutions leverage a variety of finger print solutions for desktop authentication.

Finger print is a proven technology capable of high levels of accuracy. The finger print has long been recognized as a highly distinctive identifier, and classification, analysis, and study of finger prints has existed for decades. The combination of an innately distinctive feature with a long history of use as identification sets finger print apart in the biometric industry. There are physiological characteristics more distinctive than the finger print (the iris and retina, for example), but technology capable of leveraging these characteristics has only been developed over the past few years, not decades.

Strong finger print solutions are capable of processing thousands of users without allowing a false match, and can verify nearly 100% of users with one or two placements of a finger. Because of this, many finger print technologies can be deployed in applications where either security or convenience is the primary driver. Reduced size and power requirements, along with finger print's resistance to environmental changes such as background lighting and temperature, allow the technology to be deployed in a range of logical and physical access environments.

ASAT (Axis Semi Automated Transaction)

ASAT is a biometric based semi automated transaction system for Banks, Financial Institutes, Government organizations and Corporate. ASAT allows banks to automate branch operations without investing in huge electronic network infrastructure like ATMs. ASAT consists of a biometric authentication terminal installed outside the teller counter.

Customers enter account number and verify biometric to withdraw money instead of going through the manual process of filling withdrawal slips, signature verification and repetitive cash counting by the teller.

Features

- Single device providing options of biometric authentication tools like Iris, finger print and face.
- Multiple units can be serviced by the same teller
- Can be fully automated by integration with cash dispensing machine
- Paperless transactions
- Optional Printer attached provides facility of written proof of transaction
- User friendly, full graphical illuminated LCD Display with audio output
- Tactile alpha-numeric keypad
- Video output for CCTV monitoring
- Intelligent audio, visual & silent alerts
- Built in data encryption for secure data transfer across the network
- Easy Updates by software downloads (through Ethernet or parallel port)
- Unlimited users can be enrolled
- Highly robust, fault tolerant and secure

Applications

- Banks
- Credit Societies
- Government Organizations
- Large Corporate

Benefits

- Customer convenience
- Increased efficiency
- Low costs (Cost effective as compared to all other options like Manual or ATM systems)
- Short transaction time
- No queues
- No need to fill withdrawal slips
- High security (human error in signature verification eliminated)
- Works under supervised environment
- Portable
- Compact

ACC (Automated Cheque Clearance)

Axis provides an innovative patent pending product that offers a secured, efficient platform for corporate banking. The current cheque clearance authentication process is manual, time consuming and prone to human errors. It is also very tedious as it involves checking authentication directives (Business Logic) and matching signatures on the cheque with that in the database in order to grant clearance. Axis Automated Cheque Clearance (ACC) adds another layer to signature authentication with an annotation, which is coupled with biometric authentication. In ACC an annotation is printed on the cheque, which stores confidential information such as signatory details, cheque information and finger prints of the signatories. When a cheque comes in for clearance the Axis System with the banker just scans the annotation and matches the data with that in the database and authentication is done. At the same time other authorizations are also ascertained like whether signatories are authorized to sign, whether the amount they are authorized to sign is not exceeded, etc.

Features

- Uses advanced technology to store data on the cheque/ instrument
- Controls entire cheque signing process at client end
- Annotation is tamperproof; cannot be transferred i.e. is married to the cheque/ instrument and data is stored in an encrypted form
- The annotation fits very well on cheque having 1"X 3" size
- All the information such as signatory details, finger print of signatories and cheque details are stored in the Annotation
- Fast and accurate automated reading and confirmation of cheque information at banks end
- Complex business logic can be applied instantaneously
- Biometric authentication required to print the annotation onto the cheque/ instrument
- The signature of the signatories remains on the cheque/ instrument as per legal requirement.

Deployment

- It is quickly and easily deployed with no end user downtime
- Supports all major platforms (Windows, Unix, Novell)
- Solution is software intensive, no special H/W required.

Benefits

- Since all the data pertaining to the cheque is stored on the cheque itself it becomes very convenient
- It is very secure as finger print of the signatories is used for authentication instead of signature, hence there is no question of forging of signature

- Errors due to manual authentication process eliminated thus reducing frauds
- Time required for cheque clearance process is much shortened thus increasing efficiency.

Applications

- Banks
- Financial Institutions
- Stock Exchanges

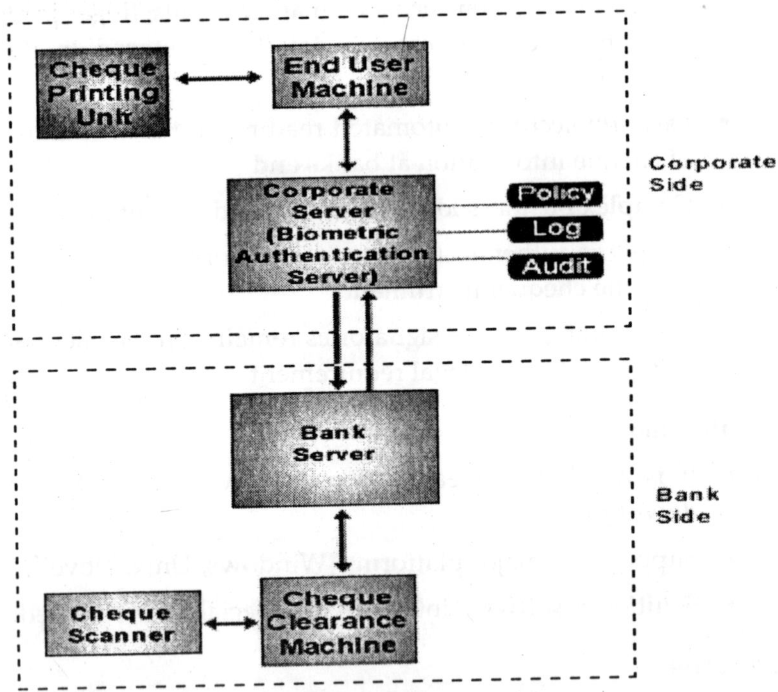

AUTHENTICATION KIOSKS

Goal

- Help to authenticate with biometric controls
- To authenticate pre-registered authorized entry

Advantage

- We understands the importance of addressing the authentication needs of customers to create a comprehensive, security-rich environment
- Authentication kiosks help to improve performance and data security, privacy protection for user biometric data & highest degree of accuracy. It has customizable modules to meet various requirements.

Benefits

Authentication kiosk is designed to provide:

- Enhance security
- Biometric security control with finger print scanning
- Online application and registration
- Qualification checks
- Background investigation
- Identification / Verification
- Biometric capture
- Checks against law enforcement watch lists
- Smart card issuance
- Smart card management service
- Smart card reader
- Membership database
- Authentication at access points
- Authentication with Barrier devices
- Video surveillance.

DEVICES USED IN BIOMETRIC TECHNOLOGY

1. Identix DFR Series

Axis provides the world's leading optical finger print recognition technology, products tools and platforms.

Consistently captures higher quality images for more accurate matching and faster processing. The Identix® DFR® Series single finger readers combine superior image capture and an easy-to-use design for more accurate matching performance and faster processing, making these readers the perfect choice for all types of large-scale finger print programmes - enrollment, verification and identification. Identifying hundreds or thousands of people on any given day requires a finger print reader that is not only durable and dependable, but one that consistently captures high quality images, time and time again. The DFR Series readers enable you to increase security, minimize identity fraud and help protect the assets of citizens and employees. DFR Series Single Fingerprint Readers are ideally suited for:

- Border crossings
- Payment processing
- Department of Motor Vehicle registration
- Social benefit distribution centers
- Employee registration
- Validating transactions at financial institutions

The DFR® Series Single Finger Readers are designed to perform in large-scale, heavy traffic environments.

2. Secugen

SecuGen® Hamster III is the next generation model of SecuGen's popular and versatile finger print reader product line. Packaged in a comfortable, ergonomic design, Hamster III features the industries most rugged and advanced optical sensor using patented SEIR finger print biometric technology. Use SecuGen Hamster III with your choice of compatible biometric software for authentication, identification and verification functions that let your finger prints act like digital passwords that cannot be lost, forgotten or stolen.

Features

SecuGen Hamster III

- USB connection
- Removable weighted stand
- Compact, lightweight and portable
- Integrated finger guide
- Readily accessible for any finger
- Driver CD included

Fingerprint Recognition Sensor

- High-performance, maintenance-free optical finger print sensor
- Resistance to scratches, impact, vibration and electrostatic shock
- Fast and accurate verification
- Latent print image removal (does not accept prints left behind)
- Encryption of finger print templates (cannot be used to reconstruct finger print images).

3. Scanner >> Digital persona

The U.are.U 4000B Reader is a USB finger print reader designed for use with Digital Persona, Inc.'s enterprise software applications and developer tools. The user simply places their finger on the glowing reader window, and the reader quickly and automatically scans the finger print. On-board electronics calibrate the reader and encrypt the scanned data before sending it over the USB interface. Digital Persona readers utilize optical finger print scanning technology to achieve excellent image quality, a large capture area and superior reliability. The U.are.U 4000B Reader and Digital Persona® Fingerprint Recognition Engine have an unmatched ability to authenticate even the most difficult finger prints accurately and rapidly regardless of placement angle. The U. are U 4000B Reader can be purchased with Digital Persona Pro Workstation, Digital Persona Pro Kiosk, Digital Persona Online or Digital Persona Integrator packages. Whether you are an enterprise customer or a system integrator, Digital Persona's finger print authentication solutions provide a natural extension to your security system and applications.

4. Cross Match >> L SCANT 100R

The new L SCAN 100R scanner is a robust and cost efficient solution for capturing both rolled and flat finger prints. There are many applications for this product including: visa application checking, border control, inmate handling and background checks.

Operating the L SCAN 100R is very easy and intuitive, just place the finger on the capture platen and with a click of a button the finger print can be scanned. Features include live image display while capturing, compact form factor, modern standard USB 2.0 PC interface, no moving parts, and solid reliability in daily use. The L SCAN 100R's plastic housing is stylish yet robust and lightweight for use in all environments.

LATEST DEVELOPMENTS IN BIOMETRICS

The main issue in identification and verification through biometric devices is user acceptability. Constant / periodic authentication of the user becomes necessary when the system stores sensitive / confidential information. The recent research has made camera based non-intrusive access systems a reality. A camera based access control system periodically authenticates the user by capturing his face / iris / retina pattern without interrupting his work. If the user does not look up during predefined time period of say 30 seconds, the system could clear the screen. The system restores the screen as and when the authorized user is verified.

Vein scan is another device that captures blood vessel pattern and is currently available for commercial use. Some other technologies in R & D stage include blood pulse measurement, skin pattern recognition, gait recognition, nail bed identification, odor sensing, ear shape recognition and DNA matching. The last three technologies are in preliminary stage of development and it may take several years before these become a reality.

DEMERITS OF BIOMETRIC TECHNOLOGY

Biometric device performance

The accuracy of biometrics identification method depends on rate of false rejection of authorised and enrolled users, also called False Rejection Rate (FRR) and the rate of false acceptance of unauthorized users, also termed as False Acceptance Rate (FAR). While FRR is known as type I error, FAR is called Type II error. FRR can be attributed to system capturing unverifiable data due to incorrect positioning of organ, interference with voice recording, unstable desk for signatures, etc. High FRR/ Type I error could lead to shifting of customer loyalty and thus entail loss of income and/ or resources of a bank. Besides, it impacts the processing and verification speed of the biometric device. This speed is also called throughput rate or system response time or transaction time. Type II error / FAR is the most significant error and makes the system highly vulnerable as it permits access to unauthorized users. Poor enrolment procedure, prescribing low level of similarity for matching attribute with live template, ongoing averaging of live attribute and stored template and system manipulation could cause false acceptance of unauthorized user. The major task of an information security officer is to choose a device that minimizes errors.

The lower the sensitivity of the attribute captured by the biometric devices, the lower is the FRR while higher the sensitivity, higher is the FRR, i.e. an upward rising curve. But, there is an inverse relationship between sensitivity and FAR. In other words, FAR has a negative relationship with sensitivity.

The point at which FRR & FAR curves meet is called the cross over error rate (CER) or equal error rate that ensures optimum performance of identification and authorization system / device. The lower the CER, the higher is the accuracy of the biometric device. CER also helps in comparative analysis of different verification devices. An accurate system should effectively and efficiently isolate unauthorized persons and reject their entry to the system or at least minimize access of unauthorized persons to an acceptable level. The CER of various biometric devices ranges from 0.2% to 10%. Iris verification is found to be 100% error free biometric system or at the maximum CER is below 0.5%. Voice pattern produces maximum CER of 10% as voice changes over a period of time and requires periodical fresh enrolments to minimize error.

Issues in Biometric Verification

a) Change in physical attributes except iris pattern that hardly changes after 1 year age leads to higher level of errors. Similarly, behavioural attributes like voice, signature and keystrokes could vary with passage of time, medical condition and frequency of typing. The data / templates, therefore, need to be amended after each use. If template is an average of existing database and current input data, the higher variation could lead to higher error rates that would necessitate re-enrolment. However, periodic reenrollment reduces acceptability of device by users.

b) Device accuracy depends on its maintenance. Increase in number of users contributes to higher intermittent downtime for cleaning accumulated skin oil, dirt, sweat, etc. on sensor plates or in eye cups.

c) The accuracy rate falls with rise in database of hand geometry devices.

d) Voice device accuracy depends on level of background disturbances. Hence, performance of such devices in highly congested and busy areas declines.

e) Users fear that light may damage their eyes or even blind them during enrollment / verification process. Besides, retinal pattern devices capture changes in health conditions. This raises privacy issue, i.e. an entity using biometric device for authorization gets unauthorized access to user's medical condition.

f) The signature device contains tiny, super accurate sensors to capture or detect even marginal variation in signature direction, speed of writing instrument and pressure thereon. Hence, accuracy rate of signature device declines over time with rough use. Although signature and thumb impression are not very accurate and reliable for the purpose of access controls, these physical attributes have a long history of legal acceptance to authenticate legal papers and financial instruments.

g) User acceptability of biometric devices is comparatively low owing to their intrusive nature, health hazards and slow speed. Privacy violation is another issue especially in continuous recording of physical or behavioural attributes like keystroke pattern, facial recognition, etc.

h) Injuries, burns, diseases, rings, nail polish, stress level, etc. also affect the performance of a biometric device.

CONCLUSION

Biometrics technology is evolving very fast with rise in losses from increased number of security breaches. Uniqueness of physical attributes make biometric authentication foolproof. As per Fujitsu Services Survey reported on CNET News.com in May 2005, one third of the English banking customers are willing to adopt biometric technology to bring down financial losses. Implementation of biometric based devices has also commenced in India with ICICI Bank and Jalgaon Peoples Cooperative Bank taking the lead. The ongoing global research and development in this area is expected to find cost effective and user-friendly devices that would secure even mobile / telephone banking besides internet banking.

Reliable personal recognition is critical to many real world applications where security is of paramount interest. Since, the conventional knowledge or token based methods rely on the surrogate representation of a person's identity; it is quite obvious that a security system must involve a biometric component for recognition. However, there exist several challenges with the successful implementation of a biometric system for real world applications. Some of these challenges are handling noise present in the image, variation in deformation present in the image at different instance of image capture, and variation in features with time. Researchers are working on these challenges to design algorithms which can handle these variations. ■ ■ ■

4

SECURITY CHALLENGES IN E-BANKING–AGENDA FOR FUTURE

ABSTRACT

E-banking is the use of a computer to retrieve and process banking data and to initiate transactions directly with a bank via a telecommunications network (even the Internet). Electronic banking offers many advantages to the consumer and the business world. It provides a powerful and convenient way to strengthen existing customer's relationships and acquire new customers by allowing the user to get his account information, balances, wire transfers, loans and credit issues, and other value added services at any hour of the day and at any location in the world. It also offers the confidentiality that many people want.

Away from the traditional security issues of robberies and frauds some serious risks mar the present-day E-banking practices. These are operational or transactional risk, security risk, reputation risk, legal risk, money laundering risk and cross-border risk apart from the traditional risks of banking like credit risk, liquidity risk, etc. Banks should have a rigorous analytic risk management process to enable them to identify, measure, monitor, transfer and control their technology risk exposure. Security of the account numbers credit card numbers and passwords and different levels of service, uses of different software by banks and bearing the full cost of designing and managing its online system are the other critical issues among many that can be listed. For E-trust to work there needs to be a substantial technological and commercial infrastructure in place. This is best described in terms of a three-layered framework as follows: E-trust Services, Trusted Digital Identity Infrastructure and PKI Technology. The Reserve Bank of India had set up a 'Working Group on Internet banking' to examine different aspects of Internet banking. The group is focusing on three major areas of Internet banking i.e., (i) technology and security issues, (ii) legal issues and (iii) regulatory and supervisory issues. RBI has accepted the guidelines of the group that provide a good insight into the security requirements of Internet banking.

The paper discusses some of the issues related to E-banking and the underlying risk management principles that should be considered by banks that believe in strengths of information technology and giving a new dimension to contemporary banking.

INTRODUCTION

Electronic banking is the use of a computer to retrieve and process banking data and to initiate transactions directly with a bank via a telecommunications network (even the Internet). In other words, e-Banking of the wave of the future. It provides enormous benefits to consumers in terms of the ease and cost of transactions. But it also poses new challenges for country authorities in regulating and supervising the financial system and in designing and implementing macroeconomic policy.

E-banking is a hygiene product today and enhances customer value proposition. It is essential to get customers to use it because of delivery services electronically is much lower. Largely on the strength of these electronically channels, the banks cost of operations have increased only incrementally even as it grew its retail customer base by 50% a year over the past two years to 3,50,000 (According to COO, ABN Ambro Bank).

E-banking also makes it easier for customers to compare banks' services and products, can increase competition among banks, and allows banks to penetrate new markets and thus expand their geographical reach. The primary drivers of E-banking include improve cost access facilitate the offers of more services, increase customer loyalty, attract new customer, provide services offered by competitors, reduce customer activities, etc.

Advantages of Electronic E-banking

E-banking offers many advantages to the consumer and the business world. It includes:

Easy access

Allow you to be able to get your account information, balances, wire transfers, loans and credit issues, at any hour of the day and at any location in the world.

Offers the confidentiality that many people want. You never have to go to a bank again. All you have to do is sit by your computer and do whatever you need to do.

Enhances the banks image and it also increases customer loyalty.

Automated teller machine (ATM) and ATM machine, is one of the first offered electronic devices that allow you to withdraw money, and check on other account information.

One could basically pay bills, or retrieve account information from a phone in the mourning, from a PC in the afternoon or from a phone booth at the airport later that day.

In addition to above, successful E-banking solution offers:

- Exceptional rates on savings
- Checking with no monthly fee, free bill payment and rebates on ATM surcharges
- Credit cards with low rates
- Easy online applications for all accounts, including personal loans and mortgages
- Twenty four hour account access
- Quality customer service with personal attention

Disadvantages of E-banking

E-banking has is the security of your account numbers credit card numbers and passwords. However many companies are doing many things to end the online theft. The one major thing that they tell you to do is to change your password or passwords on a regular basis. They also stress keeping your pin number to yourself, and like passwords change them often. Unfortunately it is not all that simple. With electronic banking, people will be dealing with a lot of money over the computer where anyone can get access.

A second problem of online banking right now is that each bank offers different levels of service, uses different software, and has to bear the full cost of designing and managing its online system. Regardless, if you are making transactions or checking your account you should always feel the security you need. So every bank is doing what it can to allow you that privacy.

Idealistic Bank

Idealistic bank expectations to define the mature branch computerization need are:

Priority	*Ideal Banking*
Counter	Automation: Faster Service to on-hand customers
Perfect	Counter Transaction Handling: Controls integrated into the system
	Keep Up Daily Action Figures: Back office load taken care of by the system
	Inter Branch Exchange Of Data: Inter-branch transactions
	Total Computerization: Statistical information

Idealistic bank should provide the services. All counter departments like savings, current, cash credit and cash all linked. The voucher flow to be redesigned and not to merely replicate the manual system.

Back-office also linked to daily transactions demanding only the minimum of input at the end of the day.

Advances department with special modules to take care of each of the products of the Bank taking into the unique control and audit requirements of each.

Advances department to have special link to documentation requirements and their follow-up to ensure the documents are not time barred.

A proposal evaluation system to offer quicker answer to prospective borrowers instead of the world record of a quarter to answer a simple proposal requirement.

Inter branch transactions linked via a modem to reduce reconciliation to not more than a week.

Remittances of inter branch funds to take seconds instead of days.

Head Office statistical requirements to be served by the system directly also via a modem or preferably by a 'dial-in-query' by the head office.

The idealist view can be achieved provided the management has the will and the guidance to do so. Merely replacing the calculator by a computer does not mean computerization.

Driving forces to E-banking Emerging

According to IT analyst firm, by coming years, a large sophisticated and highly competitive E-banking market will develop will be driven by:

- Demand side pressure due to increasing access to low cost electronic services.
- Growing customer awareness and need of transparency.
- Global players in the fray.
- Close Integration of bank with web based E-commerce or even disintegration of services through direct electronic payment.

- More convenient international transaction due to fact that Internet along with general deregulation trends eliminates geographic boundaries.

Elements of an Internet Banking System

The main elements of an Internet banking system are:

Hardware: the servers, storage devices, communication channels and links, gateways and remotely located devices.

Software: the operating systems, database management systems, E-banking applications and security application programmes.

Data: the content of the databases containing customer and account information.

Personnel: clerical staff, administrative staff and computer operations staff.

ISSUES RELATED TO E-BANKING

Authentication of E-banking Customers

Authentication of Transaction by the customer is a key risk area from an operational perspective. As a precautionary measure, some banks have installed a multi-level process, whereby customers can perform E-banking transactions only if they are valid account holders, and then by using a combination of a unique Customer ID, and a unique randomly generated password known only to the customer, which he can change to his/her convenience. Further, customers can only do financial transactions between accounts where they already possess normal operational rights.

Besides technology itself, there are at least three areas of requirements that must be considered when choosing a customer authentication system for E-banking:

1. **Legislation**: In a large number of countries, there are specialized and sometimes very strict legal regulations for the financial services industry and its software applications. In many of these countries, an application that is not compliant with legal regulations can either not be used at all or only as an interim solution.

2. **Internal regulations and guidelines**: There will be internal bank regulations and guidelines. Consequently, an internal auditing function is able to create a lot of pain and work for a bank's IT department with application systems that are not fully compliant with internal and legal regulations.
3. **Customer perception**: Internet banking solutions are not based on such proprietary combinations of software and network. The (potential) customers have much more knowledge and opinion about software solutions than in the past, based on press activity in this area, both in the way of awareness raising and panic mongering. For customer perception, authentication within Internet applications in general is a very critical architecture and design element because it can cause or dispel doubts with respect to, for example, the safety of personal data and to data protection.

The Reserve Bank of India had also set up a 'Working Group on Internet Banking' to examine different aspects of Internet Banking. The group focused on three major areas of Internet banking i.e., Technology and security issues, Legal issues and Regulatory and supervisory issues.

RBI has accepted the guidelines of the group and they provide a good insight into the security requirements of Internet banking.

E-banking, apart from opportunities, also brings with it new risk control challenges. Some of these risks are operational or transactional risk, security risk, reputation risk, legal risk, money laundering risk and cross-border risk apart from the traditional risks of banking like credit risk, liquidity risk, etc. Although security is not a new problem facing banks, Internet transactions provide new different security concerns, away from the traditional security issues of robberies and frauds. Banks should have a rigorous analytic risk management process to enable them to identify, measure, monitor, transfer and control their technology risk exposure.

E-banking include operational and internal control measures as given below (they vary from bank to bank)

Access to Internet banking provided only based on application and valid customer ID.

Password - issued to customers only on specific request.

The password generated using an internationally validated algorithm.

Access to customer information - given based on a combination of a unique Customer ID and password. (Account Holder).

Financial transactions such as Fund Transfer, Demand Draft request, Bankers Cheque request - allowed only to account holders individually authorized to operate the accounts, and not to Authorized Signatories / Mandate holders or even Jointly operated accounts.

All correspondence on account of transactions originating from E-banking is sent to the customer's address registered with the Bank and not to any third party address.

Customer instructions regarding address change, account closure, Nomination, etc. are not accepted through E-banking.

Customer logins and activities are tracked and the same are available for future investigation.

There are limits on the monetary transactions that customers are allowed to do on Internet Banking.

Secure connection: When consumers are accessing the online information, their connection is automatically converted into a secure Internet communications session.

Data encryption: When consumers access their account information or any other sensitive data, an encryption system is automatically activated to protect the transmission of information from unauthorized sources.

Despite of the efforts, the relative infancy of the Internet as a broad-based communication medium when combined with the "open" nature of the Internet make it impossible to guarantee absolute confidentiality in all circumstances. A Bank should monitor and review the security procedures that it has in place to protect customer information. These measures are updated as practices change and new technology becomes available.

Cross – Border E-banking

According to recommendations made by the Basel Committee of Banking Supervision (BCBS) through the Bank for International Settlement (BIS), In case of home country institutions providing banking services to customers outside the country, the home country supervisor should be responsible for oversight of the banking organization on a consolidated basis. The host supervisor's oversight is limited to the bank's activities conducted in the local market. The BCBS also recommends that the home country supervisor should provide host supervisors with information on how they oversee the activities.

Providers outside banks increasingly provide and operate E-banking technology. The reliance on these providers not only adds another dimension of risk that needs to be considered by banks and supervisors, but can also necessitate further cross-border cooperation among supervisors if these providers are located outside home country.

Risk Management in E-banking

The Basel Committee on banking supervision formed a working group, the Electronic Banking Group (EBG), to work in the area of E-banking risk management. The EBG's report on risk management and supervisory issues arising from E-banking developments was released in May 2001. The E-banking risk management principles identified are broadly fall into three categories: Board and Management Oversight; Security Controls and Legal and Reputation Risk Management. The report inventoried and assessed the major risks associated with E-banking, namely strategic risk, operational risk, reputation risk, and credit, market and liquidity risks. The group also noted that strategic risk; operational risk and reputation risk are certainly heightened by the rapid introduction and underlying technological complexity of E-banking activities.

Principles

The Basel Committee on Banking Supervision expects such risks to be recognized, addressed and managed by banking institutions in a prudent manner according to the fundamental characteristics and challenges of E-banking services. These characteristics include the unprecedented speed of change related to technological and customer service innovation, the ubiquitous and global nature of open electronic networks, the integration of E-banking applications with legacy computer systems and the increasing dependence of banks on third parties that provide the necessary information technology.

Based on these conclusions, the Committee considers that while existing risk management principles remain applicable to E-banking activities, such principles must be tailored, adapted and, in some cases, expanded to address the specific risk management challenges created by the characteristics of E-banking activities.

The Risk Management Principles fall into three broad, and often overlapping, categories of issues that are grouped to provide clarity: Board and Management Oversight; Security Controls; and Legal and Reputation Risk Management.

Board and Management Oversight

Because the Board of Directors and senior management are responsible for developing the institution's business strategy and establishing an effective management oversight over risks, they are expected to take an explicit, informed and documented strategic decision as to whether and how the bank is to provide E-banking services. The initial decision should include the specific accountabilities, policies and controls to address risks, including those arising in a cross-border context. Effective management oversight is expected to encompass the review and approval of the key aspects of the bank's security control process, such as the development and maintenance of a security control infrastructure that properly safeguards E-banking systems and data from both internal and external threats. It also should include a comprehensive process for managing risks associated with increased complexity of and increasing reliance on outsourcing relationships and third-party dependencies to perform critical E-banking functions.

Security Controls

While the Board of Directors has the responsibility for ensuring that appropriate security control processes are in place for E-banking, the substance of these processes needs special management attention because of the enhanced security challenges posed by E-banking. This should include establishing appropriate authorization privileges and authentication measures, logical and physical access controls, adequate infrastructure security to maintain appropriate boundaries and restrictions on both internal and external user activities and data integrity of transactions, records and information. In addition, the existence of clear audit trails for all E-banking transactions should be ensured and measures to preserve confidentiality of key E-banking information should be appropriate with the sensitivity of such information.

Although customer protection and privacy regulations vary from jurisdiction to jurisdiction, banks generally have a clear responsibility to provide their customers with a level of comfort regarding information disclosures, protection of customer data and business availability that approaches the level they can expect when using traditional banking distribution channels. To minimize legal and reputation risk associated with E-banking activities conducted both domestically and cross-border, banks should make adequate disclosure of information on their websites and take appropriate measures to ensure adherence to customer privacy requirements applicable in the jurisdictions to which the bank is providing E-banking services.

Legal and Reputation Risk Management

To protect banks against business, legal and reputation risk, E-banking services must be delivered on a consistent and timely basis in accordance with high customer expectations for constant and rapid availability and potentially high transaction demand. The bank must have the ability to deliver E-banking services to all end-users and be able to maintain such availability in all circumstances. Effective incident response mechanisms are also critical to minimize operational, legal and reputation risks arising from unexpected events, including internal and external attacks that may affect the provision of E-banking systems and services. To meet customers' expectations, banks should therefore have effective capacity, business continuity and contingency planning. Banks should also develop appropriate incident response plans, including communication strategies that ensure business continuity, control reputation risk and limit liability associated with disruptions in their E-banking services.

Risk

Risk categories mostly affected by specific nature of E-banking activities are:

Operational Risk: The central use of new technology to provide E-banking services has important implication on banks' operation risk. This new technology may require changes in procedures supervisors use to ensure that banks properly manage their E-banking risks in the areas of security, data confidentiality, data and system integrity, system availability and outsourcing. These facts are also linked to reputation and legal risks for banks since breaches in security can have damaged reputation of banks.

Reputation Risk: Reputation risk is considerably increased through E-banking. If bank fails to deliver source, accurate and timely services on a consistent basis, its reputation is at risk. In addition to system availability and integrity, breaches in data confidentiality and any other problems related to security operations can damage a banks' reputation.

Legal Risk: E-banks are expanding geographical scope of their services faster than traditional banks. Important sources of legal risk are: First the legislation of jurisdiction in which the bank is licensed or services are offered. Second, enforcement of emerging areas of law is uncertain.

Strategic and Business Risk: As rapid technological development and the lack of importance of borders for banking activities and competition, distinguish the risk nature of E-banking from other strategic decisions. Therefore prediction regarding business opportunities is also highly uncertain.

Credit Risk: Lack of personal relationship between customer and bank can have important implications for credit risk.

Consumer Education and Training

In order to provide consumer protection and for limiting reputation risk, E-banking should provide training and education to its customer's Effective awareness and training programme should include:

- Business objectives of security programmes
- Management expectations from programme

Educating basic concepts of Information System and their controls, role based access, virus and other potentially harmful entities. Knowledge security organization structure with the roles and responsibilities.

Money Laundering

E-Banking can be misused for money laundering due to lack of face to face contact with customers. Therefore, E-banking should has potential to create new opportunities for criminal activities and facilitate others.

IDENTITY AUTHENTICATION SYSTEM

E-trust Services

For E-trust to work there needs to be a substantial technological and commercial infrastructure in place. This is best described in terms of a three-layered framework as follows:

PKI Technology: The technology underlying E-trust is known as public key encryption or Public Key Infrastructure (PKI). PKI works by means of cryptographic keys issued in the form of digital certificates, which enable parties to communicate securely over an insecure network such as the Internet. Specifically, digital certificates can be used to prove beyond reasonable doubt:

> ***Authentication:*** someone is who they claim to be.
>
> ***Message integrity:*** a message has not been tampered with in any way.
>
> ***Non-repudiation:*** a message can be digitally signed to prove that it originated from a particular party, even if that party denies it.
>
> ***Confidentiality:*** a message can be encrypted so that only the intended recipient can read it.

Trusted Digital Identity Infrastructure: A digital certificate can be trusted if it is issued by trusted organization. This represents a good opportunity for highly trusted institutions to set themselves as Certificate Authorities (CAs) for issuing digital certificates to customers on the basis of a stringent registration process. If two or more CAs are involved, then there needs to be a trusted relationship between the CAs as well as between each CA and its customers. In fact there needs to be a whole commercial and legal infrastructure or "scheme" with well defined rules governing roles, responsibilities, risks and liabilities if digital certificates issued by one CA are to be interoperable with those issued by another. This is where banks really come into their own, by virtue of belonging to an international banking community whose members trust each other and are used to participating in similar schemes (for payments for example). Currently, the most important bank E-trust scheme is probably Identrus, a global trust authority backed by some of the biggest banks in the world. Identrus operates according to a "four box model", illustrated in figure.

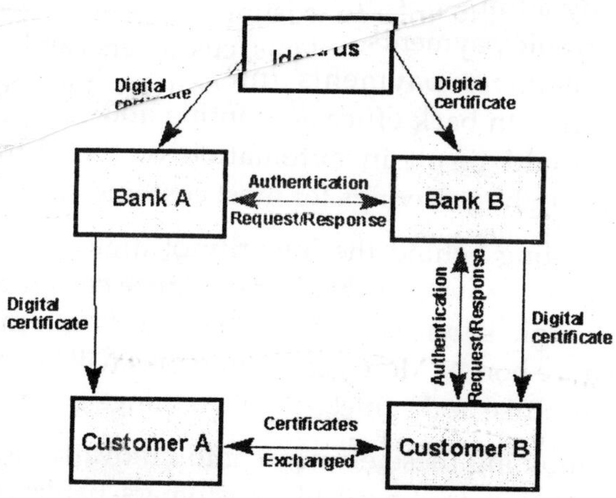

Customer B, on receipt of Customer A's digital certificate, can validate that certificate with Bank A, which issued the certificate, by means of an authentication request/response routed via its own issuing bank, Bank B. Banks A and B validate each other by reference to a "root key" held by Identrus. Provided Banks A and B issue interoperable certificates and adhere strictly to a set of well defined rules (governing, for example, registration criteria and service levels) then customers A and B, previously unknown to each other, can have a very high degree of trust in each others digital identities.

E-trust Services: Once an infrastructure of trusted digital identities is in place, banks can develop, on top of it, all sorts of added value E-trust services for their customers, for example: By combining identity validation with digital signing of electronic documents (and encryption, if necessary), together with an audit trail, banks can offer a secure messaging service. By using information about the financial standing and credit history of their customers, banks can offer on-line credit reference services, effectively upgrading digital identity to "digital status". By adding links to existing or new electronic payments systems, customers can be provided with a seamless payments integration service; further integration with back office accounting and order processing systems could result in automation of the entire trading process, with huge savings for most customers.

E-trust Services
Trusted Digital Identity Infrastructure
PKI Technology
ADDED-VALUE

By standing behind the integrity of digital identities and their supporting systems, banks can reduce customers' trading risks through services such as payments guarantees and performance bonds. More generally, banks will be in a position to offer recourse and comeback when things go wrong.

By combining these elements into innovative applications based on the needs of particular customers, banks can develop a whole new range of products and services in areas such as trade finance, or electronic auctions electronic procurement.

Implications for banks: Each individual bank needs to consider carefully its strategic positioning in the marketplace. Three principles, corresponding to the three layers in the framework above, are worth emphasizing in this respect:

Infrastructure: Banks wishing to offer E-trust services will need to build an appropriate technology and commercial infrastructure to enable it to act as a CA and issue digital certificates. This is technically quite straightforward but complex in terms of scale and scope.

Interoperability: E-trust services only work if there is interoperability between banks. Individual banks need to be quite sure that they adopt digital certificate standards and processes, which enable interoperability on a global scale.

Backing the wrong horse at this stage could be an expensive strategic mistake.

Cooperation: Banks need to cooperate if they are to dominate the E-trust market as an industry. Individual banks will, of course, compete vigorously with each other to offer superior services to their customers, but by definition, if two banks are required at either end of a transaction, then such competition must occur within a context of a cooperatively developed scheme.

Digital Signatures

Digital signatures are computer-based personal identities, which is founded on the public key cryptographic method. The basic characteristic of this secure encryption technology is that two different but mathematically related keys, the private and the public key (the so called 'key pair'), are used in order to create a digital signature and encode the data and to verify the signature and decode the data. In practical terms, the sender of an e-document can sign it by using his private key, which must be kept secret. Thus, the signature can only be verified with the public key of the sender, which is available to the public. A process strongly associated with the public key encryption and applied both in creation and verification of a digital signature is the hash function, which when applied to a particular message creates a unique number in the form of a hash value (message digest).

The process of creating, using and verifying a digital signature provides important functions for legal purposes:

> The asymmetric cryptography (PKI) ensures a high level of security in e-communications and of confidentiality of the context of a message sent over an open network like Internet.

Digital signatures provide authentication of the identity of the signer by attributing the message to the signer; so it is known who participated in a transaction. The rationale of this function is based on the fact that digital signatures cannot easily be forged, unless the signer loses control of his private key either accidentally or intentionally.

The digital signature protects the integrity of the transmitted data so the recipient can be sure that comparing the two message digests has not altered the message.

Even though these functions of digital signatures can guarantee security over open networks and strengthen consumer trust in E-commerce, another challenge is how can it be proved who participated in a particular transaction, as it cannot be identified who the sender and the recipient of the data was?

Password and Biometrics

Passwords (in combination with user names) have been the mainstay of identity authentication systems since multi-user information systems came into being. Threats to password-based authentication are:

- External disclosure
- Guessing
- Replay attacks

Password authentication systems are so notoriously insecure that they are nearly always combined with other methods of identity authentication.

Physical tokens are frequently used to enhance the security of identity authentication systems. Physical storage tokens are used by banks to corroborate an account number (held on a magnetic stripe card) with a password (PIN). More recently, tamper-proof integrated circuit cards (ICCs) allow the physical token to interact dynamically with the verification hardware.

Biometric techniques include finger print recognition, retinal scanning, hand-geometry scanning, and handwriting or voice recognition. These techniques are all, currently, extremely expensive to implement effectively and are therefore only worth considering in big-budget, high-security applications. As the drawbacks (including high cost, poor ergonomics, reliability, speed, and data storage requirements) are mitigated by improvements in technology, biometric techniques could emerge as the most secure method of automated identity authentication.

GUIDELINES FOR OFFERING E-BANKING SERVICES

The basic guidelines to offer E-banking services are:

The concerned board or approprite committee should have approved the electronic systems based on written strategic plan and risk analysis.

The analysis address should include issues like functioning of electronic delivery channels within the strategic or operating plan and risks associated with each.

Guidelines for accepting account applications and other relevant policies and procedures been updated to address activities beyond the traditional trade area.

Experienced individuals should be designated to develop and implement electronic banking services. Check duties/ responsibilities individuals.

Each system is being adequately tested by:

Volume stress testing (to ensure system capacity),

Screen testing (to review content), and

Pilot program (to evaluate feasibility).

Has management provided adequate training for all officers and staff affected by electronic banking systems, including those responsible for products, services, information systems, audit, compliance and legal issues?

For each system that interacts with any of the institution's operating systems or databases, does management require a review of the interactive components and processes to ensure compatibility and security?

If applicable, does management verify the accuracy and content of financial planning software, calculators, and other interactive programmes (between the institution and its customers) available through the systems?

As appropriate, has the institution developed a backup system or method for users to conduct normal activity in the event the system is not available for an extended period of time? Does the institution has procedures to notify users in the event of a problem?

Does the institution ensure that physical access to computer hardware, software, communication equipment and communication lines are restricted to appropriate personnel to ensure security?

CONCLUSION

This paper is an effort made by the authors in identifying issues and functioning of E-banking in general for persuing research work in identifing challenges to E-banking. Undoubtedly, electronic banking provides ample avenues to customers and new business oppurtunities to banks. But it also posses new challenges for banking regulators and supervisors:

The cross-border nature of activities require cross-border coopearation between supervisors. Supervisors should ensure that risk management principles should become integral part of banks' risk management policies as the traditional banks are facing problems with varios risk associated with changing technology. The dependence on small number of technology providers and customer satisfaction for technology and security for banks are amplified risk in E-banking.

Efforts have been made to Identify important issues, three-layered framework for E-trust Services and guidelines for oferring E-banking services.

BIBLIOGRAPHY

Kalakota, Whinston, "Electronic Commerce – A Manager's Guide", Addison Wesley, Edition 2000.

Greenstein, Feinman, "Electronic Commerce", Tata-McGraw Hill Publishing Company Ltd., Edition 2000.

Nsouli, Saleh M. and Andrea Schaechter, Challenges of the "

E-Banking Revolution", http://www.imf.org/external/pubs/ft/fandd/2002/09/nsouli.htm

Spyrelli, Christina, "Electronic Signatures: A Transatlantic Bridge? An EU and US Legal Approach Towards Electronic Authentication", http://elj.warwick.ac.uk/jilt/02-2/spyrelli.html

Ford, Matthew D., "Identity Authentication and 'E-Commerce'", http://elj.warwick.ac.uk/jilt/98-3/ford.html

"Banking Technology Trends Worth Watching"; http://www.ncollin.demon.co.uk/E-trust.html

Hoppermann, Jost, "Authentication in online banking", PC Quest 12/3/2001, www.ciol.com

Nanda, Rohit, "Security challenges in E-banking" PC Quest 1/4/2002, www.ciol.com

Trilokekar, Nitant P., "Banking Computerisation - a qualitative concern", www.bankindia.com

Mishra, A. K., "Internet Banking in India", www.bankindia.com

"Banking Security Framework In the Light of RBI Guidelines", www.banglorelabs.com

"Risk Management Principles for Electronic Banking", Basel Committee Publications No. 82 May 2001, http://www.bis.org/publ/bcbs82.htm

■ ■ ■

5

E-BANKING – PROBLEMS AND PROSPECTS

INTRODUCTION

"Why walk in, just log in".

Dynamism of modern man's life style is fast changing with the move of time. A new Technological Revolution – Computer Revolution is ushering by the turn of this century. It is leading the world to the integrated phenomenon of information Age, through growth and expansion of internet.

As a matter of fact, the world at large is rapidly entering in to the 'Net Age' by the new millennium. Indeed, unprecedented and profound charges in all walks of man's life are promised and anticipated with the extensive and intensive use of global communication networks. Internet or simple 'Net' is an interconnection of computer communication networks covering the whole world. It is a true reflection of advanced information technology of the modern century that has turned out time And space as single variable since internet system has crossed all geographical boundaries at the stroke of time. The net is changing everything everywhere: methods and mode is communication, work, education, research interface, ideas and perceptions, entertainment, health, habit, taste and preference, lifestyle, so also trade, commerce and finance.

Eventually, on of the global economic atlas banking is at the cross-road. In the new millennium, with the rapidly changing economic scene owing to emergence of E-commerce facilitated by the growth and expansion of Internet and information technology, banking scenario and financial activity everywhere is going to change rapidly and remarkably.

The cutting edge of banking business in near future is likely to be E- banking tuned with E-commerce. Electronic banking the backbone of business. When the business and commerce tend to be on the electronic modes, banking can never remain isolated. Growth of internet and the emergency of E-commerce will be bound to change the landscape of banking business world over.

E-commence imply the ability to conduct business electronically which apparently covers any form of business including banking. But for a logical distinction between commodity transactions and financial transactions, we prefer to use the term E-banking to reefer to banking business executed using and information and communication technology (ICI).

In 21st century banking will no longer be a business restricted to 'cash' and 'risk.' It is going the business related to transmission of knowledge of information on finance and risk management. Modern banking will tend to be more information based, speedy and boundary-less as an impact of e-Revolution. Banks have to well-versed in information (IT)-its use and applications. The IT should be effectively used for enhancing managerially skills and ability in banks. Banking division will have to be IT based, with the spread of digital economy.

E-banking essentially involves Electronic funds transfer [EFT] network technologies of the IT framework. This is, however not a novel idea in the modern banking, in the UK

For example the interbank electronic clearing was launched upon by the Bankers Automated Clearing House [BACH] Ltd. In 1971 a Clearing House for Automated Payment [CHAPS] in 1984 to handle high value transactions. By 1990, BACS and CHAPS, the two electronic clearing House, Processed over 40% of all cleared items in value terms 90% of all cleared payments are processed through CHAPS.

Banking is an art. But E-banking is more of a science than art. E-banking is Knowledge–based and mostly scientific in using electronic devices of the computer revolution. New paradigms of E-banking have to be visualized when the business of finance is internationally on a wider scale. Universal access to information facilitated by the internet. Internet and extranet and the web domestically as well as internationally on a wider scale. Universal access to information facilitated by the internet. Internet and extranet is the hub of new E-banking business to develop. When most business and commercial enterprises tend to become internet working organizations, banking has a to be E-banking in new century.

E-Banking is characterized with several aspects of E-power Such as :

- Power of information
- Power of execution
- Power of choice
- Power of speed
- Power of convenience
- Power of economy

The first bank of the Internet [FBOI] and Security First Network Bank [SFNB] were the pioneer bank of internet banking, i.e. E-banking in the United States. Presently, the SFNB is the world's largest commercial online service bank with an asset worth US$41 million and a customer base of 6 million. Incidentally, Industrial Credit and Investment

Corporation of India [ICICI] has come up as the first Indian bank on the internet. Asian banks need to recognized and grade the emerging opportunities of banking business on the internet.

As E-commerce essentially means conducting business electronically, the E-banking apparently means the conduct of banking electronically. It involves elimination of paper –based transaction and radical charge in the change in the operation of the banking service. E-banking is expected to result in high productivity and efficiency gain for the bank. E-banking will operate through intranet, extranet and over the internet. E-banking is banking on the information superhighway on the frontier of the internet. E-banking is essentially the internet bank of new millennium, with no lines, no teller, no ques, and no restricted office house.

Apparently, E-banking has unique advantages, such as:

- Conveniences to full banking service
- Low cost banking
- JTI (Just in Time)
- Better customer retention
- World-wide 24 hours, 7 days a week banking services
- Cost saving on infrastructure
- Highly beneficial to corporate sector and E-commerce owing to its cost effectiveness.

CONCEPT OF E-BANKING

Electronic banking is an umbrella term for the process by which a customer may perform banking transactions electronically without visiting a brick-and-mortar institution. The following terms all refer to one form or another of electronic banking: personal computer (PC) banking, Internet banking, virtual banking, online banking, home banking, remote electronic banking, and phone banking. PC banking and Internet or online banking is the most frequently used designations. It should be noted, however, that the terms used to describe the various types of use electronic banking are often used interchangeably. The Internet banking is changing the banking industry and is having the major effects on banking relationships. Even the Morgan Stanley Dean Witter Internet research emphasized that Web is more important for retail financial services than for many other industries. Internet banking involves use of Internet for delivery of banking products and services. It falls into four main categories, from Level 1 - minimum functionality sites that offer only access to deposit account data - to Level 4 sites - highly sophisticated offerings enabling integrated sales of additional products and access to other financial services- such as investment and insurance. In other words a successful Internet banking solution offers:

Exceptional rates on Savings, CDs, and IRAs.

- Checking with no monthly fee, free bill payment and rebates on ATM surcharges
- Credit cards with low rates
- Easy online applications for all accounts, including personal loans and mortgages
- Twenty four hour account access and Quality customer service with personal attention.

DEFINITION OF E-BANKING

E-banking is defined as the automated delivery of new and traditional banking products and services directly to customers through electronic, interactive communication channels. E-banking includes the systems that enable financial institution customers, individuals or businesses, to access accounts, transact business, or obtain information on financial products and services through a public or private network, including the Internet. Customers access E-banking services using an intelligent electronic device, such as a personal computer (PC), personal digital assistant (PDA), automated teller machine

(ATM), kiosk, or Touch Tone telephone. While the risks and controls are similar for the various E-banking access channels, this booklet focuses specifically on Internet-based services due to the Internet's widely accessible public network.

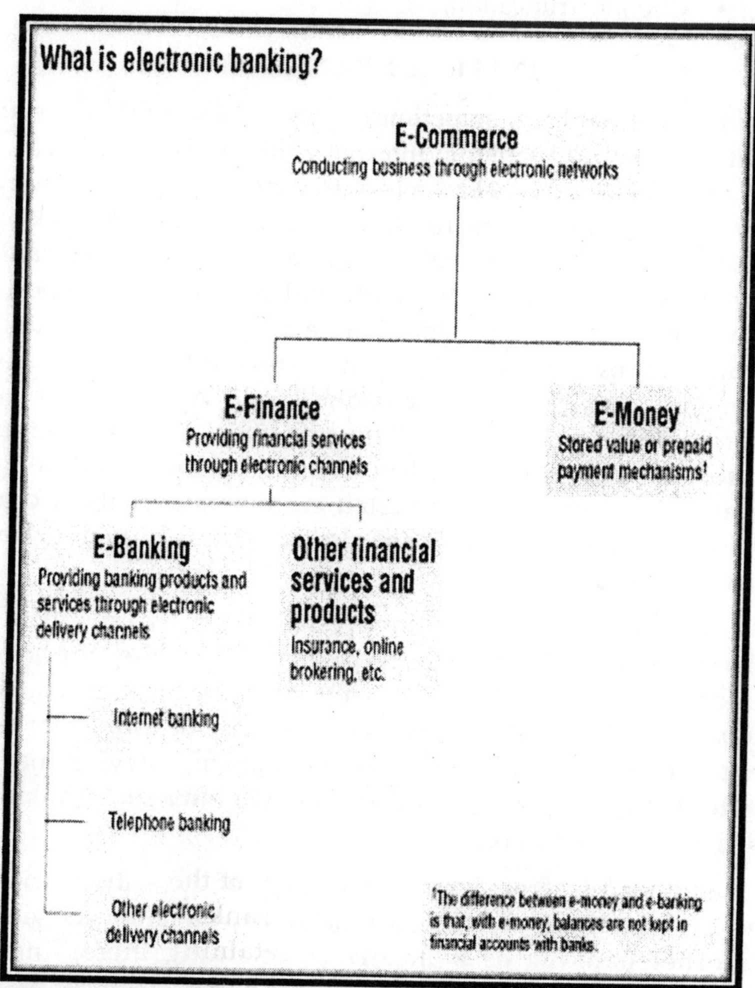

Types of E-banking

- Internet banking
- Mobile banking

- Personal digital assistant (PDA)
- Automated Teller Machine (ATM)
- Kiosk
- Cheque Truncation.

INTERNET BANKING

Internet banking, sometimes called online banking, is an outgrowth of PC banking. Internet banking uses the Internet as the delivery channel by which to conduct banking activity, for example, transferring funds, paying bills, viewing checking and savings account balances, paying mortgages, and purchasing financial instruments and certificates of deposit. An Internet banking customer accesses his or her accounts from a browser— software that runs Internet banking programmes resident on the bank's World Wide Web server, not on the user's PC. Net Banker defines a "true Internet bank" as one that provides account balances and some transactional capabilities to retail customers over the World Wide Web. Internet banks are also known as virtual, cyber, net, interactive, or web banks.

To date, more banks have established an advertising presence on the Internet—primarily in the form of informational or interactive websites—than have created transactional websites. However, a number of banks that do not yet offer transactional Internet banking services have indicated on their websites that they will offer such banking activities in the future.

Although Internet banks offer many of the same services as do traditional brick-and-mortar banks, analysts view Internet banking as a means of retaining increasingly sophisticated customers, of developing a new customer base, and of capturing a greater share of depositor assets. A typical Internet bank site specifies the types of transactions offered and provides information about account security Because Internet banks generally have lower operational and transactional costs than do traditional brick-and-mortar banks, they are often able to offer low-cost checking and high-yield Certificates of deposit. Internet banking is not limited to a physical site; some Internet banks exist without physical branches, for example, Telebank (Arlington, Virginia) and Banknet (UK). Further, in some cases, web banks are not restricted to conducting transactions within national borders and have the ability to make transactions involving large amounts of assets instantaneously. According to industry analysts, electronic banking provides a variety of attractive possibilities for remote account access, including:

- Availability of inquiry and transaction services around the clock;
- worldwide connectivity;
- Easy access to transaction data, both recent and historical; and
- Direct customer control of international movement of funds without intermediation of financial institutions in customer's jurisdiction.

MOBILE BANKING

Mobile banking (m-banking) is a service offered together by banks and mobile operators to put forward a new way for their customers to perform remote banking. The idea of this joint operation is to provide a convenient service for account owners to perform banking anytime and anywhere using their mobile phone.

PERSONAL DIGITAL ASSISTANT (PDA)

Personal digital assistants (PDAs) are handheld computers that were originally designed as personal organizers, but became much more versatile over the years. PDAs are also known as pocket computers or palmtop computers. PDAs have many uses: calculation, use as a clock and calendar, accessing the Internet, sending and receiving E-mails, video recording, typewriting and word processing, use as an address book, making and writing on spreadsheets, scanning bar codes, use as a radio or stereo, playing computer games, recording survey responses, and Global Positioning System (GPS). Newer PDAs also have both color screens and audio capabilities, enabling them to be used as mobile phones (smart phones), web browsers, or portable media players. Many PDAs can access the Internet, intranets or extranets via Wi-Fi, or Wireless Wide-Area Networks (WWANs). One of the most significant PDA characteristics is the presence of a touch screen.

AUTOMATED TELLER MACHINE (ATM)

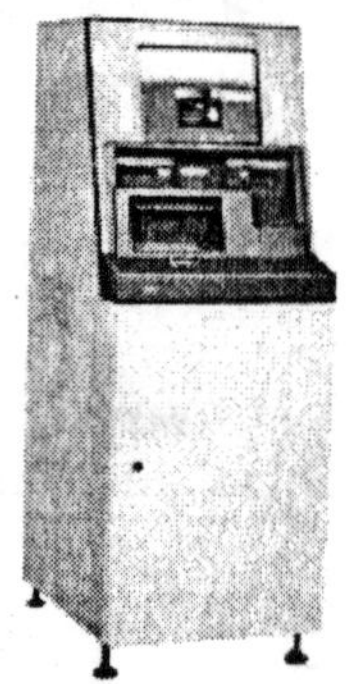

An ATM (Automatic or Automated Teller Machine) is a computerized machine designed to dispense cash to bank customers without need of human interaction. The ATM can also take deposits, transfer money between bank accounts and provide other basic financial services.

Most banks feature one or more "on premises" ATMs so that customers have access to services 24 hours a day, seven days a week. During banking hours the ATM can reduce long lines inside the bank by providing an alternative to a human teller. Even better, the ATM continues to be available long after the bank is closed. If you need cash in the evening, on a holiday or Sunday, the ATM is there to serve.

To use an ATM, the customer feeds it a bankcard, sometimes called a debit card. This resembles a credit card but is issued from the bank to use with an ATM. Once the machine reads the magnetic strip on the card, it requests a personal identification number, or PIN. The PIN provides security in case the card is lost or falls into the wrong hands.

Upon entering the associated PIN correctly, the customer will see a list of choices on the ATM screen. Through touch-screen or buttons, the customer navigates through the ATM screens to complete the desired transaction. If the customer chooses to withdraw cash, the cash is dispersed through a feeder slot. If making a deposit, the customer feeds the deposit envelope into a deposit slot when cued by the machine. Receipts are optionally printed for the customer, but the ATM retains a record of all transactions. Tied into the bank's computer system, the ATM can automatically deduct withdrawals or add deposits to the customer's account(s).

Many banks do not charge a fee to customers for using their own ATMs. However, if you withdraw cash from an ATM that does not belong to your bank, you will likely incur transaction fees. ATMs normally have posted information about non-customer fees, though this will not include fees that your own bank might charge.

Patents for ATMs were reportedly filed as early as the 1930s, but the first actual ATM is credited to Barclays Bank of London in 1967. The latest incarnations the latest incarnations of these now-ubiquitous machines include Linux and Microsoft-based screens, and talking ATMs for the blind.

KIOSK

An Interactive kiosk is a computer terminal that provides information access via electronic methods. Interactive kiosks sometimes resemble telephone booths, but can also be used while sitting on a bench or chair. Interactive kiosks are typically placed in high foot traffic settings such as hotel lobbies or airports.

Integration of technology allows kiosks to perform a wide range of functions. For example, kiosks may enable users to enter a public utility bill account number in order to perform an online transaction, or collect cash in exchange for merchandise. Customized components such as coin hoppers, bill acceptors, card readers and thermal printers enable kiosks to meet the owner's specialized needs.

Types of Kiosks

Banking Kiosk

A banking kiosk can provide the ability for customers to perform transactions that may normally require a bank teller and may be more complex and longer to perform than desired at an ATM.

Digital Minilab

A kiosk that functions as a digital minilab allows users to insert a memory card to print photographs.

Internet Kiosk

An Internet kiosk is a terminal that provides public Internet access. Internet kiosks sometimes resemble telephone booths, and are typically placed in settings such as hotel lobbies or airports for fast access to E-mail or web pages. Internet kiosks sometimes have a bill acceptor or a credit card swipe, and nearly always have a computer keyboard, a mouse Some Internet kiosks are based on a payment model similar to vending machines or Internet cafés, while others are free. A common arrangement with pay-for-use kiosks has the owner of the Internet kiosk enter into a partnership with the owner of its location, paying either a flat rate for rental of the floor space or a percentage of the monthly revenue generated by the machine.

Movie Ticket Kiosk

Many movie theater chains have specialized ticket machines that provide information about the movies that are being show now or in the future.

Vending Kiosk

An excellent example of a vending kiosk is that of McDonald's Red box kiosk.

CHEQUE TRUNCATION

Almost every individual and business has used, and possibly still uses, checks to initiate payment for goods or services. A trend currently in development is called check truncation. In this payment processing method, a payment starts as a check and ends up as an electronic payment transaction. These transaction services operate as follows:

- At the point of sale (POS), the merchant's clerk rings the sale and swipes the customer's check in a magnetic ink code reader (MICR).
- The MICR information and the related transaction (sale) information are transmitted to a site where the MICR information is converted into electronic transaction format.
- A request is sent to the paying bank for verification, and an approval transaction is returned from the bank to the store POS system.
- The customer signs the authorization document, and the clerk voids and returns the customer's check

FACETS OF E-BANKING

Electronic Banking may have dimensions, at least:

- Customer to bank electronic banking
- Bank- to- Bank electronic banking
- Electronic Central Banking.

Customer to bank electronic banking

Electronic banking is internet based. Banking transaction such as deposits, remittances credit cards etc. Banking product and service as well as relevant banking information can be made available with easy access to customers on internet.

Several network innovations for E-banking can be visualized such as smart card, electronic data interchange (EDI) and electronic house and office banking (EHOBS). Needless to say that banking operations and transactions have to be secured against unauthorized access by intruders

Bank to bank electronic banking

This from of electronic banking comprises the bulk of intra-bank transaction such as money –at-call, etc. this segment of E-banking is driving extranets, which is restricted to banks only as well-secured.

Electronic central banking

Central bank is the apex institution in the financial system. It is the leader and regulator of banking sector. Under E-central banking all banks within the purview of the central bank are interconnected on extranet to facilitate transactions such as cheque clearing, cash reserves management, open market operations, bill discounted and other aspects of credit control. Indeed, central bank is also to be connected with government treasury on extranet to carry on its functions as an agent to the government. Furthermore, through extranets, the central banks of countries should be inter-linked with the IMF, World Bank, etc. international financial instructions.

BENEFITS OF E-BANKING

Benefit for customer	Benefit for Banks
▪ Convenient banking	▪ Lower cost transaction
▪ Tailored	▪ Increase customer knowledge
▪ Easy Access	▪ Ability to tailor products and services as per customer's requirements.
▪ Ease of shopping around for best price.	▪ Ability to access a large market.

▪ Ease of changing supplier	▪ Increase customer relationship
▪ Law cost and save time	▪ Reduces errors, time consumed and overhead cost
▪ Financial planning capacity	▪ Minimum physical infrastructure requirement
▪ Privacy.	▪ Reaching new segment of the population.
▪ Elimination of waiting time	▪ Create customer loyalty
▪ Information gateway	▪ Achieve better cross-channel productivity and performance
▪ Offers new value of customers	▪ Increase in flexibility and opportunities for improved service
▪ Round the clock availability	▪ Eliminate the waste of paper

DRAWBACK OF E-BANKING

- The biggest concern is of securities and confidentiality, apart from the shifting customer loyalty due to multiple accounts with banks and the ease at which a customer can change their banks.
- Transparency, disclosure requirement, anti-money laundering adherence to know your customer norms, privacy and outsourcing concern all banks around the world apart from the development of public key infrastructure and security standards.

Sub-Drawback is as follow:

- Disadvantages include security, recent phishing attacks, all transaction not being possible online, slow adoption to Internet banking, lack of human interface, loss of opportunity in potential business leads, hung capital requirement, disproportionate level of penetration and customer education.

- Trust of customer in a web venture is an important concern. Many customers hesitate to deal with an E-bank as they are not sure of the quality of products and services they will receive.
- There are various banking products like loans and mortgages, withdrawal of cash, etc. that requires to be delivered in the physical form after proper authentication of the customer. These issues can drive the customer away from E-commerce.

BOARD AND MANAGEMENT OVERSIGHT

E-banking strategy

Financial institution management should choose the level of E-banking services provided to various customer segments based on customer needs and the institution's risk assessment considerations. Institutions should reach this decision through a board-approved, E-banking strategy that considers factors such as customer demand, competition, expertise, implementation expense, maintenance costs, and capital support. Some institutions may choose not to provide E-banking services or to limit E-banking services to an informational website. Financial institutions should periodically re-evaluate this decision to ensure it remains appropriate for the institution's overall business strategy. Institutions may define success in many ways including growth in market share, expanding customer relationships, expense reduction, or new revenue generation. If the financial institution determines that a transactional website is appropriate, the next decision is the range of products and services to make available electronically to its customers. To deliver those products and services, the financial institution may have more than one website or multiple pages within a website for various business lines.

COST-BENEFIT ANALYSIS AND RISK ASSESSMENT

Financial institutions should base any decision to implement E-banking products and services on a thorough analysis of the costs and benefits associated with such action. Some of the reasons institutions offer E-banking services include:

- Lower operating costs,
- Greater geographic diversification,
- Improved or sustained competitive position,
- Increased customer demand for services, and
- New revenue opportunities.

The individuals conducting the cost-benefit analysis should clearly understand the risks associated with E-banking so that cost considerations fully incorporate appropriate risk mitigation controls. Without such expertise, the cost-benefit analysis will most likely underestimate the time and resources needed to properly oversee E-banking activities, particularly the level of technical expertise needed to provide competent oversight of in-house or outsourced activities. In addition to the obvious costs for personnel, hardware, software, and communications, the analysis should also consider:

- Changes to the institution's policies, procedures, and practices;
- The impact on processing controls for legacy systems;
- The appropriate networking architecture, security expertise, and software tools to maintain system availability and to protect and respond to unauthorized access attempts;
- The skilled staff necessary to support and market E-banking services during expanded hours and over a wider geographic area, including possible expanded market and cross-border activity;
- The additional expertise and MIS needed to oversee E-banking vendors or technology service providers;

- The higher level of legal, compliance, and audit expertise needed to support technology-dependent services;
- Expanded MIS to monitor E-banking security, usage, and profitability and to measure the success of the institution's E-banking strategy;
- Cost of insurance coverage for E-banking activities;
- Potential revenues under different pricing scenarios;
- Potential losses due to fraud; and
- Opportunity costs associated with allocating capital to E-banking efforts.

MONITORING AND ACCOUNTABILITY

Once an institution implements its E-banking strategy, the board and management should periodically evaluate the strategy's effectiveness. A key aspect of such an evaluation is the comparison of actual E-banking acceptance and performance to the institution's goals and expectations. Some items that the institution might use to monitor the success and cost effectiveness of its E-banking strategy include:

- Revenue generated,
- Website availability percentages,
- Customer service volumes,
- Number of customers actively using E-banking services,
- Percentage of accounts signed up for E-banking services, and
- The number and cost per item of bill payments generated.

- Without clearly defined and measurable goals, management will be unable to determine if E-banking services are meeting the customers' needs as well as the institution's growth and profitability expectations.

- In evaluating the effectiveness of the institution's E-banking strategy, the board should also consider whether appropriate policies and procedures are in effect and whether risks are properly controlled. Unless the initial strategy establishes clear accountability for the development of policies and controls, the board will be unable to determine where and why breakdowns in the risk control process occurred.
- An important component of monitoring is an appropriate independent audit function. Financial institutions offering E-banking products and services should expand their audit coverage commensurate with the increased complexity and risks inherent in E-banking activities. Financial institutions offering E-banking services should ensure the audit program expands to include:
  - Scope and coverage, including the entire E-banking process as applicable (i.e., network configuration and security, interfaces to legacy systems, regulatory compliance, internal controls, and support activities performed by third-party providers);
  - Personnel with sufficient technical expertise to evaluate security threats and controls in an open network (i.e., the Internet).

■ ■ ■

6

CHEQUE TRUNCATION

Cheque Truncation is a process in which the image of the relevant data of a cheque is electronically captured and transmitted to enable payment of that cheque to the payee's account and simultaneously debiting the account of the drawer without the physical movement of the cheque itself.

Payment systems and payment services play a key role in the efficient functioning of the financial system within a country. The payment system needs to ensure that financial transactions are settled in a timely manner and complimented with reliability and security, which is vital to the maintenance of market confidence and to the safe and sound functioning of financial market. Even though there are various cashless payment instruments in the country, cash still exists as the most popular retail payment due to convenience in settling small value transactions and ready acceptance to the legal tender for payment of any amount in any part of the country.

Cheques are mainly used for retail payments. More than 90 per cent of the total value of cashless retail payments is done through cheques. This statistic alone highlights the importance of cheque-based transactions in the national payment system. To reduce the time taken in clearing and settlement of cheques, and to avoid physical transportation of cheques, and to enhance the reliability and the security of the retail payment system, cheque truncation/ imaging technology is introduced.

Cheque Truncation System (CTS) is an image-based cheque clearing system, which replaces the physical cheque flow with electronic information flow throughout clearing cycle. This process eliminates the actual cheque movement involved in clearing and hence reduces the delays associated with the movement of cheques. This in turn increases the efficiency, reduce the operational cost and expedite the clearing process.

CTS provide benefits across the board by providing the financial industry with a means for shorter clearing cycles and a centralized image archival system. Banks experience cost savings in the handling, transportation and storage of physical cheques. CTS also increase operational efficiency by giving bank staff easy access to real-time information on cheque status.

ROLE OF TECHNOLOGY IN REVOLUTION OF INDIAN BANKING SYSTEM

Technology is the current state of knowledge of how to combine resources to produce desired products, to solve problems,to fulfill needs or to satisfy wants. The history of Indian Banking had been 'brick and mortar' based but the future would be 'click and mouse' oriented.

The future of banking will be technology driven. For customers, it would be a new experience, as they would have the facility of home banking. The Utility bills will be paid without any hassles like cutting a cheque, or filling in the cover form or mailing it by courier or post. These things will happen by single click of a button through products like 'bill-pay'. A part of the technology costs shall have to be borne by customers for the accurate and prompt services offered by banks.

Implementation of technology in any industry is to have a business case i.e., it must enhance its business value and increase its competitiveness. The new environment will require a complete paradigm shift –new styles of conducting business with technology, people and processes. Indian Banking, Indian IT vendors and Indian consulting firms will be dominating players in the global banking scenario in coming years and that will surely be boom time for all.

Technology has also changed the functioning of clearing system. The settlement process has improved and is now faster & more accurate with Cheque Truncation it is expected that there will be further increase in the efficiency. It is apparent that technological advancement is not going to stop.

Since the beginning of mankind has been constantly improving its life through adoption of newer and better technologies. In the history of mankind, there have been some revolutionary technological changes, which radically changed the lifestyle and living standards of human beings and started a new era. Today it is unthinkable for us to imagine life without computers, internet, cellphones, tv, etc.

The technological revolution started in a small way in Indian Banks in the second half of the twentieth century starting from Mainframe computers facilitating inter-office reconciliation, the technology transformation journey has taken us through Automated Ledger Posting Machines,back office automation, full branch computrisation and now to Core Banking. We now have the ability to process millions of transaction in a very short time with great accuracy.

Technology will facilitate the transactions but it will be the man or woman behind the technology who will matter the most & have the last word. Any project or initiative which we venture into is full of challenges, but after we meet the challenges and overcome them, one can savour the taste of success.

Ultimately, it is a question of hardwork, application of mind and a will to succeed, which transforms any new venture into a success. Today' success mantra for achieving excellence lies in the optimal use of technology in a manner where the process of change is managed well enough to blend with customer expectations of excellent customer service. This in turn would result & improved bottom lines for the banks & above all in overall systematic efficiency. 'A person who is willing to learn a better asset than one who is technology savvy but refuses to change'.

BENEFITS OF THE CHEQUE TRUNCATION SYSTEM

- Minimize risks and introduce a secured cheque clearing system. Make cheque clearing process more efficient through electronic transmission of cheque images. This will reduce the time to complete the clearing cycle of cheque presenting, returning as well as cheque realization time.
- The existing cheque realization time span varies from 1 to 10 days. The new cheque imaging system will try to minimize this to T + 1, where the T is the cheque receiving date.
- Cheque imaging will result in cost savings due to lower cost in physical transportation of cheques.
- More importantly this would result in minimizing bottlenecks and delays due to the couriers of cheques. Customer's point of view, the new system will reduce the time lag between cheque presentation and realization time.

RISKS IN CHEQUE TRUNCATION

- The introduction of the truncation process will change the roles and the responsibilities of the various participants in the truncation process and may lead to introduction of certain risks that will have to be mitigated. These are documented below.
- At the presenting bank level, the responsibility to verify the genuineness of the cheque based on the apparent tenor or the visible features of the cheque presented for

collection may lead to banks refusing to accepting a genuine cheque or accepting a forged cheque based on a manual scrutiny. Images and MICR data to be sent to the clearing house have to be matched before they are released to the Clearing House.

- The Clearing House will have to assume that the data given by the banks is the data meant for that day's clearing and will have to arrive at the settlement based on this assumption. If the MICR data given by the bank is not that matching with the day's image the bank has sent for collection, it may lead to erroneous settlement and large returns.
- Truncating cheques entails additional operational risks. Banks will have to take adequate measures to ensure that all necessary safeguards are provided for – in consonance with legal requirements and banking practice while making payments, especially for high value instruments.
- The drawee bank has to verify the signature on the image of a cheque. If a drawee bank chooses to verify signatures on the images of cheques above a cut-off amount only, then it runs the risk of paying some forged instruments.
- The Warehousing Agency for images and physical storage of cheques might not be able to produce the image or the physical cheque demanded by the bank. This may lead to legal complications and assignment of liabilities. These will have to be covered by suitably drafted agreements and service level agreements between the banks and the Warehousing Agency.

THE CHEQUE TRUNCATION SYSTEM PROCESS FLOW

Process Flow

Banks worldwide spend millions of dollars each year to process cheques. The Cheque Truncation System (CTS) from

BCS Information Systems Pte Ltd is the recommended solution to high-cost cheque processing. In June 1999, BCS/BCSIS was granted approval by the Singapore Clearing House Association to develop and implement a nationwide Cheque Truncation System for the banking industry in Singapore.

The Cheque Truncation System (CTS) replaces physical cheques with electronic images on all four legs of a clearing cycle. It is an online image-based cheque clearing system, where the cheque images and the Magnetic Ink Character Recognition (MICR) data are captured at the collecting bank/ branch and transmitted electronically to the Singapore Automated Clearing House (SACH) via a secure broadband data communications network.

The CTS is protected by comprehensive PKI-based security architecture. On top of the PKI technology, the security architecture also incorporates basic security and authentication controls such as dual access control; user ID and passwords with cryptobox and smart card interfaces. Smart card device is used to activate system access to the CTS Backend Host (BeCTS) at SACH. Encrypted password using asymmetric keys is checked by BeCTS. Once access is granted, all transactions transmitted over the network are digitally signed and authenticated by both parties.

The Cheque Truncation System supports flexible connectivity options for the participating banks ranging from distributed branch capture through the use of a Front End Cheque Truncation System (FeCTS) to regional/ centralized approach through the banks' existing cheque imaging system.

At the SACH, the BeCTS continuously receives and processes this cheque information transmitted from the presenting banks throughout the clearing window. Successfully processed outward data is sorted immediately and made available as inward data for downloading and processing by the paying banks instead of having to collect the physical cheques from the clearing house. The cheque images and

MICR of the inward clearing cheques can be downloaded from the BeCTS throughout the day as soon as the outward batch is processed (real-time batch processing). This continuous inward download feature allows the banks to perform inward verification as soon as the items are ready for retrieval from clearing house. This information can then be used by the banks'/branches' signature verification system for the inward clearing process. The same unique features also apply to the return legs.

With these powerful features, the BeCTS is able to compute its members' clearing statistics and positions in a real-time mode instead of the conventional batch mode at the end of each clearing cycle. With the CTS, real-time net settlement between settlement banks will be a possibility.

At suitable intervals, both images and data received are also archived into a National Archive for storage and future retrieval by members.

The CTS & the National Archive were launched successfully on a nation-wide basis in July 2003.

LAWS RELATING TO THE CHEQUE TRUNCATION SYSTEM

There are basically three issues which need to be considered:

- Does our existing law permit cheque truncation?
- Does the advantage of cheque truncation outweigh the accompanying risk involved in the process?
- What changes are called for in law, at this stage of development of technology in India, for following cheque truncation system?

Under the Negotiable Instruments Act, 1881 (NI Act), cheques have to be presented for payment to the bank on which these are drawn. Without such presentment, no cause of action arises against the drawer. Section 64 of the Act ibid declares that in default of presentment of a cheque to the drawee for payment, other parties to the cheque are not liable to the holder. A collecting bank, by implied contract assumes an obligation to present the cheque at the drawee bank and that obligation is discharged only when the cheque is so presented. The fact that the presentment for this purpose means physical presentment is clear from the following addition made to Section 64 by an amendment in 1885.

"Where authorised by agreement or usage, a presentment through the post office by means of registered letter is sufficient."

By banking practice, both in India and in England it is open to banks to agree to presentment at any place other than the branch, such as at a clearing house.

The right of the paying bank to require physical presentation and possession of the cheque is designed to provide it with an opportunity to examine the signature or other authentication of the cheque, to examine the "apparent tenor" for its accord with the formal requirement of law, to be sure that there is no material alteration and that a paid cheque is not presented for second time. In large measure the existing requirements are designed for the protection of the drawer.

If a customer claims that the payment by his bank against the cheque was without proper mandate, the paying bank can rebut his claim only by producing the paid cheque (in original), and showing that it had discharged its obligation under law by verifying the signature and apparent tenor and that the payment was in due course. In the absence of such proof, the paying banker is bound in law to recredit the amount. In the UK., banks have tried to reduce the risk by obtaining customer consent agreements to enable them to waive physical presentment of cheques. Section 76 of the N I Act in India, which deals with waiver of presentment, specifically recognises the drawer's right to waive the presentment.

The requirement of physical presentment is a legal requirement but this is meant for the benefit of the drawer. Courts in India have held that an individual can waive his legal right if there is no public policy behind the right conferred by law. On this basis also it should be possible for the banks in India, like the banks in U.K. to introduce the cheque truncation process on the basis of customer agreements. But in the long term, unless the law is changed, the process of truncation of cheques may not make such headway. The definition of "presentment" in Section 64 of the NI Act may have to be suitably amended to permit electronic presentment of essential data or image of the cheque. This, however, involves a greater probe into the status of technology at the branch level and the extent of dishonour of cheques for alteration/forgery, etc.

Section 1(4)(a) of the IT. Act, 2000 provides that the Act shall not apply to a negotiable instrument as defined in Section 13 of the N.I. Act, 1881. In order to bring conformity between I.T. Act and N.I. Act and also to facilitate evolution and use of payment instruments in electronic mode as well as hybrid instruments, the Government of India, Ministry of Finance by its order dated 9th January 2001 constituted a working group with Shri N.V. Deshpande, Principal Legal Adviser, RBI, as Chairman to suggest inter-alia amendments to Negotiable Instruments Act, 1881 to conform it with provisions of I.T. Act.

The Working Group has made recommendations and also given the draft of Negotiable Instruments and Other Connected Laws (Amendment) Bill, 2001 in its report which covers *inter alia:*

(*a*) Amendment to Section 6 of N.I. Act to include electronic image of a truncated cheque and a cheque in electronic form in the definition of "cheque" and also included Explanation (*i*) and Explanation (*ii*) to define "truncated cheque" and "cheque in electronic form".

b) Amendment to Section 64 of N.I. Act by adding new sub-section (2) providing that notwithstanding anything contained in Section 6, where an electronic image of a truncated cheque is presented for payment, the drawee bank is entitled to demand any further information regarding the truncated cheque from the Bank holding the truncated cheque in case of any reasonable suspicion about the genuineness of the apparent tenor of instrument, and if the suspicion is that of any fraud, forgery, tempering, or destruction of the instrument, it is entitled to further demand the presentment of the truncated cheque itself for verification. Provided that the truncated cheque so demanded by the Bank shall be retained by it, if the payment is made accordingly.

c) Amendment to Section 81 of N.I. Act by adding new sub-sections (2) and (3) providing that where a cheque is the electronic image of a truncated cheque, even after the payment the banker who receives the payment shall be entitled to retain the truncated cheque; and a certificate issued on the foot of the print out of the electronic image of a truncated cheque, by the banker who paid the instrument, shall be prima facie, proof of such payment.

d) Amendment to Section 89 of N.I. Act by adding new sub-sections (2) and (3) providing that any difference in apparent tenor of the electronic image of the truncated cheque and the truncated cheque shall be a material alteration and it shall be the duty of the bank or the Clearing House, as the case may be, to ensure the exactness of the apparent tenor of the electronic image and the truncated cheque while truncating and transmitting the image; and any bank or a Clearing House which receives a transmitted electronic image of a truncated cheque, shall cross verify from the party who transmitted the image to it, that the image so transmitted to it and received by it is exactly the same.

e) Amendment to Section 131 of N.I. Act by adding Explanation (ii) providing that it shall be the duty of the banker who receives payment based on an electronic image of a truncated cheque held with him, to verify the prima facie genuineness of the cheque to be truncated and any fraud, forgery or tampering apparent on the face of the instrument that can be verified with due diligence and ordinary care. Amendment to Section 1 of IT. Act to delete clause (a) of sub-section (4) of Section 1.

WORKING GROUP ON CHEQUE TRUNCATION

Introduction

1. Processing of paper based cheques constitutes an important segment of the payment and settlement scenario of the India. Settlement of cheques is arrived on the basis of the physical presentation of paper based cheques to the clearing houses of the country (currently 1047 in number) for transmission to the drawee banks and for payment thereafter. In view of the need to transport the paper based cheques and the time involved in their processing at various intermediary levels, the total time taken for realisation of cheques has tended to be rather long. The problem gets compounded when cheques are tendered for collection by customers at a branch in a city which is not the actual place of the drawee branch. These are called outstation cheques and these cheques typically take longer realisation periods especially in a geographically large country like India and cases of delays in credit – by more than a fortnight are not uncommon.
2. The entire processing of cheques and their payment are all governed under the covenants of the Negotiable Instruments Act, 1881, which necessitate that these instruments are in writing and have to be physically presented for payment in due course. The attendant

delays on account of not being able to exploit technological alternatives available have been engaging the attention of the Reserve Bank of India for some time. After the passage of amendments to the Negotiable Instruments Act 1881 and the IT Act 2000 in the last quarter of 2002 to provide a legal framework for the implementation of cheque truncation and e-cheques in India, the Governor of the Reserve Bank of India, in the mid-term review of the Monetary and Credit Policy Statement of October, 2002 had suggested that a Working Group on Cheque Truncation be constituted to suggest an appropriate model suitable to Indian conditions, in view of various models of truncation available the world over.

3. These apart, it was also felt necessary to consider several operational aspects relating to the processing cycle, technology requirements and the approach to implementation for the introduction of cheque truncation in the country. Further, in order to facilitate debit transfers also in electronic mode, feasibility of e-cheques was also required to be studied.

4. In order to examine such issues closely, the Reserve Bank of India decided to constitute a Working Group. The composition of the Working Group is as under:

   i) Dr R B Barman, Chairman, Executive Director, Reserve Bank of India

   ii) Shri N V Deshpande, Member, Principal Legal Adviser, Reserve Bank of India

   iii) Shri M R Srinivasan, Member, Chief General Manager-in-charge, Department of Banking Operations and Development, Reserve Bank of India

   iv) Shri Ashok Kini, Member, State Bank of India, Mumbai

   v) Dr. D B Phatak, IT Specialist, K R School of Information Technology, IIT Powai, Mumbai *vi*) Shri S K Awasthi, Member, Punjab National Bank, New Delhi

vii) Shri Pravir Vora, Member, ICICI Bank, Mumbai

viii) Shri C N Ram, Member, HDFC Bank, Mumbai

ix) Ms. U A Dharadhar, Member, Saraswat Co-operative Bank Ltd, Mumbai

x) Shri K C Chowdhary, Member, Indian Banks' Association, Mumbai

xi) Shri R Gandhi Member-Secretary, Chief General Manager-in-charge, Department of Information Technology, Reserve Bank of India.

The Working Group was entrusted with the task of studying the various aspects of cheque truncation and e-cheques and work out the models which could be adopted for the country. The memorandum of constitution of the Working Group is given in Annexure 1. As cheque truncation and e-cheques are two independent though related issues, the Group decided to offer their views and recommendations on these issues in separate parts. Accordingly, in this part (Part I), the Group examines the issues relating to cheque truncation and will address e-cheques in the subsequent part (Part II).

The Group is thankful to Shri S Ganesh Kumar, General Manager and Shri Vipin K Surelia, Asst. General Manager, Dept. of Information Technology, Reserve Bank of India for conducting extensive studies of the cheque truncation the world over, in performing various costing options and in various inputs to the Group. The Group acknowledges the inputs provided by NCR Corporation, Unsisys Ltd., and BCSIS, which provided insight into various options available from a technology perspective. The valuable inputs of the Sveriges Riksbank, Sweden and the Monetary Authority of Singapore, Singapore to the members of the study teams are also appreciated by the Group.

Methodology

1. The Group had deliberations on its terms of reference in the various sittings. Vendors who had experience in providing cheque truncation solutions and implementation exposure internationally were invited to make presentations to the Working Group. M/s. NCR Corporation, Unisys and BCSIS shared their implementation experience. In addition, two teams of the members of the Working Group visited Sweden (where cheque truncation had been in vogue for more than two decades) and Singapore (which is at the threshold of introduction of cheque truncation) for studying various facets of the processes, requirements and other issues including legal aspects; they share their experience with the other members.
2. The deliberations of the Working Group focussed on the following issues in the context of its terms of reference:
   - Point of truncation of the cheque
   - Cheque Issuance or Generation Process
   - Security Features required in e-cheques and e-cheque clearing and settlement process
   - Defining Inter-bank Clearing and Settlement Process for e-cheques
   - Conduct of e-cheque clearing with normal paper clearing with the data for the two consolidated or altogether a separate clearing
   - Frequency of Clearing per day
   - Centralised Clearing House for the entire country for e-cheques or e-cheque clearing to be the part of the local Clearing House Jurisdiction
   - Cost Benefit Analysis for putting in place the infrastructure
   - At the customer and bank interface levels

- Within Banks: at the branches and service branches
- Between the Banks and the Clearing Houses
- Between the Clearing House and the Settlement Banks
- Roles and Responsibilities and Rights and Obligations of various participants
- Legal framework required for enabling e-cheques
- The changes required in Uniform Regulations and Rules Governing Bankers' Clearing Houses (URRBCH) for implementing e-cheque clearing and settlement
- Return cycle to be a separate cycle or whether it can be merged with the subsequent settlement

Cheque Truncation

1. The cheque is currently the most visible and significant mode of payment in India. In view of the importance of cheque to the retail segment, Magnetic Ink Character Recognition (MICR) technology was introduced by the Reserve Bank of India. MICR technology enabled the banking system to handle the growth in the cheque volumes and to provide faster and efficient clearing services to customers and to do straight through processing using MICR data. Over a period of two decades, a number of MICR Clearing Houses have evolved.
2. The entire clearing cycle is dependent on the movement of the physical paper cheque from the presenting bank to the drawee bank (branch) as was mandated by the NI Act prior to its amendment. This bottleneck had an over-riding impact on any consideration for improvements or reduction in the cycle time for clearing.
3. Until very recently, legal covenants in India required the cheque to be presented to the paying branch for payment. The paying branch is the last node in the

clearing cycle as it exists in the country, and thus the paper cheque is on the move through the entire cycle from the bankbranch of the collecting bank where it is first deposited to the service branch of the collecting bank, onward to the Clearing House, which acts as a focal point for the cheques of all the banks, and from the Clearing Centre to the paying bank service branch and lastly the paying branch. If the cheque is returned unpaid, it has to re-trace the entire path back to the presenting branch.

4. Cheque Truncation is one of the ways to compress the clearing cycle to provide faster clearances of local and intercity cheques. Cheque truncation, very loosely defined, is the process in which the physical movement of cheque within a bank, between banks or between banks and the clearing house is curtailed or eliminated, being replaced in whole or in part, by electronic records of their content (with or without the images) for further processing and transmission.

INTERNATIONAL SCENARIO OF CHEQUE TRUNCATION SYSTEM

1. Truncation straddles many count rise across the globe on either side of the hemisphere. These include countries like Denmark and Belgium which were the pioneers in the truncation process, having introduced complete cheque truncation *(dokumentiase clearings)* in the early 1980s itself to the island state of Singapore which is in the final phase of implementation.

2. Retail payment analysts make a two-fold classification —countries like England, US and France where cheque has always dominated non-cash payments on one hand and the others like Sweden, Norway where giro transfers have been the dominant modes of non-cash payments. Cheque volumes in the second group have historically been low and from the point of view of

truncation, manageable, and these countries have been successful in introducing truncation in the clearing process. Sweden is the extreme example of achievement of complete truncation where all cheques can be presented and encashed at any bank branch, irrespective of the bank on which they are drawn.

3. Secondly, the implementation of truncation has invariably been preceded by either the amendment of the existing laws governing cheques and other payment instruments or by the introduction of new laws.
4. Many countries such as Spain, Italy and Luxemburg have an amount ceiling for the cheques that can be truncated. Cheques which are considered low value are eligible for truncation whereas the higher value instruments still follow the traditional clearing route.
5. Under most implementations the cheques are truncated early on in the clearing cycle, typically at the collecting branch level or the collecting bank level. Ireland stands out as an example of late truncation, where 95 per cent of the cheques are truncated at the paying bank stage.
6. International experiences with cheque truncation show that the geographically smaller countries are the ones that have been able to implement the process of truncation, be it Greece or Singapore or Belgium. Cheque truncation has been less than a complete success in larger countries. USA, for example, is still a laggard in this respect despite having the maximum number of cheques written (237 per head in a year). Nonetheless, it is making progress towards implementation of cheque truncation.

CHEQUE TRUNCATION MODEL FOR INDIA

1. The Group deliberated on the point in the clearing cycle, where the movement of the physical paper should be stopped i.e. - whether cheques should be truncated at the Presenting Bank, the Clearing House or the Drawee

Bank. The Group is of the view that full benefits of truncation will be available only when the truncation takes place at the Presenting Bank; otherwise, the clearing process will again be slow and the clearing cycle will be inefficient to that extent. Within a bank, the Group is of the view that the bank should have a choice, depending upon its individual efficiencies, resources and cost considerations, where it wants to truncate the cheque. Whether a bank wants to truncate the physical cheque at its' service branch or whether it wants to truncate it at the branch of the first deposit or even outsource the truncation process should be left to the decision of the bank concerned. Truncating the cheque after the Clearing House does not entail any advantage to the current clearing process and therefore, truncation at the drawee bank is not suitable. Therefore, the Group recommends that in India the cheques should be truncated at the Presenting Bank itself and within the Presenting Bank it should be left to the individual banks whether cheque is truncated at the branch or at the service branch or whether the truncation process is outsourced, depending upon the individual efficiency, resources, facilities and cost considerations of the bank.

2. The Group deliberated on the mode of truncation i.e. whether the truncation is to be based on electronic image of the cheque or based on the MICR code line only. However, the amendment to NI Act facilitates payment on the basis of an image of the cheque only. As payment based on the MICR code line exchange would not provide opportunities for signature verification (which is a legal requirement as on date), the Group recommends electronic image based cheque truncation.

3. The preservation period of the physical cheques was considered by the Group. Presently, the preservation period of the physical cheque leaves is eight year as

mandated by the "Banking Companies Preservation of Records" Rules 1985. Under the amended Negotiable Act, the certificate from the drawee bank on the print out of the image of the physical cheque is a proof of payment. Therefore, the Group debated whether the present period of eight years is suitable or whether it can be reduced. The Group was of the opinion that the preservation period should be governed by the reconciliation period between the customers and the banks. Large Corporates in the country take almost six months to reconcile the cheques issued by them and in the case of Government cheques the period is extensible up to a year. Therefore, the Group concludes that the even though the period for which the physical cheques should be preserved can be brought down below one year, in view of the reconciliation requirements, the preservation period of paper instruments should be one year. The Group accordingly recommends that suggestion to change the existing statutory preservation period of eight years under "Banking Companies Preservation of Records" Rules 1985 to one year should be made to the Government.

4. The Group considered the issue of the storage location of cheque images and the preservation period for the cheque images. On the storage location, the Group debated on the idea of the cheque images being stored at by a Central Image Warehousing Agency or by the presenting banks/drawee banks themselves. As per the amended NI Act, it is the drawee bank that has to certify the printout of the image of the cheque as a proof of payment. Going by this consideration, the images should be stored at the drawee bank. On the other hand, the physical cheques are with the presenting bank and it is the presenting bank which initiates the process of truncation and hence the images as well as paper instruments are available with it and the presenting bank should be responsible for storage of images. A

third alternative that was considered by the Group was that of a Centralised Image warehouse. The drawee bank can always request the central agency for any image and certify that image for the purpose of proof of payment. Also, having a Centralised Agency will give the member banks the benefit of having to approach a single agency in case it requires images of any instruments rather than to approach multiple presenting banks. From the point of view of efficiency and control, the Group concludes that Centralised Agency per clearing location should act as an image warehousing facility for the banks. However, given the challenges involved in setting up a single agency in the Indian context, the Group recommends that the choice could be either a single agency or individual drawee banks as the points of storage.

5. A concurrent question that was discussed was which entity should act as a Centralised Image Warehousing Facility or what kind of entity should be given permission to act as one. The Group considered various issues like the cost required to set-up such an agency, whether any existing agency or institution can set up an image warehouse, what will be considerations while setting up such an agency, how will vendor proposals for setting up such agency evaluated and against what benchmarks will they be compared, etc. The group decided to lay down broad guidelines for the suitability of any entity to provide image warehousing facilities. The Group recommends that for the entity that will act as a Centralised Image Warehousing Facility should meet the following criteria:

   i) The entity should have the technical competency

   ii) The entity should have an efficiency orientation

   iii) The entity should be sizeable in terms of resources

   iv) If the entity is an existing organisation, it should be well reputed *v*) It would be preferable for banks to have ownership stakes in such entities

vi) It should be subject to supervisory and regulatory controls of the Reserve Bank of India or any other agency that may be authorised for this purpose by the Reserve Bank of India.

6. The Group also considered that storage requirement of the electronic image of the physical cheques and deliberated that technology places no limitation on the period the images can be stored. The Group recommends that the preservation period of the electronic image of the cheque should be eight years. The Group also recommends that Government may be approached to amend the "Banking Companies Preservation of Records" Rules 1985 to enable image preservation for eight years.

7. Imaging of cheques can be based on various technology options, the cheque images can be black and white, Grey Scale or coloured. The Group considered all the three options. Black and White images do not reveal all the subtle features that are there in the cheques. Coloured Images increase storage and network bandwidth requirements. Therefore, the Group recommends that the Grey Scale technology which helps capture finer features on cheques and also have relatively lesser storage and network bandwidth requirements will be suitable for India.

8. A question that arose was whether cheques should be standardised as has been done in Singapore from security and image friendliness perspective. In Singapore, a common format for cheque has been designed and is used by all the banks. The Group suggested that the same can be done but the introduction of truncation process should not be made to wait till the process is complete and old cheques are

fully withdrawn. Also, it would entail a cost to the banks that have already printed large number of cheques and the withdrawal of old cheques is a time consuming process with non-MICR cheques still being presented by customers. Therefore, the Group recommends that truncation and standardisation of cheque format should be independent initiatives with the latter being implemented after even after the introduction of cheque truncation.

9. The Group also considered the issue of changes to the MICR line as has been done in Singapore. In Singapore, a check digit has been introduced in the MICR line. This change enables verification of the genuineness of the cheque at the presenting bank itself and provides an additional level of control in case of image misreads. The Group was of the opinion that any change in the existing MICR line structure in a vast country like India will lead to a delay in implementation and additional costs as hardware and software changes will be required at all processing points in the clearing cycle-presenting bank/branch, clearing house and the drawee bank/ branch, apart from printing costs of cheques to accommodate modified MICR Code line. Therefore, the Group recommends that the truncation should be introduced in India for settlement to be generated on the basis of the current structure of the MICR fields.

10. The Group also considered the issues related to the security requirements for the flow of cheque data and images over the network from the presenting bank to the clearing house and onwards to the drawee bank, etc. and the handling of data and images at the various processing nodes in the clearing cycle. The Group was of the view that digital signatures should be used but encryption may not be essential. The Group also deliberated on the security requirements during storage of the images of the cheques either by banks or at the

Centralised Image Warehousing Facility and recommended that these should be in consonance with the requirements of IT Act 2000. The Group accordingly recommends that use of Public Key Infrastructure (PKI) should be adopted to protect data and image flow over the network and to establish authenticity, non-repudiation, integrity, etc. and suggested that digital signatures should be used. The Group also recommends that the security requirements for the storage of images by the banks or the Centralised Warehousing Agency should be in consonance with the requirements of the IT Act 2000.

11. Another question that arose and deliberated by the Group was whether various participants in the truncation process should be subjected to a certification process and based on that certification process they should be allowed as members in the truncation process. The members were of the opinion that the certification process would ensure that the participants adhere to the minimum requirements of security and efficiency and recommends that the members in the truncation based clearing system should be subjected to a certification process based on prevalent Information Security Audit Guidelines of the Reserve Bank of India.

12. On the issue of implementation, the Group considered two approaches - big bang *versus* phased approach to implementation. The advantage of the big bang approach is that once a cutoff date is decided for truncation at a centre, all the processes and members will be geared towards meeting the date. If a phased approach is adopted, full benefits of truncation will not be available. Also, the group was of the opinion that if truncation process is to be phased out, say, for ready banks by one cut-off date and remaining banks by a second cut-off dates, there will be duplication of efforts and confusion and operational issues like sorting out

and transportation of cheques for banks which are not ready and imaging and transmission of cheques for banks which are truncation ready. Therefore, the group recommends that truncation should be introduced for all banks and all clearings at a centre from a cut-off date for all participants at that centre.

13. A related question that arose was whether truncation should be based on a cut-off amount as is a practice prevalent in some countries. The Group felt that truncation should not be based on amount as it will require cheques to be sorted out at the presenting branch itself and there will be two separate channels and two separate clearing requirements both in terms of infrastructure required and process definitions. Therefore, the Group recommends that there should be no amount based cut-off for truncation and all cheques should irrespective of value, should be truncated.

14. The Group also considered the issue of from which city the city cheque truncation should be commenced. Should the centres with lower volumes be targeted first, where implementation process will be smooth in view of smaller number of cheques, smaller number of participants. etc. or should the efforts be concentrated on centres with large cheque volumes where the efficiency and customer service impact will be much larger? The Group recommends that the truncation initiatives should be targeting larger cities viz. the four metros which account for the major chunk of the cheque volumes in India and once the truncation process is established in these centres, rolling it out to the other centres will be a relatively easier task. Therefore, the Group recommends that in view of large number of cheque volumes and the benefit derived by introduction of truncation the four metro centres should be targeted first in the first phase. Before that, pilots at two small centres near the metros will be done within a time frame of one year.

15. The issues relating to the countermanding and stop payments were discussed by the Working Group. The Group recognised that in clearings based on cheque truncation, the cycle time for the entire process will be compressed, compared to the clearing based on physical movement of paper cheque, especially the inter-city clearing cycle. The Group felt that even in the context of the compressed clearing cycle, countermanding payments and stop recordings should be allowed till the time payment has been made as is the current practice. Therefore, The Working Group recommends that countermanding payments and recording stops should be allowed till the time of payment as is the existing practice.

LEGAL ISSUES RELATED TO CHEQUE TRUNCATION SYSTEM

1. The Working Group also examined the major recommendations that had been made by an earlier Working Group on legal issues in cheque truncation chaired by Shri N V Deshpande, Principal Legal Adviser, Reserve Bank of India.
2. The recommendation made by the above mentioned Working Group that institutions will have to obtain Reserve Bank of India approval to ensure uniform standards/practices are implemented in India is also being recommended by this Group by way of members in the truncation process being subjected to a certification process as per the IS Audit Guidelines of Reserve Bank of India.
3. On the additional responsibility on the collecting bank under a truncated environment, to verify the genuineness of the cheque based on visible features, the same has been assigned as per the amended NI Act and the drawee bank will continue to verify the signature, availability of funds.

4. The Deshpande Group had also recommended that the Clearing House cannot be held responsible for fraud, forgery, etc. As per the recommendations of the current Working Group, the Clearing House will be doing settlement based purely on MICR data and will act as a pass through for the images. Therefore, the Clearing House cannot be held responsible for the fraud, forgery of cheques as it cannot even open the images sent in by the banks.
5. On the issue of the earlier recommendation, on drawee bank having accepted the image in case no protest is lodged within 24 hours, the Group clarified that it will be as per the timings of the existing return cycle.
6. On the right of the drawee bank to seek further information on the veracity/genuineness of the cheque, the amended NI Act already provides for the same. The drawee bank can seek not only further information but can also seek the physical instrument for verification and can retain it if the payment has been made accordingly.
7. The earlier Group had recommended an eight year period for retention of the images and the same is being recommended by the current working group.

DEPARTMENT OF INFORMATION TECHNOLOGY MEMORANDUM

Working Group on Cheque Truncation and E-cheques

1. The current process of reforms in Payment and Settlement Systems in the country is aimed at ensuring the establishment of a safe, secure, efficient, robust and Integrated Payment and Settlement System, with thrust on electronic modes of payment and settlement. Presently, the paper based cheque clearing system is the most predominant system in the country. In addition to the international sound practices in the form of the

"Core Principles" of the Bank for International Settlements and technology being at the base of improvements in payment and settlement systems, various legal requirements provided for in the form of amendments to the Negotiable Instruments Act, 1881 have further speeded up the reforms. These initiatives have heralded new processes to ensure, safe and secure payments. Cheque truncation is one such facility, while e-cheques could replace paper based cheques.

2. Cheque Truncation reduces the physical movement of cheques and consequentially, the dependence on the infrastructure therefore, facilitates shorter clearing and settlement cycle through straight through processing, dispatch of the cheque images and the associated data electronically and faster realisation of funds. With the accordance of legal validity to an electronic cheque as a negotiable instrument, the introduction of Cheque Truncation in the cheque clearing process can now become a reality in the country. In the Mid-term Review of Monetary and Credit Policy for the year 2002-2003, the Reserve Bank announced that it would form a Working Group to suggest an appropriate model of Cheque Truncation, suitable to the Indian conditions. Cheque Truncation can happen at the presenting bank branch level, presenting bank service branch level, Cheque Processing centre or the clearing house or at the drawee bank service branch level.

3. E-cheques reduce the dependency on paper based cheques for transfer of money. They provide for electronic presentment, endorsement and delivery-subject to adequate security and other requirements being put in place.

4. In order to examine the various aspects pertaining to cheque truncation and e-cheques and their implementation in India, a Working Group for Cheque Truncation and e-cheques is being constituted with representation as under:

1. Dr R B Barman, Chairman, Executive Director, Reserve Bank of India, Mumbai
2. Shri N V Deshpande, Member, Principal Legal Adviser, Reserve Bank of India, Mumbai
3. Shri M R Srinivasan, Member, Chief General Manager-in-charge, Department of Banking Operations and Development, Reserve Bank of India, Mumbai
4. Shri Ashok Kini, Member, Deputy Managing Director, State Bank of India, Mumbai
5. Shri S K Awasthi, Member, General Manager, Punjab National Bank, N Delhi
6. Shri Pravir Vora, Member, General Manager, ICICI Bank, Mumbai
7. Shri C N Ram, Member, HDFC Bank, Mumbai
8. Ms. U A Dharadhar, Member Saraswat Co-operative Bank Ltd., Mumbai
9. Shri K C Chowdhary, Member, Indian Banks' Association, Mumbai
10. Prof. D B Phatak, Member, Head, (IT-Specialist), K R School of Information Technology Indian Institute of Technology, Mumbai
11. Shri R Gandhi Member-Secretary, Chief General Manager-in-charge, Department of Information Technology, Reserve Bank of India, Mumbai

5. The terms of reference of the Working Group are as follows:

i) **Cheque Truncation:**

a) To examine the existing models of cheque truncation in other countries, review the same and recommend the optimal model for the Indian context.

b) To assess the infrastructural requirements, including the hardware and software for cheque truncation, for all participants including the cheque processing centre / Clearing house.

c) To lay down the standards and procedures for cheque clearing in a cheque-truncated environment, including a uniform procedure for cheque truncation.

d) Applicability of the provisions of the IT Act, 2000 to cheque truncation

ii) E-cheques:

a) To examine the existing models of E-cheques in other countries and other experiences in India and to recommend a model for India.

b) To lay down the standards and procedures relating to E-cheque-both from a technology and an operational perspective apart from security and other aspects.

c) Applicability of the provisions of IT Act, 2000 to E-cheques.

d) To provide for broad rules and regulations for issue of E-cheques, processing, clearing and settlement, and other related issues.

The Group may co-opt members from the industry, depending on their areas of expertise as and when necessary or arrange for interactive sessions with such industry members. The Working Group may submit its report within 3 months.

RESERVE BANK OF INDIA- CHEQUE TRUNCATION PROCESS

Cheque Truncation - Pilot Implementation

1. The Reserve Bank has been taking several reform measures to improve safety and efficiency in the payment modes. Though the thrust has been towards a move to the safer and more efficient electronic modes of payment, it is necessary that we take measures to

improve efficiency in the paper based modes of payments as well. The introduction of the Magnetic Ink Character Recognition (MICR) technology for cheque processing and the creation of imaging capabilities helped bring in efficiency improvements in handling volume and reconciliation of clearing differences. However, beyond a point the MICR technology could not speed up the collection process thanks to the logistics involved in the requirement that the cheques have to physically transported all the way from the collecting branch of a bank to the drawee bank branch. The way several countries have sought to solve this problem is by introducing a process called cheque truncation in which the movement of the physical instruments is curtailed at a point in the clearing cycle beyond which the process is completed purely based only on the electronic data and images of the cheques.

2. The question of introduction of cheque truncation in India has been engaging the attention of the Reserve Bank for quite some time. In order to provide legal basis for payment of truncated paper based instruments, we took up with the Government to amend the Negotiable Instruments Act, 1881 and accordingly the Act was suitably amended in December, 2002. A Working Group for Cheque Truncation and e-cheque was constituted by the Reserve Bank in January 2003 under the chairmanship of Dr. R. B. Barman, Executive Director, Reserve Bank of India to, among other things, draw a road map for introduction of cheque truncation for the country. The Working Group recommended the suitable cheque truncation model for India.

3. The recommendations of the Working Group have been accepted. Accordingly, it has been decided that an Image based Cheque Truncation Pilot Project be inititated by the Reserve Bank for the Bankers Clearing House of the National Capital Region of Delhi and its nearby areas.

4. Several preparatory steps are required to be undertaken by both the Reserve Bank and the banks for implementation of the project. The Reserve Bank has initiated steps to procure the required hardware and software systems for the central system. The steps to be taken by the banks primarily revolve around the procurement and/or outsourcing of truncation capabilities and adopting related changes in the systems and procedures.
5. A request was made to initiate action as described above within the prescribed timeframe to ensure launching cheque truncation in the National Capital Region smoothly.

REPORT OF THE WORKING GROUP ON CHEQUE TRUNCATION AND E-CHEQUE

Salient Features

To introduce a system of cheque truncation in India, a Working Group on Cheque Truncation and e-cheques (Chairman: Dr. R B Barman, Executive Director) was constituted by the Reserve Bank. The Working Group submitted Part I of its report in July 2003 and suggested a model for the cheque truncation in India. The major recommendations of the Working Group are as under:

- The physical cheque will be truncated within the presenting bank.
- Within the presenting bank the point of truncation could be decided by each individual member bank providing for Service Bureau models where banks can approach or set up Service Bureaux for capturing images and MICR data.
- Settlement will be generated on the basis of current MICR code line data.
- Electronic images will be used for payment processing.

- Grey scale technology will be deployed for imaging.
- Images will be preserved for eight years.
- A centralised agency per clearing location will act as an image warehouse for the banks. Group recommended norms for agencies to provide the service.
- Public Key Infrastructure will be deployed to protect images and data flow over the network.

IMPLEMENTATION OF CHEQUE TRUNCATION-TIMEFRAME FOR PREPARATORY MEASURES

1. Formation of a Cheque Truncation Implementation Policy Group within the bank at the highest level (to be headed by the Executive Director or the Chief Operating Officer or similar functionary) with due representations (at HOD level) from banking operations, systems and procedures, audit, legal, IT and other related functions to guide implementation of cheque truncation within the bank.
2. Formation of a Cheque Truncation Implementation Group in New Delhi.
3. Nomination of two Nodal Officers, one each from the Policy Group and the Implementation Group to interact with the Reserve Bank.
4. Deciding point/s of truncation within the bank.
5. Deciding point/s of truncation within the bank.
6. Undertaking Business Process Reengineering required for introduction of cheque truncation.
7. Organising Cheque Truncation Awareness Programmes within the bank to sensitise staff about the new system, its rules and procedures among other things, i) for outward and inward processing of cheques and images, and ii) changed responsibilities as a collecting and paying banker including preservation of cheques as the collecting bank and paying cheques based on images of cheques.

Advantages of the Cheque truncation Sytem

- No need to visit RBI
- Cheque has to undergo a system which will capture the image of the cheque electronically & the same will be circulated to respective bank.
- Service branch will only have this system.
- In Delhi & Nagpur Cheque Truncation System has been started.

Process of cheque truncation Sytem

- In service the image of cheque will be captured.
- Image will be sent to respective branch.
- Content of the cheque will be inspected e.g. amount of the cheque, etc.
- Communication will be done with concerned branch.
- According to that Cheque will be cleared or passed within 1 day or few minutes.
- As in general it takes two and half day to clear the cheque.

Disadvantages of the cheque truncation process

- Huddle to start the system in Mumbai
- In Mumbai technology is not much improved.
- Banker are not ready for the technology to be introduced.
- It is taking crores of Rupees to introduce.

CONCLUSION

The history of Indian Banking had been 'brick and mortar' based but the future would be 'click and mouse' oriented.

The future of banking will be technology driven. The cheque truncation system will speed up banking procedures and processes. For customers, it would be a new experience, as they would have the facility of home banking. The utility bills will be paid without any hassles like cutting a cheque, or filling in the cover form or mailing it by courier or post. These things will happen by single click of a button through products like 'bill-pay'. A part of the technology costs shall have to be borne by customers for the accurate and prompt services offered by banks.

The new environment will require a complete paradigm shift –new styles of conducting business with technology, people and processes. Indian Banking, Indian IT vendors and Indian consulting firms will be dominating players in the global banking scenario in coming years and that will surely be boom time for all. Non-awareness among the customers is the main reason for the scheme not picking up among them. Hence there is an urge that the customers use this mode of payment system. More and more people are to be made aware of the functioning of the cheque truncation system and its benefits because even though banks have many branches they have not yet touched the common man.

"Start by doing what is necessary , then what is possible, and suddenly you are doing the impossible."

BIBLIOGRAPHY

Professional Banker (The ICFAI University Press, 2007 Publication).

Interview with Mr. Pradeep. R. Arolkar, Assistant Manager, Clearance Department, Reserve Bank of India, Fort Branch, Mr. A. K. Rathod, Assistant General Manager, SBI Bank, Madame Cama Road Branch, Mrs. Nayna Shah (Customer Care Officer), Punjab National Bank, Malad (E) Branch.

■ ■ ■

7

TRANSFORMATION IN INDIAN BANKING THROUGH E-BANKING SERVICES–AN EMPIRICAL STUDY

ABSTRACT

In the post-LPG era and information technology, transformation is taking place in Indian banks with different parameters and in this era contours of banking services dynamically altering the face of banking services and the banks are stepping towards E-banking from traditional banking.

On the basis of five point likert type scale, the present paper empirically analyzes the quality of E-banking services in the changing environment. With different statistical tools like weighted average method, ranking, etc. the paper concludes that most of the customers of e-banks are satisfied from the different e-channels and their services but lack of awareness is a major obstacle in the spread of more E-banking services. At the end, the paper suggests some measures to make E-banking services more effective in the future.

INTRODUCTION

In the post-reforms period, Indian banking is passing through crucial stages. There is a paradigm shift in different parameters of transformation. Many internal and external factors are responsible for this bank transformation. A huge competition (inter and intra-bank group), global forces are compelling the banks to make radical changes in their day-to-day functioning. WTO, another dimension forcing the banks to make internal and external changes to meet the e-age challenges.

IT is a crucial parameter for transformation in structure, work-culture, functioning, HRD and business re-engineering. E-banking services are replacing traditional services and creating a new scale in transformation. In the initial stage, e-channels were introduced in metropolitan cities and urban areas but recently some banks have start capturing rural and semi-urban areas. New private sector banks are taking a lead to capture rural and semi-urban sector.

The different E-channels like ATMs, Credit & Debit Cards, Tele-banking, Mobile-banking, Online-banking, Smart Cards, etc. are changing the face of the Indian banks. New private sector banks and foreign banks are attracting the customers in a different way. The potential customers and big companies are shifting their accounts from traditional banks (not fully computerized) to e-banks (fully computerized and provide different e-channels). If traditional banks, mostly public sector banks, will not transform their business with introduction of IT, their survival will become difficult as now days IT is not a matter of convenience but a survival factor. Therefore, E-banking services are potent factor for transformation in this e-age.

E-banking has also affected the customer's expectations as they prefer to deal with the banks offering better, efficient and innovative services. To face and survive in this cutting edge competition, the banks have to deliver better quality services to the customers because it is only a customer who can evaluate quality of services. Hence, the service quality is conformance of services to customer's specifications and expectations. The banks must know what type of services the customers expect to have and then accordingly serve them the products and services that meet their expectations. The banks should not be adamant to accept changes otherwise their survival will become difficult in the emerging competition. Therefore, there is a need to evaluate the customer's perceptions regarding the recent E-banking services too, which will help to further improve the services if they are not satisfied with their services. In this context, this paper has much significance because it will help the banks to know their customer's perception regarding their E-banking services and they can further modify and make these services more efficient.

ORGANIZATION OF THE WORK

The work is organized into five sections. After the brief introduction, section II makes a review of the literature. Section III fixes the objectives and methodology. Section IV discusses the findings and suggestions and last section provides the concluding observations along with future areas of research.

REVIEW OF LITERATURE

Hasanbanu (2004), studied customer services in rural banks. He found that the rural customers are not aware for what purpose the loans are available and how they can avail. Customers do not know the complete rules, regulations and procedures of the banks as they preserve them for themselves and do not take interest in educating them.

Husain, (1988), also highlighted the importance of IT in various sectors. In the introduction of any new technology or system various organizational, financial and functional problems are faced in the initial stages. People are generally reluctant to accept new system, howsoever beneficial it may be. Such various issues, which are involved in computerization, have been critically & vividly discussed.

Heggade (2000), studied bank customer relationship in India. He analyzed responses of 11 different classes of bank customers like businessmen, salaried, advocates, peasants, etc. He analyzed customer's views on the one hand and employees view on the other hand. It concludes that there is a low correlation among the different occupations and satisfaction from services in the PSBs.

Pathrose, (2001), banking the world over is undergoing a rapid and radical transformation due to the all- pervasive influence of IT and breath taking developments in the technology of telecommunications and electronic data processing. The winds of change are blowing in India too. The IT which implies the integration of information system with communication technology has radically altered the traditional ways of doing banking business and allowed banks to wipe out the difference in time as well as distance. It is in this context his article attempts to trace the present status of hi-tech banking in India, visualize its prospects and look at the challenges and problems in the tracks to be traversed. He concludes that in the scenario of severe competition and escalating expectation of customers for newer products and alternative delivery channels, the contours of banking are being redefined. The key to survival of banks therefore is retention of customer's loyalty by providing them with value added services tailored to their needs, using state-of- the-art IT. There is no way a bank can remain lukewarm to hi-tech and yet hope to grow. It is a choice between survival and extinction.

Sharma & Singh (1993), analyzed the quality of customer services produced by Standard Charted Bank (SCB) and Punjab National Bank (PNB) (one branch of each bank situated in Hall Bazaar, Amritsar) with the sample of 40 respondents in total. They concluded that the quality of customer services of PNB branch is very poor in comparison to that of SCB branch. But the main limitation of the study is that it is related to two banks only.

Singh & Malhotra (1993), analyzed customer satisfaction in banking services in the Amritsar city. They concluded that public sector banks should improve their services to attract the new customers. Bank management should prepare the list of existing and prospective customers and carry out detailed studies on customer satisfaction in order to improve their services. But this study is limited to only one district of Punjab.

Singh (2004), explained the appraisal of customer service of PSBs and concluded that level of customer services and satisfaction is determined by the branch location, design, variety of services, rates and changes, systems and procedures and attitude and responses. His study is purely concerned with the customers of PSBs.

Sharma & Kaur (2004), studied strategies of customer satisfaction in rural banks. This study is concerned with Hoshiarpur district of Punjab. They used five-point likert scale and found that the rural customers are not satisfied from the strategies adopted by Gramin Bank.

Singhal's, (1987), is yet another important study about customer services in Indian banks. This study is based on a research project of Sushila Singhal's, sponsored by Shri Ram Center for Industrial Relations, New Delhi. The study itself two objectives: (a) " an adequate and systematic description analysis and explanation of customer services by the bank." This study is based on a broad sample of 528 bank employees (both officers and clerks) and 1,427 customers selected by a purpose-wise procedure. She had adopted a stage-wise methodology to select banks for the case study. In the first stage, she has chosen six banks and in the second stage five branches of the six banks for a more intensive study. The most important findings of this study are: (a) there are considerable differences between different banks in regard to employees job involvement and motivation, customer loyalty and identification of banks and branches employees attitudes towards bank customers and colleagues, etc. (b) the demographic and psychologicai variables were identified and their relationship with employees job performance and customer service is explained (c) it is also found that there is no correlation ship between'service efficiency' and' customers satisfaction'; further she has also not found any systematic relationship between the size of bank branch and customer satisfaction. She also elaborately discusses the implications of her findings for efficient bank management. The important merit of her study is that it is based on multi-method and multi-variable approach to explain the bank employee's job behaviour.

Shastri, (2001), he analyzed the effect and challenges of new technology for banks. Technology has brought a sea change in the functioning of the banks. The earlier manual system of preparation of vouchers, etc. is slowly being automated thereby saving a lot of time & effort. The use of ATMs and introduction of IT more than in the past, especially in the Post- VRS Scenario.

Shanti, (1984), has made a pioneering attempt to examine the issues relating delivery of customer services in Indian banks as against the backdrop of a sound conceptual framework. She has provided as empirical analysis of bank employee's job behavior and its relationship with bank services delivery. She has found that lack of job motivation, lack of freedom at branch level, lack of leadership qualities among bank managers, job security, etc. have resulted in poor quality customer services in Indian banks.

Uppal (2006), with stratified sampling of 500 bank customers, explained the impact of computerization on the satisfaction of customers of all bank groups and concluded that customer services are quite better in fully computerized banks and further in e-banks as compared to that in partial or non-computerized banks. The study was concerned only with the urban sector of Punjab. But the study is only concerned with the urban sector of Punjab.

Varghese & Ganesh (2003), analyzed customer services in PSBs and old private sector banks based on the responses of 776 customers of 10 PSBs and 13 old private sector banks operating in Kerala. They found regarding 'time' spent on a transaction where there is no difference in the two types of the bank branches.

Verma (2000), analyzed the impact of IT on PSBs & NPSBs in her article 'Banking on Change'. The IT is a threat for the PSBs. It has to be a complete face off for the PSBs. With the business per employee, even for the front-run PSBs, a mere fraction of that of NPSBs, the PSBs have to do a lot on improving their productivity & efficiency. NPSBs are fully computerized & providing services on Internet. Especially ICICI bank, HDFC bank is very active on this front and is concentrating on Internet & E-commerce to offer their clientele a whole range of products under one roof. New banks like GTB, BOP, IDBI & UTI bank are not lagging behind. While some of them are concentrating on expansion & modernization, some are focusing on mergers and acquisitions for their growth.

From the brief review of related literature, it can be concluded that not even a single study is related to recent bank transformation through e-delivery channels and the present study is an attempt to fulfill this gap.

Objectives

- To study and analyze the perceptions of bank customers using e-delivery channels in the context of recent bank transformation.
- To analyze and determine the future of e-delivery channels.
- To suggests some remedial measures to further aware about and improve e-channel services.

DATABASE AND METHODOLOGY

The present study is concerned with the Indian banking industry in general and particularly with those banks that are providing services through e-channels i.e. e-banks. Universe of the study is customer of e-banks. The sample size of the bank customers is 25. These customers are selected at random holding saving or current account in the e-banks and using e-channels from last 3 to 4 years.

The data is collected through pre-tested and well-structured questionnaire in the Ludhiana district of Punjab. The survey was conducted in the month of May, 2006. Weighted average scores (WAS) are calculated from the five point likert scale. The weights of 2 to most reasonable/strongly agreed/most important, 1 to reasonable/agreed/important, 0 to undecided status, -1 to unreasonable/disagreed/unimportant and –2 to most unreasonable/strongly disagreed/most unimportant.

The weights are given to ranks of the different statements. The highest weight is given to the first rank and the lowest weight is given to the lowest rank. On the basis of these weights, total sore of each statement is calculated separately and then overall rank is given to each statement.

RESULTS AND DISCUSSION

As we know, recent bank transformation is taking place with IT and this all affects customer's perceptions regarding E-banking services. In the present paper an attempt has been made to know the perceptions of e-bank customers (who are using e-delivery channels).

Table-I: Responses About the Status of Annual Income, Education Level & Occupation Level of the Respondents.

Income Range (Rs.)	Number of Responses	Level of Education	Number of Responses	Occupation Level	Number of Responses
Less than 1 lakh	2 (8)	High School	2 (8)	Service Class	11 (44)
1 to 2 lakhs	13 (52)	Graduates	3 (12)	Business Class	4 (16)
More than 2 lakhs	10 (40)	Post Graduates	16 (64)	Industrialists	1 (4)
		Doctorates	4 (16)	Agriculturists	2 (8)
				Professionals	4 (16)
				Others	3 (12)

Note: Values in parenthesis show percentage.

The economic status like age, income, family size, education level and occupation level all affect the customer's thinking. Table-I reveals that out of the total 25 respondents, 52 per cent are those having income between one to two lakhs and 40 per cent are those having more than two lakhs income. Similarly, it is concluded that 64 per cent of the 25 respondents are highly educated with master degree and 16 per cent with doctorate degree. The table also shows the occupation level of the respondents, where 44 per cent respondents are under service class, 16 per cent are businessman and 16 per cent are professionals. Only 4 per cent are industrialists.

Overall, we can say that the customers with middle-income level, high education, serviceman & businessman use e-delivery channels more and aware about the concept E-banking. Industrialists and agriculturist, even 8 per cent of the respondents having income below one lakh and only high school educated are also using these e-channels to some extent.

Table-II: Factors Influencing the Selection of E-Channels.

Factors	Most Imp.	Imp.	Un-Decided	Un-Imp.	Most Un-Imp.	WAS
Convenient accessibility of e-channels	12	11	1	-	1	1.32
Convenient location of ATMs	18	6	-	1	-	1.64
Easy availability of e-channels	7	16	2	-	-	1.20
Low hidden cost for services	14	6	3	1	1	1.24
Number of facilities provided by e-channels	8	12	2	2	1	0.96
Security/less risk to use	16	8	-	-	1	1.52

Here, it can be concluded that WAS of all the factors the one factor i.e. 'number of facilities provided by e-channels' is more than 1 i.e. the respondents feel all factors much important in selecting their e-channels but among all these factors, convenient location with first priority and then security are the main factors affecting their e-channel selection decision.

Table-III: Responses Regarding Preferences for E-Channels.

E-Channels	R-1	R-2	R-3	R-4	R-5	R-6	R-7	Total Scores	Overall Ranks
ATM	17	5	1	1	-	-	1	159	1
Credit Cards	2	8	6	2	1	4	1	112	2
Debit Cards	-	6	8	1	4	4	2	102	4
Mobile Banking	1	3	4	6	8	2	1	98	5
Online-Banking	5	1	5	7	4	2	1	111	3
Smart Card	-	-	-	1	3	6	15	40	7
Tele-Banking	-	2	1	6	5	7	4	74	6

It is evident from this table that out of 25 respondents, most of them prefer ATMs as compared to other channels. ATMs got first rank in preference of e-channels by the respondents where second most preferred e-channel is Credit Cards and then Online-banking but Smart Cards and Tele-banking are least preferred among the respondents. The basic reason for the popularity of e-channels is these are convenient, easy to access and easy to operate.

Table-IV: Motivational Factors Encouraging Customers to Prefer a Particular E-Channel.

Motivational Factors	SA	A	UD	DA	SDA	WAS
Cost-effective	10	14	1	-	-	1.36
Convenient accessibility	13	9	1	2	-	1.32
Provide accurate information	14	9	-	1	1	1.36
Provide efficient services	18	5	-	1	1	1.52
Provide security for threats to loose information	13	8	-	-	4	1.04
Time-saving	17	8	-	-	-	1.68

This table analyzes the motivational factors encouraging the customers to prefer a particular e-channel against others. Here the strongest factor is time saving and secondly efficient services. Cost-effectiveness and accurate information are another factors, which attracts them to choose a particular e-channel. Most of the respondents are preferred e-channels mainly due to time saving and which provide efficient services.

Table-V: Awareness About Hidden Cost of E-Channels.

Status	**Respondents**
Yes	12 (48)
No	13 (52)

Note: Values in parenthesis show percentage

T-V shows the awareness level of the respondents about hidden cost of the e-channels. It is examined that 48 per cent are aware about the hidden cost but 52 per cent are not may be due to their ignorance or inadequate information provided by the banks.

Table-VI: Responses Regarding Cost-Effectiveness of E-Channels.

E-Channels	**Most Reasonable**	**Reasonable**	**Un-Decided**	**Un-Reasonable**	**Most Un-Reasonable**	**WAS**
ATM	13	10	2	-	-	1.44
Credit Card	6	9	4	5	1	0.56
Debit Card	5	8	9	3	-	0.60
Internet - Banking	6	8	9	2	-	0.72
Mobile - Banking	5	7	7	6	-	0.44
Smart Card	3	3	12	4	3	0.44
Tele - Banking	5	4	11	2	3	0.24

T-VI analyzed that whether the service charges of e-channels are reasonable or not and which e-channel is most cost-effective. Majority of the respondents are in favour of ATMs that means ATMs are most cost-effective and secondly they are in favour of Internet-banking that also provide services at reasonable cost. Here important to note is most of the respondents are not aware about these charges, therefore, these results are on the basis of the views of just those respondents having knowledge about these charges. Hence, out of all the e-delivery channels, ATMs and Internet-banking is considered as most cost-effective as compared to other channels, whereas Debit & Credit Cards are also cost effective as these come after ATMs & Internet-banking.

Table-VII: Responses Regarding Problems Faced by the Customers while Using E-Channels.

Problems	R-1	R-2	R-3	R-4	R-5	R-6	R-7	R-8	Total Score	Overall Rank
Inadequate knowledge	6	10	1	2	2	2	2	-	152	2
Lack of knowledge reg. use of e-channels	9	5	2	3	3	3	-	-	155	1
Lack of infrastructure	2	-	7	5	7	2	2	-	121	4
Unsuitable location of ATMs	-	4	4	7	4	3	1	2	116	6
Insufficient Number of ATMs	8	1	2	5	4	3	2	-	137	3
Poor Network	1	3	7	3	2	8	-	1	119	5
Time consuming	-	-	2	-	1	2	18	2	60	7
No problem at all	-	1	-	-	2	2	-	20	41	8

T-VII examined the problems faced by the respondents while using e-channels. Here, it is examined that lack of knowledge regarding use of e-channels and inadequate knowledge about e-channels are the most dominating problems faced by the majority of the respondents where problem of insufficient number of ATMs and lack of infrastructure are also major ones faced by the respondents.

T-VIII analysis the most effective solutions preferred by the respondents out of the given list. Information/demo at the counter is most preferred solution to make them aware about e-channels and secondly they prefer demo-fares regarding e-channels and after that personal contact programmes. Therefore, we can conclude and suggests the banks that make personal contacts with demo at the counter and any other information to make more and more customers aware about E-banking services as they think these methods are most effective to cover this path.

Table-VIII: Responses Regarding Suggestions to Make the Customers Aware about E-Channels.

Suggestions	R-1	R-2	R-3	R-4	R-5	Total Score	Overall Rank
Conduct more training programmes for bank customers	5	4	5	5	6	72	4
Demo-fares regarding e-channels	9	3	2	5	6	79	2
Information/demo at the counter	5	6	7	4	3	81	1
More advertisements	2	5	6	9	3	69	5
Personal contact programmes	4	7	5	2	7	74	3

Table-IX: Frequency of Customer's Monthly Physical Visits in the Banks in Addition to Accessing E-Channels.

Number of Bank Visits	Number of Responses
Occasionally once	11 (44)
2 to 5 times	11 (44)
6 to 10 times	2 (8)
11 to 15 times	1 (4)
More than 15 times a month	-

Note: Values in parenthesis show percentage.

T-IX analysis the frequency of physical visits of the customers in banks even they are using e-channels. Majority of the respondents (44 per cent) visit the banks occasionally once a month and 44 per cent visit 2 to 5 times within a month. Only 12 per cent respondents visit more than 5 times.

We can see that majority of the respondents visit banks less than 5 times within a month even they are accessing E-channels.

Table-X: Purpose of Customer's Physical Visits in the Banks in Addition to Accessing E-Channels.

Purpose	R-1	R-2	R-3	R-4	R-5	R-6	R-7	Total Score	Overall Rank
Mega-size deposits	7	9	1	5	1	1	1	134	2
Mega-size withdrawals	9	7	3	4	2	-	-	142	1
Making Complaints	-	1	4	3	7	5	5	74	7
Getting Loans/advances	2	2	2	4	2	8	5	79	6
To access lockers	3	2	6	1	5	3	5	93	3
To get new information	1	5	2	7	1	3	6	90	4
Any other	3	-	6	1	7	5	3	89	5

T-X analysis that those who visit the banks physically even accessing e-channels, for what purpose they do so. It is concluded that majority of the respondents visit banks for mega-size withdrawals & deposits or otherwise to get loans/ advances. Some of them visit to access lockers or to get new information.

T-XI shows that respondents are strongly agreed with some aspects of e-channels as their WAS is more than 1 that are E-channels have bright future, these improve quality of customer services, these are necessary in the competition and global era, make online purchase/sale of goods/services easy, online-banking helps to manage transformation but with other aspects like privacy, etc. either they are disagree or cannot decide. It is important to note that they are strongly disagreed that E-channels are creating more confusion. That means they don't think so. Hence, from their views, it can be concluded that E-channels are necessary in future and helps in managing business efficiently and timely.

Table-XI: Responses Regarding Different Aspects of E-Channels.

Statements	SA	A	UD	DA	SDA	WAS
E-channels do not ensure privacy	2	12	2	7	2	0.20
E-channels ensure more transparency	3	15	3	3	1	0.64
E-channels are creating more confusion for customers	5	4	5	7	4	-0.04
E-channels have bright future in global age	17	6	1	1	-	1.56
E-channels improve the quality of customer services in banks	13	12	-	-	-	1.52
E-channels are necessary in the competitive, global and new economy of India	19	5	1	-	-	1.72
E-channels make online purchase of goods and services easier	12	11	1	1	-	1.36
E-channels are creating more social relations among the bank customers and bank employees	4	10	3	6	2	0.32
E-channels are fulfilling our all requirements in e-age	6	10	3	2	4	0.48
E-banks charge more hidden cost	1	14	7	2	1	0.48
More formalities are required to get e-channels issued from the banks	3	10	7	5	-	0.44
Online banking helps to manage transformation in banks more efficiently	8	13	2	2	-	1.08
Smart card sometime creates technical hurdles to make payments	1	15	6	2	1	0.52

T-XI shows that respondents are strongly agreed with some aspects of e-channels as their WAS is more than 1 that are E-channels have bright future, these improve quality of customer services, these are necessary in the competition and global era, make online purchase/sale of goods/services easy, online-banking helps to manage transformation but with other aspects like privacy, etc. either they are disagree or cannot decide. It is important to note that they are strongly disagreed that E-channels are creating more confusion. That means they don't think so. Hence, from their views, it can be concluded that E-channels are necessary in future and helps in managing business efficiently and timely.

SUGGESTIONS

On the basis of the findings of the study, we may put some suggestions to make E-banking services more effective, which will further accelerate the process of transformation in banks.

Convenient accessibility of E-channels

The banks should make the availability of ATMs and accessibility of other e-channels convenient and make these channels secure from fear of lost of information by increasing the number of ATMs as these factors are most important concluded from their perceptions. They should start to introduce mobile ATMs as these are time saving and became more popular in these days.

Popularity of E-channels

As ATMs, Credit Cards and Internet banking are most preferred by the customers due to time and cost utility and efficient services where other channels are not much popular. So the banks should make efforts like arrange demo-fares or provide information at counters to make the channels popular and easier to the customers.

Transparency

The banks should disclose the full information to the customers to win their confidence like service charges, service tax, interest, penalty, if any, etc.

Awareness regarding E-delivery channels

As E-banking is a new concept and more than 50 per cent respondents are not aware about E-channels and their operating system, so the banks should provide appropriate information and demo to operate these channels and solve their any problem regarding these channels on priority basis in a polite manner. Besides the channels, the customers should also be make aware about the type of services provided by a particular e-channel. The banks should provide operational knowledge of e-channels with their each function to the customers, separately to the different age groups and occupation-wise as well.

Rural and Semi- urban sector

In India more than 60 per cent of the population is residing in the rural areas. Therefore, it is the need of the hour to capture this market through e-delivery channels. Hence, banks should make e-delivery channels popular in rural and semi-urban areas too with some practical and effective strategies.

Wider scope of E-channels

The banks should make the area of e-delivery channels wider by providing the facility of draft making, mega-size withdrawals and deposits and even provide loans to the customers. This will further make these channels popular and help to earn more income by charging more charges on mega-size deposits and withdrawals.

Infrastructure Facilities

Every branch of a bank should provide sufficient and proper vehicle parking, sitting arrangement, water and sanitary facilitates, etc. Posters of existing schemes should also be displayed in the appropriate places.

Improvement of HRD systems

The employees of E-banks should be given training time to time to match their skill level with the requirements of changing environment at least they should make aware about all the schemes provided by the banks.

Social rapport with customers

It is suggested that bank officials should make full rapport with customers, this will develop a social banking environment.

CONCLUSION

It is evident from the above discussion that the majority of the customers of e-banks are highly satisfied from E-banking services. The customers prefer e-channels with time and cost utility and which provide efficient services. The customers are not fully aware about the operational part of each channel and their transactional facilities. On the basis of the observations of the respondents, the future of E-banking services is bright and we may determine that in the coming years, these e-channels will definitely help to manage the bank transformation with positive results. On the basis of the findings, paper suggests that awareness regarding operating system and facilities provided by e-channels should be highlighted to each age group and also to the customers of each occupation. It will awaken the customers regarding the E-banking services through these e-delivery channels.

Future Areas of Research

- Per transaction cost in traditional banking and in E-banking system.
- Quality of E-banking services in rural and semi-urban areas.
- Comparative study of quality of services of the entire Indian bank groups and even at bank level.
- Feasibility of e-shopping in the rural and semi-urban areas.

BIBLIOGRAPHY

Avasthi, G.P.M. (2000-01), 'Information Technology in Banking: Challenges for Regulators', *Prajnan*, Vol. XXIX, No. 4, pp. 3 –17.

Eapen, P.G. (2000), 'Automated Teller Machines- Security Issues', *IBA Bulletin*, Vol. XXII, No. 9 (Sept.), pp. 23-26.

Hasanbanu, S. (2004), 'Customer Service in Rural Banks: An Analytical Study of Attitude of different types of Customers towards banking services', *IBA Bulletin*, Vol. XXVI. No. 8 (August), pp. 21-29.

Husain , F. (1988), Computerization and Mechanization in Indian Banks, (New Delhi: Deep & Deep Publication).

Heggade, O.D. (2000), Banker – Customer Relationship in India, (New Delhi: Mohit Publication).

Kulkarni, R. V. (2000), 'Changing Face of Banking From Brick and Mortar Banking to E- Banking', *IBA Bulletin* (January).

Metzer, S.R. (2000), 'Strategic Planning for Future Bank Growth', *The Banker's Magazine* (July- Aug.), pp. 57-65.

Mittal, S.R. A. (2000), 'Payment Systems in High – Tech. Banking', *The Journal of The Indian Institute of Bankers*, Vol.71, No. 3, (July-Aug.), pp. 8-19.

Pathrose, P.P. (2001), 'Hi- Tech. Banking-Prospects and Problem', *IBA Bulletin*, Vol. XXIII, No. 7 (July).

Padwal, SM (2003), 'Data warehousing and CRM in Banking', Vinimaya, Vol. XXXIV, No. 2 (July- Sept.), pp. 19-30.

Shanti, S. (1984), Customer Services in Banks (Bombay: Himalaya publishing House)

Singh, S. (2004), 'An Appraisal of Customer Service of Public Sector Banks' *IBA Bulletin*, Vol. XXVI, No. 8 (August), pp. 30-37.

Sanker, G. (2004), 'Customer Service in Banks', *IBA Bulletin*, Vol. XXVI, No. 8 (August), pp. 5-8.

Sharma, R. D. & Kaur, G., 'Strategy for Customer Satisfaction (2004). in Rural Banks – A case Study of Shivalik kshetriya Gramin Bank, Hoshiarpur', Prajnan, Vol. XXXIII, No. 1 (April-June), pp. 23-45.

Shama; S.C. and Singh, J. 'Quality of Customer Service (1993), In Banks: A Comparative Study of SCB AND PNB', ed. (Radha Publication: New Delhi).

Singh, R & Malhotra, 'Customer Satisfaction in Banking A (1993), Services: A Study of Amritsar', ed. (Radha Publication: New Delhi).

Sushila, S. (1987), Banks and Customers: A Behavioral Analysis, (New Delhi: Shri Ram Centre for Industrial Relations and Human Resources).

Shastri, R.V (2001), 'Technology for Banks in India- Challenges', *IBA Bulletin*, Vol. XXIII, No. 3 (March), pp. 23-45

Uppal, R.K. (2006), Indian Banking and Information Technology (New Delhi: New Century Publications)

Vajay, K. (2002), 'Job Satisfaction Among Bank Employees: Cadre – Wise - A Case Study', *IBA Bulletin*, Vol. XXIV, No. 2 (Feb.), pp. 29-34.

Verghese, M.E.& Ganesh, 'Customer Service in Banks: C (2003), An Empirical Study', Vinimaya, Vol. XXXIV, No. 2 (July- September), pp. 15-26

Verma, D. (2000), 'Banking on Change', ICFAI Reader (May), p. 69.

■ ■ ■

8

E-BANKING SERVICES AND BANKERS' PERSPECTIVE–AN EMPIRICAL STUDY

ABSTRACT

The paper is an attempt to study the perceptions of bankers for internet based E-banking services related with important issues like collaborative culture, training & development, knowledge management. The perceptions of employees experienced in E-banking system are surveyed where the study covers 60 employees of e-banks located in selected districts of Punjab during the first half of July, 2007. The study concludes that there exists collaborative culture and employees are satisfied with the working of e-channels and training programmes organized by e-banks, but not much satisfied with the knowledge management and behavioural aspects of E-banking. The employees experienced some frustration and a major problem of lack of knowledge of e-channels and their operating ways while dealing with these channels, are the most prevalent ones.

KEYWORDS: E-services in Banks, Policy Recommen-dations and Future Areas of Research

INTRODUCTION

The process of globalization has affected each and every aspect of life where technology has become the forerunner of this dynamic change. In this changing scenario, banking sector is not an exception. Banking sector is passing through a crucial transformation stage where all vistas of working are changing at a fast pace and technology is the most dominating factor which helped the banks to have a mix of knowledge with innovative products/services to win the competitive market. Prior to the electronic era, the whole business was done manually while only a little bit business was done through computers, but now-days, every transaction is made electronically through various e-channels like, ATMs, Credit/ Debit Cards, Smart Cards, I-Banking, M-Banking, Tele-Banking, EFTs, etc, which is also known as e-channels of banks. These e-channels are becoming more popular among the entire banks world over where in India only foreign banks, new private sector banks and a few of public sector banks are fully computerized and delivering services to their customers electronically. Public sector banks are also entering this e-age banking but at very low speed.

Whether the banks are public owned or private is not the matter of concern, the main thing is the success of every business depends upon its employees. Now the working culture has been totally changed totally i.e. from manual work to computerized where the burden of paper work and delivery time is reduced, database management is improved with lesser strain of work load. The employees feel free to provide services through e-channels and can spend their saved time on other important activities. If the employees are not satisfied from their job, working conditions, work culture, management, etc. they can never make the customers satisfied with better quality services. A big question to be answered for all the banks is how to manage human resources so that optimum production in terms of best services to customers can be get along with the fulfillment of their individual goals too. There is need to analyze the perceptions of bank employees regarding their working through e-channels in this new electronic era. Some questions arisen from the above discussion are:

1. Whether the bank employees are satisfied by working through e-channels or not and to what extent they are satisfied or dis-satisfied?
2. Have they any problem in dealing through e-channels, if so, what type of problems they are facing and how to solve these problems?

3. By working with which type of banks either traditional or E-banking, they are more satisfied?

In this work, an attempt is made to examine the perceptions of bank employees dealing with internet based E-banking services so that an analysis can be made to find out the problems faced by bank employees so that an appropriate solution for their efficient performance cab be searched out.

ORGANIZATION OF THE WORK

The whole work is divided into five parts. After brief introduction about the study, section II describes the objectives and methodology. Section III exhibits the results of the survey. Section IV suggests some policy recommendations to make the E-banking services efficient and popular among the employees where last part concludes the paper.

Objectives

- To study and analyze satisfaction level of bank employees working through e-channels.
- To study and examine the effectiveness of culture, behaviour and knowledge management etc.
- To examine the problems faced by the employees, if any, while dealing with e-channels and to suggests some measures to solve these problems.

METHODOLOGY

This survey is conducted to examine the perceptions of bank employees providing E-banking services. The methodology adopted for this study was based on primary data collected through well-defined and well-structured questionnaire. The study was based on a sample of 60 employees working with e-channels and having experience in dealing with customers through e-channels. The survey was conducted in the first half July, 2007 in different cities of Punjab as Ludhiana, Bathinda, Jalandhar, Patiala and Sangrur. A sample size of only 60 bank employees taken due to shortage of time, finance and the employees of only e-banks having experience in dealing with e-channels were surveyed for the study.

Data was analyzed with the help of percentage method; ranking and weighted average score (WAS) methods. The respondents were asked to respond on a five-point scale i.e. strongly agree, agree, undecided, disagree, strongly disagree regarding various statements. Weights of 2, 1, 0, -1, -2 were assigned to these scales respectively for calculating the weighted average score. On the other hand for the purpose of ranking, the following step-by-step methodology has been followed:

First Step: Firstly, in respect of each aspect (Collaborative Culture, Training & Development, Knowledge Management etc.) the number of times a factor occupied the 1st, 2nd, ... Nth ranks were computed in terms of frequency.

Second Step: Weights were assigned to each rank in the descending order. For example in collaborative culture aspect, there were three factors with three ranks, weightage pattern was as follows: 1st rank was assigned with 3 weight, 2nd rank with 2 weight and 3rd rank with 1 weight.

Third Step: The sum of the above given weights, for all the ranks, were calculated which was denoted in the tables as total score.

Fourth Step: Overall ranks were assigned on the basis of total score values for each factor calculated in the above step.

LIMITATION

The main limitation of the present study is that a few bank employees were not interested to properly fill up the questionnaire either due to lack of time or lesser interest.

FINDINGS OF THE STUDY

a) **Socio-Economic Background of the Respondents:** From the survey, it is evident that out of 60 respondents the majority of the respondents i.e. 32 per cent were under the age of 26 years and 45 per cent respondents were those having income above 2 lakhs whereas 42 per cent have annual income between 1 to 2 lakhs. From 60 respondents, 82 per cent were male members where only 18 per cent were females that indicate the women's employment in banks is still low. 58 per cent were highly qualified with master degrees where only 5 per cent were high school level educated in the banks. 42 per cent of the respondents have been employed in the banks for less than 3 years where 40 per cent employed for more than 7 years at their jobs. From total sample, 55 per cent were posted at manager level where 17 per cent were clerks. Overall, majority of the respondents were well qualified males, with rich experience and income.

Table I (a): Socio-Economic Background of the Respondents.

Age			Annual Income			Educational Qualification		
Range	Responses	%age	Range (Lakhs)	Responses	%age	Range	Responses	%age
Less than 26	19	32	Less than 1	8	13	High School	3	5
26 to 35	16	27	1 to 2	25	42	Bachelor Degree	22	37
36 to 45	11	18	2 & above	27	45	Master Degree	35	58
Above 45	14	23				Doctorate Degree	0	0

Source: Computed from Data Collected through Survey.

Table I (b): Socio-Economic Background of the Respondents.

Job Duration			Category of Job		
Range (Years)	Responses	Percentage	Category	Responses	Percentage
Less than 3	25	42	Manager	33	55
3 to 4	6	10	Executives	17	28
5 to 6	5	3	Clerks	10	17
Above 6	24	40			

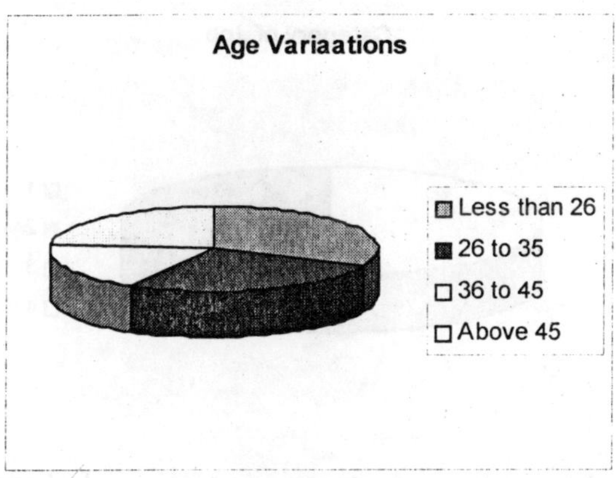
Age Variaations
Less than 26
26 to 35
36 to 45
Above 45

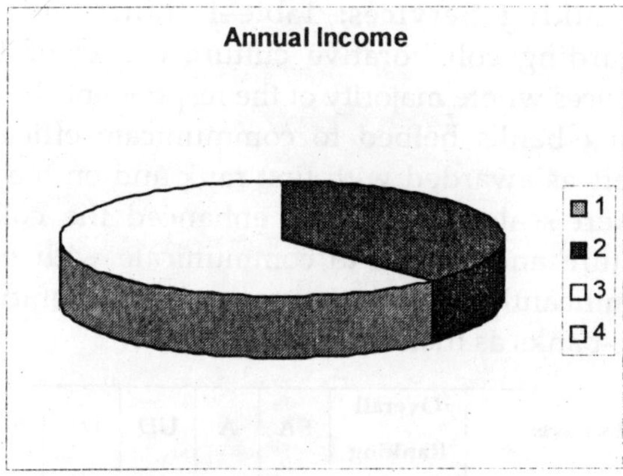
Annual Income
1
2
3
4

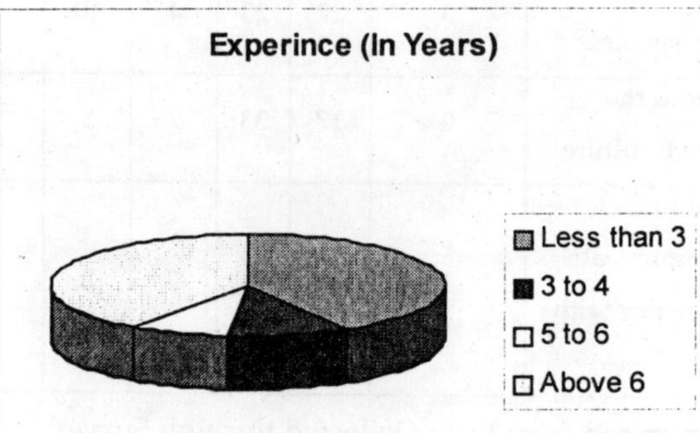
Experince (In Years)
Less than 3
3 to 4
5 to 6
Above 6

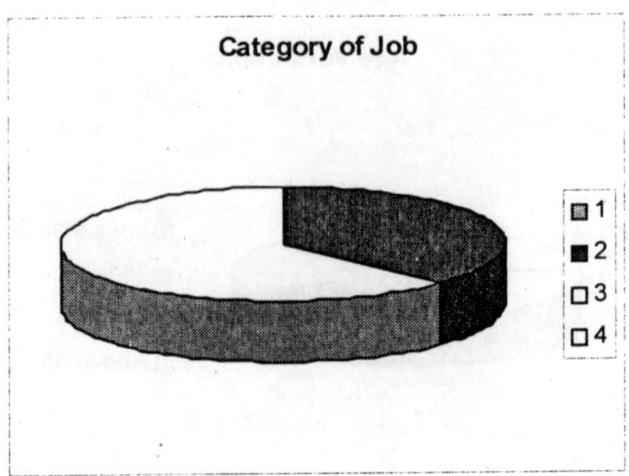

b) **Bankers' Perspective regarding Internet-based E-banking Services:** Table–I shows the responses regarding collaborative culture aspect of E-banking services where majority of the respondents have opinion that e-banks helped to communicate efficiency with peers as awarded with first rank and on the five point lickert scale, the factors, enhanced the collaborative culture and helped to communicate with peers were significantly contributing towards collaborative culture in e-banks as their WAS was above 1.

E-banks have:	Overall Ranking	SA	A	UD	DA	SDA	WAS
(i) brought about group cohesiveness	3	22	23	4	10	1	0.92
(ii) enhanced the collaborative culture	2	17	33	7	3	0	1.07
(iii) helped to communicate efficiency with peers	1	18	34	6	2	0	1.13

Source: Computed from Data Collected through Survey

Note: SA- Strongly Agree, A- Agree, UD- Undecided, DA- Disagree & SDA- Strongly Disagree.

Table-II shows the responses regarding behavioural factors where majority of the respondents (24 respondents) out of 60 awarded the factor e-bank have helped to do routine work more efficiently with first rank where increase interest in work was at second position. On the rating scale too, the respondents were strongly agreed that e-banks helped to do routine work more efficiently as its WAS was above 1 whereas other factors were not much significant as their WAS was below 1 that means employees experienced as e-banks haven't reduced work stress, confusions and they were not satisfied with their jobs too.

Table II: Reponses Regarding "Behavioural Factor" in e-banks.

E-banks have:	Overall Ranking	SA	A	UD	DA	SDA	WAS
(i) helped in reducing work stress	4	24	23	1	8	4	0.92
(ii) helped in educing chaos and confusions	5	17	23	10	10	0	0.78
(iii) helped to do routine work more efficiently	1	30	28	2	0	0	1.47
(iv) increased interest in work	2	14	33	8	4	1	0.92
(v) increased level of motivation	3	15	28	8	9	0	0.82
(vi) increased level of job satisfaction	6	17	28	4	8	3	0.80

Table–III exhibits the responses regarding Training & Development where all the factors like training enhanced confidence, help to work more efficiently, etc. have got WAS more than 1 hence, all were contributing significantly in training and development policies of e-banks.

On the basis of ranking method, factor that training enhanced the confidence was awarded with first rank and increased effectiveness at the job was awarded with second rank. We may conclude that employees were satisfied with the training programmes organized by the e-banks to improve their efficiency and confidence in working.

Table III: Responses Regarding "Training and Development Factor" in e-banks.

E-banks have:	Overall Ranking	SA	A	UD	DA	SDA	WAS
(i) enhanced the skills	3	27	28	1	4	0	1.30
(ii) increased the confidence level through training	1	27	28	1	4	0	1.30
(iii) increased effectiveness at job due to training	2	36	20	2	2	0	1.50
(iv) organized training programmes to match changing technical skills	4	17	33	9	1	0	1.10
(v) provided adequate training in handling e-banks services	5	23	27	5	4	1	1.12

Table–IV examines the responses regarding Knowledge Management where majority of the respondents were strongly agree with the only statement that e-banks have empowered with better access to information as its WAS was above but others were not having significant contribution towards knowledge management as their WAS was below 1. On the basis of ranking too, the same statement was awarded with first rank and others like control over work, enhanced creativity were at second and third positions respectively. Hence, it is concluded that knowledge management was still not according to the desired level.

Table–V examines that to what extent the respondents were satisfied with the ways of working through e-channels. It is evident that 36 out of 60 respondents were satisfied where only 15 were highly satisfied with the ways of working through e-channels. Overall its WAS was above 1 i.e. 1.07 hence, it can be said that employees were satisfied by working through e-channels.

Table IV: Responses Regarding "Knowledge Management Factor" in E-banks.

E-banks have:		Overall Ranking	SA	A	UD	DA	SDA	WAS
(i)	empowered with better access to information	1	40	17	1	2	0	1.58
(ii)	empowered with more control over work	2	19	27	2	9	3	0.83
(iii)	enhanced creativity	6	12	23	9	12	4	0.45
(iv)	empowered to solve problems	5	14	27	4	10	5	0.58
(v)	enhanced capacity to contribute in research & development activities	4	9	37	13	0	1	0.88
(vi)	increased involvement in decision – making	3	14	30	4	8	4	0.70
(vii)	magnified abilities to think and articulate thoughts	7	7	31	9	5	8	0.40

Source: Computed from Data Collected through Survey.

Table V: Responses Regarding the Satisfaction Level Among the Bank Employees Regarding the Way of Working through e-channels.

Highly Satisfied	Satisfied	Undecided	Dissatisfied	Highly Dissatisfied	WAS
15	36	7	2	0	1.07

Source: Computed from Data Collected through Survey.

Table–VI examines that out of 60 respondents, 41 were agreed with the statement that with the downsizing of employees efficiency has increased but overall, its WAS was below 1 and hence, we can say that all the employees were not experienced with that downsizing increased the efficiency.

Table VI: Responses regarding the statement, "There is a downsizing of employees due to the emerging technology but efficiency in terms of productivity has increased.".

Strongly Agree	Agree	Undecided	Disagree	Strongly Disagree	WAS
12	41	0	5	2	0.93

Source: Computed from Data Collected through Survey.

Table – VII exhibits the responses regarding various negative effects of E-banking system. Only 32 per cent of the total respondents felt that there was no frustration while dealing electronically but others found that they get frustrated some times. Majority of the respondents were in favour that e-banks have increased their work-efficiency whereas 32 per cent feels little strain due to E-banking system and 22 per cent experienced very much strain.

Table VII: Responses Regarding the Negative Effects of e-channels.

Effects of e-channels	Very Much	Some What	A Little	Very Little	Not at all
(i) frustration in getting work done electronically	7 (11.67)	12 (20.00)	8 (13.33)	14 (23.33)	19 (31.67)
(ii) increased work efficiency but reduced personal efficiency	15 (25.00)	13 (21.67)	14 (23.33)	11 (18.33)	7 (11.67)
(iii) strain, if any, due to e-banking as compared to manual banking	13 (21.67)	10 (16.67)	10 (16.67)	19 (31.67)	8 (13.33)

Source: Computed from Data Collected through Survey.

Table–VIII tested the responses for problems faced by the respondents while dealing with customers electronically. It is evident that only three problems were the most dominating problems as their WAS is above 1 these were illiteracy, increasing expectations of the customers and lack of knowledge regarding how to use/operate various e-channels, while others like lack of trust and problem of security, etc. were not much important in the opinion of majority of the respondents.

Table VIII: Responses Regarding the Problems Face by the Employees while dealing through e-channels.

Effects of e-channels	Very Much	Some What	A Little	Very Little	Not at all
(i) frustration in getting work done electronically	7 (11.67)	12 (20.00)	8 (13.33)	14 (23.33)	19 (31.67)
(ii) increased work efficiency but reduced personal efficiency	15 (25.00)	13 (21.67)	14 (23.33)	11 (18.33)	7 (11.67)
(iii) strain, if any, due to e-banking as compared to manual banking	13 (21.67)	10 (16.67)	10 (16.67)	19 (31.67)	8 (13.33)

Source: Computed from Data Collected through Survey.

Table-IX examines that how many problems the respondents face when they work through e-channels. It is evident that 50 per cent of the respondents experienced that the problem of lack of knowledge about these channels was interrupting the work to a large extent while 35 per cent experienced its effect to some extent. Lack of proper training was also affecting the work very much in the opinion of 43 per cent respondents, and they experienced that this problem was a major obstacle and obsolete technology, etc. were the other ones affecting the working of bank employees negatively.

Table IX: Responses Regarding the Difficulties Faced by the Employees to Work with e-channels.

Problems	SA	A	UD	DA	SDA	WAS
(i) illiteracy	32	20	4	4	0	1.33
(ii) increasing expectations of customers	19	36	3	2	0	1.20
(iii) lack of trust	8	33	7	11	1	0.60
(iv) lack of knowledge regarding how to use/operate	30	26	3	1	0	1.42
(v) problem of security	24	20	6	7	3	0.83
(vi) resist to change	13	30	9	7	1	0.78
(vii) unawareness among the customers	26	25	4	3	2	0.12

Note: Values in the parenthesis show percentage of responses.

Glaring Issues

1. Behavioural aspect towards E-banking is not developed to the desired extent.
2. Knowledge management is also not developed properly.
3. Frustration and strain is still prevalent among the employees due to technical faults or poor network, etc.
4. E-channels are less popular mainly because of problems of illiteracy, increasing expectations of customers, lack of security and knowledge, lack of proper training, etc.

POLICY RECOMMENDATIONS

E-banking is a major issue for all the banks especially in the current transformation era. Therefore, special care is needed to manage these services efficiently to make the bank employees satisfied with the working conditions, culture, etc. so that they can further provide best services to the valuable customers. As we all know that satisfied customer is an asset for the banks and the whole prestige of an organization is attached with the working of employees in a manner that how they make their customers delighted. Due to E-banking system, work culture is totally changed and there are some problems due to which employees feel uncomfortable to work electronically. Hence, there is a need to solve these problems with effective implementation of some practical strategies to make E-banking more popular and friendly among the employees. In this context, below some suggestions are given in the light of deficiencies experienced during this survey.

- Teamwork is a need of the hour, so create collaborative culture for work by motivating the employees to work together. For this purpose, organize the people in different task groups with specified targets and time period, it will definitely result in collaborative work culture and help in timely achievement of the desired goals.
- Effective training especially on the job, should be given to al the employees engaged in E-banking system and are in need to work efficiently so that their stress and confusions can be eliminated.
- To access training needs, it will be more effective to fix meeting for every last day of the month to listen their problems, confusions. It will help to eliminate their frustration due to some difficulties and technical problems occurred during their working hours.
- Research and development is an important task to grow and lead in today's competitive market. So every bank should establish separate department by involving all the employees with creative brains and by welcoming their suggestions to motivate them, which will help to provide innovative services to the customers.
- Make all the employees up to date by providing every current information for any aspect of banking services

and products to develop knowledge management concept.

- As downsizing have negative and wrong concept in the minds of employees, make it clear and implement in renewed ways and effectively, so that productivity cannot be affected negatively.
- From the survey it is observed that the problem of lack of knowledge regarding new channels and how to operate and use these channels is a major bottleneck in the way of progress of E-banking channels. So firstly trained the employees about each and every new concept of E-banking system only then they can provide right information to the customers to make them aware about these e-channels. Customers prefer to know anything better on the counter, so arrange demo for how to use e-channels at the counter rather through advertisements in newspapers and television, etc. More particularly, separate cell should be established for the queries of the customers, which will be more helpful for awareness about this new system among the masses.
- Every bank should establish separate HRD department, which can control all the aspects/issues, related to human resources. It is necessary, because now it has become a continuous and full time process to create, develop and then maintain the human resources in a way to make them more efficient and adaptable to the changing environment.

FUTURE AREAS OF RESEARCH

1. Comprehensive study is required to know the employee's satisfaction level in the E-banking working environment as compared to that of traditional banking at bank group level and at individual bank level.
2. Comparative study to examine the perceptions of employees of e-banks in rural areas as compared to that of urban areas especially the problems they

generally face while working through computers and proving customer services electronically.

3. In-depth survey of the E-banking related all aspects adopted by the various banks and to what extent these are efficient.

CONCLUSION

From the survey, it is concluded that although the employees are satisfied with the working of e-channels, but still they are facing some problems. To make the employees more efficient and getting their services to the desired goals, it is necessary to make them satisfied with their jobs by providing proper training, friendly work environment, collaborative culture and up to date knowledge about all customer's demands/queries. E-banking is at infant stage in Indian banking industry but have enveloped the whole banking industry into a single net. Hence, there is a need to improve and make some effective and practical efforts to bring the banks out of the wood.

BIBLIOGRAPHY

Adhivarahan, V., 'Information Technology Act, (2001), 2000 – The Legal Viewpoint', *IBA Bulletin,* Vol. XXIII, No. 12 (December).

Akter, Md. Shahriar, 'Customer's Expectations and & Ghosh, S.K. (2006), Perceptions Toward Banking Services Through SERVQAL Model – An Evaluation of a Multinational Bank's Services in Bangladesh', Strategies of Winning Organizations, Ed. by Upinder Dhar, S. Dhar & V.S. Chauhan, Excell Books, New Delhi, pp. 491-502

Al-Tamimi & 'Service Quality & Bank, Jabnoun, N. (2006), Performance: A Comparison of the UAE National and Foreign Banks', Finance India, Vol. XX, No. 1 (March), pp 181-197.

Arora, Kalpana, 'Indian Banking: Managing (2003), Transformation through IT', *IBA Bulletin,* Vol. XXV, No. 3 (March), pp 134-38.

Avasthi, G.P.M., 'Information Technology in (2000-01), Banking: Challenges for Regulators', Prajnan, Vol. XXIX, No. 4, pp. 3 –17.

Jaski, B. (2002), 'Unleashing Employee Productivity: Need for a Paradigm Shift', *IBA Bulletin* Vol. XXIV, No. 3 (March).

Chachadi, A.H. 'HRD as a Strategic Tool in (2003), Organizational Transformation in Indian Banks', *IBA Bulletin,* Vol. XXV, No. 3 (March), pp 114-120.

Consumer Voice 'Banking Sector: India's First (2006), Survey of Customer Satisfaction Study', Consumer Voice, Vol. 7, Issue 1 (July), pp 14-20.

Das, S.C. (2003), 'Managing Transformation in Indian Banking Through HRD', *IBA Bulletin,* Vol. XXV, No. 3, (March).

Dhillon, J.S., Batra, 'Pradigm Change: Relationship G.S. & Dhyani, A. Marketing and Services Quality of (2003), Banking Services', *IBA Bulletin* (June), pp 26-32.

Eapen, P.G. (2000), 'Automated Teller Machines-Security Issues', *IBA Bulletin,* Vol. XXII, No. 9 (Sept.), pp 23-26.

Ganesh, S. (2001), 'Frauds in A Computerized Environment', *IBA Bulletin,* Vol. XXIII No. 12 (Dec.), pp 19-25 .

Garg, I.K. (2003), 'Indian Banking in Transition: Some Management Challenges', *IBA Bulletin,* Vol. XXV, No. 3, (March), pp 121-123.

Geetha, D (2005), 'A Study on the Performance of ATM Services in Malaysia and Coimbatore City', Management: Strategies and Policies, Ed. by Justin Paul and S Ganesan, Allied Publishers.

Malhotra, P. & 'New Revolution in the Indian Singh, B. (2005), Banking Industry: Internet Banking', Punjab Journal of Business Studies, Vol. 1, No. 1 (April-September), pp 75-86.

Mittal, S.R. A. (2000), 'Payment Systems in High – Tech. Banking', The Journal of The Indian Institute of Bankers, Vol.71, No. 3 (July- August), pp. 8-19.

Mohan, R. (2003), 'Transforming Indian Banking: In Search of a Better Tomorrow', *IBA Bulletin,* Vol. XXV, No. 3, (March).

Nair, S.N. (2000),'E-Commerce and The Emergence of E-banking', *IBA Bulletin,* Vol. XXII, No. 10 (October)

Niranjan, (2000), 'Internet Banking is Here', Business World, (3rd April).

Vittal. N. (2001), 'The Emerging Challenges: Strategies and Solutions for Indian Banking', *IBA Bulletin,* Vol. XXIII, No. 3 (Mar.), pp 9-15.

Pai, D.T. (2001), 'Indian Banking – Changing Scenario', *IBA Bulletin,* Vol. XXIII, No. 3 (March), pp 20-24.

Pathrose, P.P. (2001), 'Hi - Tech. Banking Prospects and Problems', *IBA Bulletin,* Vol. XXIII, No. 7 (July).

Paul, J. & 'Retail Baking, ATMs and Supply, Mukherjee, A. (2006), Chain Management in Banking: A Study of Two Banks', Prajnan, Vol. XXXV, No. 1 (April-June), pp. 47 60.

Paul, Justin (2006), 'Global Trends in Banking Sector: Analysis of High-Tech Services', Indian Bankers, Vol. 1, No. 5 (May).

Paul, Justin (2006), 'Technological Environment: Developments in the Banking Sector', Business Environment, Tata Mcgraw-Hill.

Pipreya, B.K. (2006), 'Internet Banking', The Indian Banker, Vol.1, No. 3 (March), pp 143-145.

Rangarajan, C. (2000), 'Banking in The Hi -Tech. Environment', The Journal of The Indian Institute of Bankers, (January-March) .

Ray, G., Muhanna, 'Information Technology and the W.A. & Performance of the Customer Barney, J.B. (2005), Service Process: A Resource-Based Analysis', MIS Quarterly, Vol. 29, No. 4 (December), pp 625-652.

Rao, P.K. (1999), 'IT in Financial Services Industry: Innovations and Implications', Chartered Secretary, (September).

Rao, N.V. (2000), 'Changing Indian Banking Scenario: a Paradigm shift' *IBA Bulletin,* Vol. XXIV, No. 1, pp. 12-20.

Shapiro, C (2000), 'Will E- Commerce Erode Liberty', *Harvard Business Review,* (May-June).

Shastri, R.V (2001), 'Technology for Banks in India-Challenges', *IBA Bulletin,* Vol. XXIII, No. 3 (March), pp 23-45.

Singh, S. (2004), 'An Appraisal of Customer Services of Public Sector Banks', *IBA Bulletin,* Vol. XXVI, No. 8 (August), pp 30-33.

Srivastava, D.K., 'Impact of Banking Reforms on Umesh, H. & Employees' Role Clarity: A Case of Bajpai, N. (2006), an Indian Public Sector Bank', *Prajnan,* Vol. XXXV, No. 1 (April June), pp. 39-45.

Trivedi, A. K. (2003), 'Indian Banking: Managing Transformation', *IBA Bulletin,* Vol. XXV, No. 3, (March).

Uppal, R.K. (2006), 'Indian Banking Industry and Information Technology', New Century Publications, New Delhi.

Verma, D. (2000), 'Banking on Change', *ICFAI Reader,* (May), p. 69.

■ ■ ■

9

INDIAN BANKING: MOVING TOWARDS INFORMATION TECHNOLOGY–EMERGING CHALLENGES AND POSSIBLE SOLUTIONS

ABSTRACT

The process of economic liberalization in India initiated in 1991, has significant impact on banking industry of the country. Information Technology (IT) revolution has not only changed the way banking business is done but also widened the range of products/services offered by the banks.

The present paper highlights the extent of computerization, core banking solutions, e-delivery channels in different banks and bank groups. The paper analyses the impact of computerization and e-delivery channels on the comparative performance of different bank groups. The performance of these bank groups is very high which are fully computerized and providing services through e-delivery channels. Ultimately, the paper finds some areas of bank problems in e-age and their solutions and suggests some areas of comprehensive research.

KEYWORDS: Extent of computerization, E-channels, Core Banking Solution (CBS), Problems and their solutions.

INTRODUCTION

The concept of banking has drastically changed from a business dealing with money transactions alone to a business related to information on financial transactions. This implies that IT will play a critical role in the years to come by providing better customer services, presumably at a lower cost (Uppal & Rimpi, 2006, p.7). Several innovative IT based services such as ATMs, EFT, anywhere-anytime banking, smart cards, net-banking, etc. are no longer alien concepts to Indian banking customers (Rangarajan, C., 2000, p.4). Technology has played a significant role in improving the efficiency of the financial system in recent years. It is also being viewed as an excellent tool for providing a fairly exhaustive range of products and extending banking facilities to the vast multitude of population. Indian banking sector has made a quantum leap forward in terms of switching over from paper-based transactions, which include use of currency notes, cheques or challans to electronic means. Computerization of banking business got high importance in 2005-06. Between Sept. 1999 and March 2006, public sector banks incurred an expenditure of Rs.10676 Cr. on computerization and development of communication networks (Report on Trend & Progress of Banking in India, 2005-06, p.97). Today, in India, the bank customers have done away with the old-fashioned passbook, and the customer can have a statement of his transaction from the ATMs (Banerjee, 2005, p. 73).

SCHEME OF THE WORK

After a brief introduction of the theme, Section II fixes the objectives, data base and research methodology. Section III highlights the extent of computerization, CBS and ATMs and the performance of various bank groups. Section IV finds some areas of bank problems and their solutions while section V concludes the paper and bring out some new areas for comprehensive research.

Objectives

- To study analyze the recent trends in information technology in different bank groups.
- To study the paper based verses electronic transactions in banks in IT era.
- Areas of bank problems and their solutions in e-age era.

RESEARCH METHODOLOGY

The universe for the study is Indian banking sector and five major bank groups have been consider to draw the required results such as Nationalized Banks (G-I), SBI & its associates (G-II), Old Private Sector Banks (G-III), New Private Sector Banks (G-IV) and Foreign Banks (G-V). Time period for the study is from 2004-05 to 2005-06.

DATABASE

Report on Trend and Progress in 2005-06.

IBA, Performance Highlights, 2000-06.

COMPUTERIZATION IN PUBLIC SECTOR BANKS AND CORE BANKING SOLUTIONS

The number of branches providing 'core banking solutions (CBS)' has increased significantly in recent years. The CBS provides a host of benefits such as 'anywhere banking', 'anywhere access' quick funds movement at optional costs and in an efficient manner, while new private sector banks, foreign banks and a few old private sector banks have already put in place core banking solutions, PSBs are increasingly adopting similar systems. The total number of branches providing CBs increased from 11.00 per cent as on March 31, 2005 to 28.9 per cent as on March 31, 2006. Many of the PSBs having fully computerized branches adopted CBS during the year.

More then 95 per cent branches of PSBs at end-March 2006 were fully or partially computerized. Out of 27 PSBs, branches of as many as ten PSBs were 100 per cent computerized.

Andhra Bank, Bank of Baroda, Corporation Bank, SBI, SBBJ, State Bank of Hyderabad, State Bank of Mysoor, SBP, State Bank of Saurashtra, State Bank of Travancore), while branches of another 12 banks were more than 50 per cent computerization (Allahabad Bank, Dena Bank, Vijaya Bank, Bank of India, Bank of Maharashtra, Canara Bank, CBI, IB, Indian Overseas Bank, OBC, PNB, State Bank of Indore). Branches of only five PSBs were less than 50 per cent computerization (Punjab & Sindh Bank, Syndicate Bank, UCO Bank, Union Bank of India, United Bank of India).

Table I (a): Computerization in PSBs (As on March 31st, 2006).

Technology	*(Per cent)*
1. Branches already fully computerized*	48.50
2. Branches under Core Banking Solutions	28.90
3. Fully Computerized Banks	77.50
4. Partially Computerized Branches	18.20

Source: Report on Trend and Progress in 2005-06, P. 97.
Note: *Other than branches under CBS.

Table I (b): Banks Under Core Banking Solutions.

CBS %age	*No. of Banks*	*Name of the Banks under CBS*
0-10	9	Allahabad Bank, Bank of Baroda, Canara Bank, CBI, Dena Bank, Punjab & Sindh Bank, Bank of Maharashtra, UCO Bank,United Bank of India
11-50	8	Bank of India, Indian Bank, Indian Overseas Bank, Syndicate Bank, Union Bank of India, Vijay Bank, SBI, State Bank of Mysore
50-100	5	Andhra Bank, Corporation Bank, Oriental Bank of Commerce, PNB, Sate Bank of Indore
100 per cent	5	SBBJ, State Bank of Hyderabad, State Bank of Patiala, State Bank of Saurashtra, State Bank of Tranvancore

Source: Report on Trend & Progress of Banking in India, 2005-06, p. 311.

ATMs of Scheduled Commercial Banks at the end of March, 2006

Table II indicates total number of ATMs installed by the banks were 21147 at the end of March 2006. Nationalized Banks accounted for the largest share of installed ATMs, followed by the new private sector banks, SBI group, old private sector banks and foreign banks, while SBI group, new private sector banks and foreign banks had more off-site ATMs, Nationalized Banks and Old Private Sector Banks had more on-site ATMs.

Off-site ATMs as percentage of total ATMs were the highest in case of foreign banks, followed by SBI group, new private sector banks, nationalized banks and old private sector banks.

Table II: Total Branches and Number of ATMs of Scheduled Commercial Banks.

Bank Groups	Total Banks	Number of ATMs			%age of Off-site to total ATMs
		On-site	Off-site	Total	
G-I	34185	4812	2353	7165	32.80
G-II	13831	1775	3668	5443	67.40
G-III	4566	1054	493	1547	31.90
G-IV	1950	2255	3857	6112	63.10
G-V	259	232	648	880	73.60
Total (I to V)	54791	10128	11019	21147	52.10

Source: Report on Trend and Progress of Banking in India, 2005-06, p. 97.

Retail Electronic and Card-based Payments

The convenience and easy acceptability of credit cards and technology advances have resulted in a continuous rise in retail electronic and card-based mode of payments. The volume and value of card and electronic based payments more than doubled in 2006 from the previous year.

Table III: Retail Electronic and Card-Based Payments.

(Volume in thousands, value in Rs. Crores)

Year	Retail Electronic@		Card-Based#		Total	
	Volume	Value	Volume	Value	Volume	Value
2001-02	178	6123	NA	NA	178	6123
2002-03	237	10222	NA	NA	237	10222
2003-04	290	29606	1862	35889	2152	65486
2004-05	579	77702	3615	77267	4194	154969
2005-06	832	106599	10453	236994	11286	343593

Note: @ECS (Debit & Credit), EFT & SEFT/NEFT, # Credit, Debit Cards, Smart Cards, Vol. represents number of transactions.

Paper based Vs. Electronic Transactions

Reflecting the increasing use of electronic and card-based payments in retail transactions, their share in total transactions constituted 46.70 per cent in terms of volume and 51.20 per cent in terms of value in 2006. The use of electronic mode of payments increased both in terms of volume and value during 2005-06 compared with the previous year, (table IV).

Table IV: Paper-based Vs. Electronic Transactions

Volume (Number of Transactions)			
Year	**Paper-based**	**Electronic**	**Total**
2002-03	10139	1730	11869
2003-04	10228	2152	12380
2004-05	11671	4200	15871
2005-06	12895	11300	24195
Value (Rs. Crore)			
2002-03	13424313	37536	13461849
2003-04	11595960	67461	11663421
2004-05	10120716	4221153	14341869
2005-06	11337062	11884429	23221491

Report on Trend and Progress of Banking in India, 2005-06, p. 97.

A Paradigm Shift in IT-Oriented Bank Groups

There is a paradigm shift in profitability of these bank groups (Table-V) which have the maximum computerization and using e-delivery channels. Foreign banks and new private sector banks are at the front line I this case, their profitability is higher than other bank groups and nationalized banks are following them. Even intra-bank group analysis shows only those banks have the maximum average of profitability which are using the latest technology.

Table V: Net Profits as Percentage of Total Assets.

(Per cent)

Bank Groups	1999-00	2000-01	2001-02	2002-03	2003-04	2004-05	2005-06	Average	S.D.	C.V. (Percent)
G-I	0.44	0.33	0.69	0.98	1.19	0.89	0.81	0.76	0.30	39.47
G-II	0.80	0.55	0.77	0.91	1.02	0.91	0.86	0.83	0.15	18.07
G-III	0.81	0.59	1.08	1.17	1.20	0.33	0.59	0.82	0.34	41.46
G-IV	0.97	0.81	0.44	0.90	0.83	1.05	0.97	0.85	0.20	23.52
G-V	1.17	0.93	1.32	1.56	1.65	1.29	1.52	1.36	0.27	19.85
Average	0.84	0.64	0.86	1.10	1.18	0.89	0.95			
S.D.	0.27	0.23	0.34	0.28	0.30	0.35	0.35			
C.V. (%)	32.14	35.94	39.53	25.45	25.45	39.32	36.84			

Source: IBA, Performance Highlights, 2000-06.

PROBLEM AREAS

Particularly in public sector banks and in general all the bank groups, state-of-the-art banking software may be useless if handled by an untrained or demotivated staff. Centralized banking operations hold no meaning for customer who has to wait for a queue for half an hour to know his bank balance.

Another problem area that comes up is the concept of service quality in itself. Service quality is a concept that is based on what customers perceive, which is very subjective. A number of complications may arise due to the gap between the customers' perception and the organizational perceptions.

Gap-I: Customers' Expectations Vs. management Perceptions–A result of lack of marketing research, inadequate upward communication and too many layers of management.

Gap-II: Management Perceptions Vs. Service Specifications–A result of inadequate commitment to service quality, a perception of unfeasibility, inadequate task standardization and an absence of goal setting.

Gap-III: Service Specifications Vs. Service Delivery–A Result of role ambiguity and conflict, poor employee-job fit and poor technology-job fit, inappropriate supervisory control systems, lack of perceived control and team work.

Gap-IV: The discrepancy between customer expectations and employees' perceptions–A result of the differences in the understanding of customer expectations by front line service providers.

Gap-V: The discrepancy between employee's perceptions and managerial perceptions–A result of the differences in the understanding of customer expectation between managers and service providers.

Solutions

1. Developing effective service quality: Developing service quality in banks can not be left at the stage of technological up-gradation.
2. Human resources up-gradation: Now is the stage to go for HR upgradation. This may initially add to the banks' cost and even fixed resistance amongst employees used to official slumber. But then it is better to incur costs now than to lose a customer forever.
3. System maintenance: Banks have to be as sensitive to the needs of maintenance of the new IT-based systems as a mother is to her child.
4. Brand building: With a strong online brand, banks can rejuvenate their offline strategy as well as add more

affordable and useful services to their total offering. Building strong brands will help to reduce the perceptual gaps and will not only bring the customers closer to the banks but also help managers understand their customers better.

5. Measuring the quality of service: Unless the quality of service is measured continuously andby modern scientific methods, it will be very hard to take corrective action. Many such tools and techniques are available which are widely accepted such as SERVQUAL, SERVPREF, ROQ models, etc.

   Many of these models have also been standardized for E-banking operations. Scores of such techniques should form the bases for future actions.

6. Business of process re-engineering: Because of the change in the banking system that has came in as a result of technology, customer behaviour and expectations have also changes. Banks have to start redefining their strategy and bring in structural changes to their existing form.

Issues for the future comprehensive research

1. Dimensions of IT and Indian banking industry in WTO regime
2. Feasibility and viability of E-banking in rural and semi urban areas
3. Cost efficiency of e-banks in India
4. IT & its adverse effect on banking relations and operations
5. New strategies for the E-banking awareness.

CONCLUSION

We may conclude from the ongoing discussion that technology up-gradation is taken place in all the bank groups but it is faster in foreign banks and new private sector banks. Off-site

ATMs as percentage to total ATMs is the highest in case of foreign banks, followed by SBI group. The electronic transactions have increased from 29.40 pc in 2004-05 to 51.20 pc in 2005-06. Technology is directly affecting the performance of the banks. Technological advancement has to be seen beyond hardware and machines. It has to be seen in totality with the larger socio-economic system.

BIBLIOGRAPHY

Arora, Kalpana (2003), 'Indian Banking: Managing Transformation Through IT', *IBA Bulletin*, Vol. XXV, No. 3, (March), pp. 134-138.

Avasthi, G.P.M. 'Information Technology in (2000-01), Banking: Challenges for Regulators', *Prajnan*, Vol. XXIX, No. 4, pp. 3 -17.

Bajaj, K.K. (2000), 'E-Commerce Issues in the Emerging Hi -Tech. Banking Environment', *The Journal of The Indian Institute of Bankers*, (Jan- March).

Bakshi, S. (2003), 'Corporate Governance in Transformation Times', *IBA Bulletin*, Vol. XXV, No. 3, (March).

Banerjee, S. (2005), 'Technology Upgradation Impact on Service Quality', *Chartered Financial Analyst*, (October), pp.77-78.

Bhasin, T.M. (2001), 'E-Commerce in Indian Banking', *IBA Bulletin*, Vol. XXIII, Nos. 4 & 5, (April – May).

Ganesh, S. (2001), 'Frauds In A Computerized Environment', *IBA Bulletin*, Vol. XXIII, No. 12, (December), pp. 19-25.

Garg, I.K. (2003), 'Indian Banking in Transition: Some Management Challenges', *IBA Bulletin*, Vol. XXV, No. 3, (March), pp.121-123.

Gupta, R P. (2001), 'Banking In The New Millennium: Strategic Management Issues', *IBA Bulletin*, Vol. XXIII, No. 3 (March), pp. 38-45.

Jalan, B. (2003), 'Strengthening Indian Banking and Finance: Progress and Prospectus', *IBA Bulletin*, Vol. XXV, No. 3, (March).

Kulkarni, R. V. (2000), 'Changing Face of Banking From Brick and Mortar Banking to E- Banking', *IBA Bulletin*, (January).

Mohan, R. (2003), 'Transforming Indian Banking: In Search of a Better Tomorrow', *IBA Bulletin*, Vol. XXV, No. 3, (March).

Nair, S.N. (2000), 'E-Commerce and The Emergence of E-banking', *IBA Bulletin*, Vol. XXII, No. 10, (October).

Rangarajan, C. (2000) 'Banking in the Hi-Tech Environment', *The Journal of the Indian Institute of Bankers*, (January-March), pp. 3-7.

Report on Trend and Progress of Banking in India, 2005-06.

Shapiro, C (2000), 'Will E-Commerce Erode Liberty', *Harvard Business Review*, (May-June).

Shastri, R.V (2001), 'Technology for Banks in India-Challenges', *IBA Bulletin*, Vol. XXIII, No. 3, (March), pp. 23-45.

Trivedi, A. K. (2003), 'Indian Banking: Managing Transformation', *IBA Bulletin*, Vol. XXV, No. 3, (March).

Uppal, R.K. & 'Transformation in Indian Banks Rimpi Kaur (2005),— Challenges and Opportunities', *The Journal of Commerce & Trade*, Vol. 1, No. 1 (October).

■ ■ ■

10

MOBILE BANKING– A NEW REVOLUTION

INTRODUCTION

The last technology that had a major impact in helping banks service and their customers was with the introduction of the Internet banking. Internet banking helped the customer's anytime access to their banks. Customer's could check out their account details, get their bank statements, perform transactions like transferring money to other accounts and pay their bills sitting in the comfort of their homes and offices.

However the biggest limitation of Internet banking is the requirement of a PC with an Internet connection, not a big obstacle if we look at the US and the European countries, but definitely a big barrier if we consider most of the developing countries of Asia like China and India. Mobile banking addresses this fundamental limitation of Internet banking, as it reduces the customer requirement to just a mobile phone.

Mobile usage has seen an explosive growth in most of the Asian economies like India, China and Korea. In fact Korea boasts about a 70 per cent mobile penetration rate and with its tech-savvy populace has seen one of the most aggressive rollouts of mobile banking services.

Still, the main reason that Mobile banking scores over Internet banking is that it enables 'Anywhere Banking'. Customers now don't need access to a computer terminal to access their banks, they can now do so on the go - when they are waiting for their bus to work, when they are traveling or when they are waiting for their orders to come through in a restaurant.

The scales at which Mobile banking has the potential to grow can be gauged by looking at the pace users are getting mobile in these big Asian economies. According to the Cellular Operators' Association of India (COAI) the mobile subscriber base in India hit 40.6 million in the August 2004. In September 2004 it added about 1.85 million more. The explosion as most analysts say, is yet to come as India has about one of the biggest untapped markets. China, which already witnessed the mobile boom, is expected to have about 300 million mobile users by the end of 2004. South Korea is targeted to reach about 42 million mobile users by the end of 2005. All three of these countries have seen gradual roll-out of mobile banking services, the most aggressive being Korea which is now witnessing the roll-out of some of the most advanced services like using mobile phones to pay bills in shops and restaurants.

ADVANTAGES AND BENEFITS OF MOBILE BANKING

The biggest advantage that mobile banking offer to banks is that it drastically cuts down the costs of providing service to the customers. For example an average teller or phone transaction costs about Rs. 2.36 each, whereas an electronic transaction costs only about Rs. 0.10 each. Additionally, this new channel gives the bank ability to cross-sell up-sell their other complex banking products and services such as vehicle loans, credit cards, etc.

For service providers, Mobile banking offers the next surest way to achieve growth. Countries like Korea where mobile penetration is nearing saturation; mobile banking is helping service providers increase revenues from the now static subscriber base. Also service providers are increasingly using the complexity of their supported mobile banking services to attract new customers and retain old ones.

Mobile banking solutions offer a full range of benefits for financial institutions, ranging from reduced customer support costs to improved customer satisfaction and retention as well as revenue growth. A recent Gartner Measurement study showed that an average contact centre deflects 16 per cent of its contacts to phone-based automated self-service technology, with some high-performing companies achieving deflection rates of upto 50 per cent. With typical IVR (Integrated Voice Response) calls averaging Rs. 0.95 per call, banks could reap cost savings of up to 45 per cent by deflecting half of their calls to an IVR system.

A mobile self-service alternative to both call center and IVR customer queries could reap even more cost savings. Bank-related customer support calls typically relate to routine banking inquiries, such as account balances, which are perfectly suited to a mobile self-service solution. Customer ROI studies has shown that Mobile aware can reduce the cost of simple query resolutions or transactions by up to 95 per cent. Added to that is a more satisfied customer base that is no longer faced with the frustrations of dealing with IVR systems, or waiting in line for the next available customer service representative.

Offering innovative, personalized mobile services can also assist banks to attract and retain customers. Mobile banking offers financial institutions the opportunity to target and acquire new customer segments that value mobility and real-time control of their finances, leading to increased customer growth and revenue.

MOBILE BANKING SERVICES

Banks offering mobile access are mostly supporting some or all of the following services:

1. Account balance inquiry
2. Account statement inquiries.
3. Cheque status inquiry.
4. Cheque book requests.
5. Fund transfer between accounts.
6. Credit/Debit alerts.
7. Minimum balance alerts.
8. Bill payment alerts.
9. Bill payment.
10. Recent transaction history requests.
11. Information requests like interest rates/exchange rates.

The above services are the basic services provided by a bank. However, a more systematic and thorough look at a proper banking operation providing such services could classify them in a more opt and dignified manner as shown below:

Account Information

1. Mini-statements and checking of account history
2. Alerts on account activity or passing of set thresholds
3. Monitoring of term deposits
4. Access to loan statements
5. Access to card statements
6. Mutual funds / equity statements
7. Insurance policy management
8. Pension plan management
9. Status on cheque, stop payment on cheque

Payments AND Transfers

1. Domestic and international fund transfers
2. Micro-payment handling

3. Mobile recharging
4. Commercial payment processing
5. Bill payment processing
6. Peer to Peer payments

Investments

1. Portfolio management services
2. Real-time stock quotes
3. Personalized alerts and notifications on security prices

Support

1. Status of requests for credit, including mortgage approval, and insurance coverage
2. Check (cheque) book and card requests
3. Exchange of data messages and email, including complaint submission and tracking
4. ATM location

Content Services

1. General information such as weather updates, news
2. Loyalty-related offers
3. Location-based services.

One way to classify these services depending on the originator of a service session is the 'Push/Pull' nature. 'Push' is when the bank sends out information based upon an agreed set of rules, for example your banks sends out an alert when your account balance goes below a threshold level. 'Pull' is when the customer explicitly requests a service or information from the bank, so a request for your last five transaction statement is a Pull based offering.

The other way to categorize the mobile banking services, by the nature of the service, gives us two kind of services-Transaction based and Inquiry Based. So a request for your bank statement is an inquiry based service and a request for your fund's transfer to some other account is a transaction-based service. Transaction based services are also differentiated from inquiry based services in the sense that they require additional security across the channel from the mobile phone to the banks data servers.

Based upon the above classifications, we arrive at the following taxonomy of the services listed before.

	Push Based	*Pull Based*
Transaction Based		• Fund Transfer • Bill Payment • Other financial services like share trading.
Inquiry Based	• Credit/Debit Alerts. • Minimum Balance Alerts • Bill Payment Alerts	• Account Balance Inquiry • Account Statement Inquiry. • Cheque Status Inquiry. • ChequeBook Requests. • Recent Transaction History.

TECHNOLOGIES ENABLING MOBILE BANKING

Technically speaking most of these services can be deployed using more than one channel. Presently, Mobile banking is being deployed using mobile applications developed on one of the following four channels:

1. IVR (Interactive Voice Response)-IVR service operates through pre-specified numbers that banks advertise to their customers. Customer's make a call at the IVR number and are usually greeted by a stored electronic message followed by a menu of different options. Customers can choose options by pressing the corresponding number in their keypads, and are then read out the corresponding information, mostly using a text to speech programme.

Mobile banking based on IVR has some major limitations that they can be used only for enquiry based services. Also, IVR is more expensive as compared to other channels as it involves making a voice call which is generally more expensive than sending an SMS or making data transfer (as in WAP or Standalone clients).

One way to enable IVR is by deploying a PBX system that can host IVR dial plans. Banks looking to go the low cost way should consider evaluating Asterisk, which is an open source Linux PBX system.

Asterisk, due to its open source nature has caught on in a big way and is being sold as a PBX solution by quite a few companies commercially. However there has been considerable noise on multiple Asterisk related forums over the stability of Asterisk based systems. Companies planning to use Asterisk for their IVR solutions should certainly do a rigorous evaluation of its capabilities before committing their long-term future on it.

2. SMS (Short Messaging Service)-SMS uses the popular text-messaging standard to enable mobile application based banking. The way this works is that the customer requests for information by sending an SMS containing a service command to a pre-specified number. The bank responds with a reply SMS containing the specific information.

For example, customers of the HDFC Bank in India can get their account balance details by sending the keyword 'HDFCBAL' and receive their balance information again by SMS. Most of the services rolled out by major banks using SMS have been limited to the Inquiry based ones.

However there have been few instances where even transaction-based services have been made available to customer using SMS. For instance, customers of the Bank of Punjab can make fund transfer by sending the SMS ' TRN (A/c No)(PIN No) (Amount)'.

One of the major reasons that transaction based services have not taken of on SMS is because of concerns about security and because SMS doesn't enable the banks to deliver a custom user interface to make it convenient for customers to access more complex services such as transactions.

The main advantage of deploying mobile applications over SMS is that almost all mobile phones, including the low end, cheaper one's, which are most popular in countries like India and China are SMS enabled.

An SMS based service is hosted on a SMS gateway that further connects to the Mobile service providers SMS Centre. There are a couple of hosted IP based SMS gateways available in the market and also some open sources ones like Kannel.

3. WAP (Wireless Access Protocol)-WAP uses a concept similar to that used in Internet banking. Banks maintain WAP sites which customer's access using a WAP compatible browser on their mobile phones. WAP sites offer the familiar form based interface and can also implement security quite effectively.

Bank of America offers a WAP based service channel to its customers in Hong Kong. The banks customers can now have an anytime, anywhere access to a secure reliable service that allows them to access all inquiry and transaction based services and also more complex transaction like trade in securities through their phone. A WAP based service requires hosting a WAP gateway. Mobile application users access the bank's site through the WAP gateway to carry out transactions, much like internet users access a web portal for accessing the banks services.

The following figure demonstrates the framework for enabling mobile applications over WAP. The actually forms that go into a mobile application are stored on a WAP server, and served on demand. The WAP Gateway forms an access point to the Internet from the mobile network

4. Standalone Mobile Application Clients-Standalone mobile applications are the ones that hold out the most promise as they are most suitable to implement complex banking transactions like trading in securities. They can be easily customized according to the user interface complexity supported by the mobile. In addition, mobile applications enable the implementation of a very secure and reliable channel of communication.

One requirement of mobile applications clients is that they require to be downloaded on the client device before they can be used, which further requires the mobile device to support one of the many development environments like J2ME or Qualcomm's BREW. J2ME is fast becoming an industry standard to deploy mobile applications and requires the mobile phone to support Java.

The major disadvantage of mobile application clients is that the applications needs to be customized to each mobile phone on which it might finally run. J2ME ties together the API for mobile phones which have the similar functionality in what it calls 'profiles'. However, the rapid proliferation of mobile phones which support different functionality has resulted in a huge number of profiles, which are further significantly driving up development costs. This scale of this problem can be gauged by the fact that companies implementing mobile application clients might need to spend as much as 50 per cent of their development time and resources on just customizing their applications to meet the needs of different mobile profiles.

Out of J2ME and BREW, J2ME seems to have an edge right now as Nokia has made the development tools open to developers which has further fostered a huge online community focused in developing applications based on J2ME.

Nokia has gone an additional mile by providing an open online market place for developers where they can sell their applications to major cellular operators around the world. BREW on the other hand has seen limited popularity among the developer community, mostly because of the proprietary nature of its business and because of the steep prices it charges for its development tools.

Quite a few mobile software product companies have rolled out solutions, which enable J2ME mobile applications based banking. One such product is Wireless I-banco_. The mobile user downloads and installs the wireless I-banco application on their J2ME pone. The J2ME client connects to the wireless I-banco server through the service providers GSM network to enable users to access information about their accounts and perform transactions. One of the other big advantages of using a mobile application client is that it can implement a very secure channel with end-to-end encryption.

However countries like India face a serious obstacle in the proliferation of such clients as few users have mobiles, which support J2ME or BREW. However, one of the biggest CDMA players in the Indian telecom industry, Reliance Infocomm has about 7.01 million users all of which have handsets, which support J2ME. Reliance has unveiled one of the most ambitious data services deployment programme in the country. On the other hand a country like South Korea with its tech-savvy population has a widespread adoption of the higher-end mobiles, which support application development.

THE VALUE OF MOBILE BANKING

Despite mobile phones being much more prevalent than PCs, there are more services available in the marketplace for Internet commerce rather than mobile commerce or M-commerce. It is interesting to note this phenomenon, as one would assume a marketer's interest in tapping a device that is always with the customer. While one almost always carries a mobile phone, one does not carry one's PC or laptop. The adoption of mobile technology is still slow while web technology is being used by people to offer more convenient customer services.

The same is true for banking services. Banks need to look for multiple and alternate channels to engage the customer by providing him/her with value added services. Banks also need to look for innovative means of reducing transaction costs as the per- customer transactions have increased, as banks are providing multiple services under one roof. Mobile technologies could come to the rescue of financial services in such a scenario. SMSs based through a web interface could be one such service. A web interface allows you to communicate instantly with individuals or groups via bulk text messaging. One could send SMSs to one's groups through a mobile phone.

Yet another way of improving customer service could be to inform customers better. Credit card fraud is one such area. A bank could, through the use of mobile technology, inform owners each time purchases above a certain value have been made on their card. This way the owner is always informed when their card is used, and how much money was taken for each transaction.

Similarly, the bank could remind customers of outstanding loan repayment dates, dates for the payment of monthly installments or simply tell them that a bill has been presented and is up for payment. The customers can then check their balance on the phone and authorise the required amounts for payment. The customers can also request for additional information. They can automatically view deposits and withdrawals as they occur and also pre- schedule payments to be made or cheques to be issued. Similarly, one could also request for services like stop cheque or issue of a cheque book over one's mobile phone.

There a number of reasons that should persuade banks in favour of mobile phones. They are set to become a crucial part of the total banking services experience for the customers. Also, they have the potential to bring down costs for the bank itself. Through mobile messaging and other such interfaces, banks provide value added services to the customer at marginal costs. Such messages also bear the virtue of being targeted and personal making the services offered more effective. They will also carry better results on account of better customer profiling.

Yet another benefit is the anywhere/anytime characteristics of mobile services. A mobile is almost always with the customer. As such it can be used over a vast geographical area. The customer does not have to visit the bank ATM or a branch to avail of the bank's services. Research indicates that the number of footfalls at a bank's branch has fallen down drastically after the installation of ATMs. As such with mobile services, a bank will need to hire even fewer employees, as people will no longer need to visit bank branches apart from certain occasions.

With Indian telecom operators working on offering services like money transaction over a mobile, it may soon be possible for a bank to offer phone based credit systems. This will make credit cards redundant and also aid in checking credit card fraud apart from offering enhanced customer convenience. The use of mobile technologies is thus a win-win proposition for both the banks and the bank's customers. Such services are highly personal in nature and are effective because of the same.

The banks add to this personalized communication through the process of automation. For instance, if the customer asks for his account or card balance after conducting a transaction, the installed software can send him an automated reply informing of the same. These automated replies thus save the bank the need to hire additional employees for servicing customer needs.

MOBILE BANKING IN INDIA

"The account that travels with you". This is needed in today's fast business environment with unending deadlines for fulfillment and loads of appointments to meed and meetings to attend. With mobile banking facilities, one can bank from anywhere, at anytime and in any condition or anyhow. The system is either through SMS or through WAP. (Check out for SMS Banking under different head)

Mobile Banking is the hottest area of development in the banking sector and is expected to replace the credit/debit card system in future. In past two years, mobile-banking users has increased three times if we compare the use of either debit card or credit card. Moreover 85-90 per cent mobile users do not own credit cards.

Mobile banking uses the same infrastructure like the ATM solution. But it is extremely easy and inexpensive to implement. It reduces the cost of operation for bankers in comparison to the use of ATMs.

Using compact HTML and WAP technologies, the following operations can be conducted through advanced mobile phones which can is further viewed on channels such as the Internet via the Channel Manager.

- Bill payments
- Fund transfers
- Check balances
- Any many more which is also available in SMS Banking.

In countries like Korea, two SIM Card is used in mobile phones. One for the telephonic purpose and the other for banking. Bank account data is encrypted on a smart-card chip. About 3.3 million transactions were reported by Bank of Korea in 2004.

INDIANS RECEPTIVE TO MOBILE BANKING

One of every three Indians with a bank account is ready to switch to another bank on being offered free mobile banking, states an Asia Pacific survey on mobile banking opportunities.

The survey found Indian users to be more aware of mobile banking than those in other countries. The report titled, 'Mobile Opportunities for the Financial Sector' was conducted in five countries. It was commissioned by Sybase 365, a subsidiary of Sybase, along with BDM Intelligence-a custom market research firm in Asia. It surveyed 1,818 mobile users. The survey states that 81 per cent of Indian respondents are aware they can check bank balance on a mobile phone, while 49 per cent have used these services in the last three months-the highest amongst the five countries surveyed in the region.

The survey found out that consumers in India (71 per cent) are more aware when compared to their counter parts in the other regions on the offerings their bank provides on mobile phones. Almost a half of the Indian respondents checked their bank balance on their mobile phone and 54 per cent via the Internet.

The biggest concern among the Indian user while accessing details through mobile phones is security. In line with this, they accounted for the largest percentage of survey respondents expressing an interest in the ability to report potentially fraudulent transactions and to freeze cards via their mobile phones (67 per cent for both). Indian respondents were also the most willing to pay for these services.

Kaustuv Ghosh, Country Manager Sybase 365 India said, "Indian banks needed a comprehensive view of mobile service deployment and its benefit to customer and operational expenditure alike. The survey reveals a growing culture of financial awareness as customers are becoming increasingly vigilant when it comes to their money."

BANKING ON TECHNOLOGY

Fifty per cent of the respondents use mobiles for checking their bank balance 29 per cent think mobile banking is safe 41per cent are ready to pay for services that allow them to freeze a card 35 per cent are ready to pay for reporting a potentially fraudulent transaction.

Mobile Banking in Western Europe

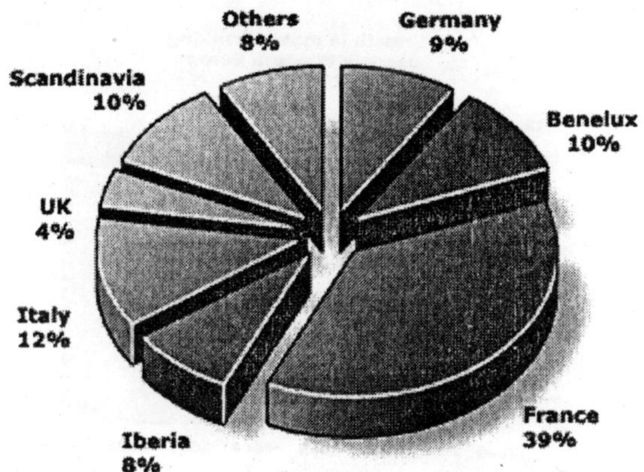

According to a recent report by Celent, there are currently about 5 million users of mobile financial services in Europe. Recently, i-mode services have been imported from Japan, and a number of banks are offering i-mode services now, hoping that it will lead to more rapid growth in terms of usage.

After the failure of WAP-based mobile financial services in 2001, new hopes for mobile banking in Europe have been awakened by a Japanese import, i-mode. A handful of banks in Western Europe have deployed mobile banking services using the Japanese i-mode standard.

However, according to Octavio Marenzi, author of the report, "there is little demand for interactive banking services via WAP or i-mode in Western Europe. However, there has been rapid growth in the use of text messages or SMS messages. We expect that future growth will continue to be driven by SMS alerts, rather than more sophisticated interactive services."

According to the study, wide variances exist between countries in Europe, with mobile banking playing a virtually non-existent role in many countries. The rather unexpected leader in terms of mobile banking penetration is the French market, which accounts for almost 40 per cent of all mobile banking users in Western Europe.

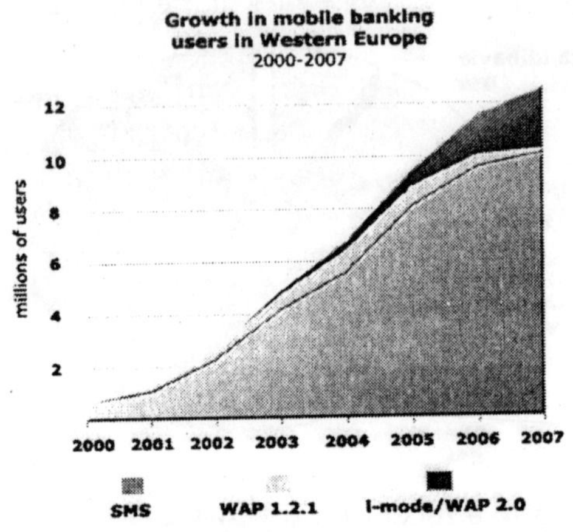

The report analyzes and compares the mobile banking offerings of the top twenty-five banks in Western Europe, compares the state of play in the major countries within Europe, examines the role of WAP, i-mode and SMS and make recommendations to banks regarding future mobile strategies.

RELATIVE ADVANTAGE

Relative advantage is concerned with the degree to which an innovation is perceived as being better than the idea it supersedes. The degree of relative advantage is often expressed as economic profitability, social prestige, savings in time and effort, immediacy of the reward or as decrease of discomfort. The construct of relative advantage is highly domain specific and thus advantage can be seen differently in context of different innovations and on other hand of different consumer. In the case of mobile banking relative advantage is mainly formed across the mobile value of the new banking service delivery medium. Mobile value signifies the value arising from the mobility of the medium, i.e. making use of electronic services while on the move/road; mobility offers the creation of choice and new freedom. As the major trigger for adopting mobile banking services regular users (85.4 per cent) and occasional users (77.8 per cent) named the accessibility and availability of services regardless of time and place. Over half of the regular users (52.1 per cent) and 43.8 per cent of occasional users mentioned also savings in time and effort as reasons to adopt as well as savings in financial costs of conducting banking.

COMPLEXITY

The perception of complexity involved when conducting financial transactions via mobile channel is often inversely related to a consumer's experience with technology in general. Adoption of complex products depends on adopter's ability to develop new knowledge and new patterns of experience. This ability can be enhanced by the knowledge gained from related products. In Finland usage of Internet banking has already diffused to masses of banking customers, it can be argued that Internet banking is sort of related service. Payments and account management products over mobile GSM phone as SMS have been available in Finland since 1992 too. When respondents were asked about problem faced with mobile banking, all the response alternatives got rather low ratings. Regular users mentioned that malfunction of service (12.5 per cent) had caused some problems, whereas occasional users complained about insufficient guidance (14.6 per cent) to using mobile banking services.

COMPATIBILITY

The degree to which an innovative channel such as a mobile device is compatible with the individuals past experiences and values appears to have a significant impact on willingness to adopt. Respondents were asked about their attitudes towards technology-based products and services. Every target segment informed with positive mean scores to mobile phone and services, Internet, personal computer, cable television, E-mail that they were pretty enthusiastic about using technology, except of electronic ID-card. Furthermore 82 per cent of the respondent had an Internet connection on use. In Finland mobile phone penetration exceeds 85 per cent, which certainly affect adoption of mobile banking services too. These results are consistent with Rogers' suggestion and previous research that compatibility of an innovation with previously introduced idea can influence the adoption of the innovation as well as the development stage of infrastructure. Further, Hirschman (1980) has suggested that prior experience with the product class, which for example in this case is usage of Internet banking, may lead to greater acceptability of a new product.

OBSERVABILITY

Observability of an innovation describes the extent to which an innovation is visible to other members of a social system, how easily the benefits can be observed and communicated. The lack of physical domain in service products may present some problems, even though in this case the service delivery medium, mobile phone itself, may enhance physical evidence of the innovation. In this survey respondents mentioned they had gained information of mobile banking services from banks' personnel via personal selling activities, and secondly from marketing communication activities, such as advertisements and mailings.

TRIALABILITY

Rogers argues that potential adopters who are allowed to experiment with an innovation will feel more comfortable with it and are more likely to adopt it. Consequently, if consumers are given the opportunity to try the innovation certain fears of unknown and inability to use can be reduced. In this survey 12.7 per cent of non-users had tested mobile banking services, but this did not lead to permanent use. However, this evidences that trial use of mobile banking services is possible.

PERCEIVED RISK

Security and trustworthiness of usage of service was mentioned to be the most important factor within every target segments when deciding on banking service delivery channel. Survey participants responded also positively to the argument "using mobile phone in banking is trustworthy."

MARKETING FOR MOBILE BANKING

Mobile banking is poised to become the big killer mobile application arena. However, Banks going mobile the first time need to tread the path cautiously. The biggest decision that Banks need to make is the channel that they will support their services on.

Mobile banking through an SMS based service would require the lowest amount of effort, in terms of cost and time, but will not be able to support the full breath of transaction-based services. However, in markets like India where a bulk of the mobile population users' phones can only support SMS based services, this might be the only option left.

On the other hand a market heavily segmented by the type and complexity of mobile phone usage might be good place to roll of WAP based mobile applications. A WAP based service can let go of the need to customize usability to the profile of each mobile phone, the trade-off being that it cannot take advantage of the full breadth of features that a mobile phone might offer.

Mobile application standalone clients bring along the burden of supporting multiple mobile device profiles. According to the Gartner Group, a leading wireless computing consulting organization, mobile banking services will have to support a minimum of 50 different device profiles in the near future. However, currently the best user experience, depending on the capabilities of a mobile phone, is possible only by using a Standalone client.

Mobile banking has the potential to do to the mobile phone what E-mail did to the Internet. Mobile Application based banking is poised to be a big m-commerce feature, and if South Korea's foray into mass mobile banking is any indication, mobile banking could well be the driving factor to increase sales of high-end mobile phones. Nevertheless, Bank's need to take a hard and deep look into the mobile usage patterns among their target customers and enable their mobile services on a technology with reaches out to the majority of their customers.

SMS BANKING

When people are hard pressed for time, the need for "anytime anywhere" banking gains utmost importance. Bearing this in mind, banks provide a novel service which gives retail customers account information and real-time transaction capabilities from their cell phones. With SMS banking the following services can be obtained:

- Get account balance details
- Request a cheque book
- Request last three transaction details
- Pay bills for electricity, mobile, insurance, etc.

SMS BANKING OVERVIEW

In order to avail the services mentioned above, a user subscribing to a wireless carrier sends an SMS with a predefined code to the bulk service provider's number.

The service provider forwards this message to the bank's mobile banking applications. The mobile banking applications interface with the core banking servers (that contain the user account information) that service the request made by the user. The response is then sent by the mobile banking applications to the bulk service provider who in turn forward it to the valid user via SMS.

There are two ways in which a bank can communicate with a customer using SMS:

In the first method the bank proactively sends data to customers in response to certain transactions. For e.g. account to account transfer, salary credit and some promotional messages. This data can be sent to the customer in two ways

- ***E-mail to mobile (E2M):*** In this method, the bank sends an email to the mobile banking application through a specific E-mail address. This E-mail may consist of the message content together with the mobile numbers of the customer. The mobile banking application in turn sends this message in a specific format (for e.g. XML tags are part of a HTTP GET message query string) to the service provider's application server. From hereon the information from the XML tags is extracted and sent as a SMS to the wireless carrier which in turn forwards this message to the customer.
- ***Database to mobile (D2M):*** Here a mobile banking application continuously polls the banks database server and whenever a relevant event happens, for e.g. an account to account transfer, it forwards the specific message to the service provider's application server. The message format may be the same as the one used in the E2M case. This message is then forwarded to the wireless carrier which in turn forwards this message to the customer.

In the second method the bank sends data in response to specific customer query such as account balance details. The customer first sends a pre-defined request code via SMS to the Bulk SMS service provider's registered mobile number. Depending on the message code, the bulk SMS provider forwards the SMS to a PULL application in the mobile banking server. The PULL application receives the request and forwards it to the core banking application for further processing. The core banking server then processes this message and sends the reply to the PULL application which in turn forwards in to the customer via the service provider. As in the above cases the request and the response for the PULL application may be a HTTP GET message with tags in the query string.

PUSH AND PULL MESSAGES

SMS Banking services are operated using both Push and Pull messages. Push messages are those that the bank chooses to send out to a customer's mobile phone, without the customer initiating a request for the information. Typically push messages could be either Mobile Marketing messages or messages alerting an event which happens in the customer's bank account, such as a large withdrawal of funds from the ATM or a large payment using the customer's credit card, etc.

Another type of push message is One-time password (OTPs). OTPs are the latest tool used by financial and banking service providers in the fight against cyber fraud. Instead of relying on traditional memorized passwords, OTPs are requested by consumers each time they want to perform transactions using the online or mobile banking interface. When the request is received the password is sent to the consumer's phone via SMS. The password is expired once it has been used or once its scheduled life-cycle has expired.

Pull messages are those that are initiated by the customer, using a mobile phone, for obtaining information or performing a transaction in the bank account. Examples of pull messages for information include an account balance inquiry, or requests for current information like currency exchange rates and deposit interest rates, as published and updated by the bank.

The bank's customer is empowered with the capability to select the list of activities (or alerts) that he/she needs to be informed. This functionality to choose activities can be done either by integrating to the Internet banking channel or through the bank's customer service call centre.

Typical Push and Pull Services offered under SMS Banking

Depending on the selected extent of SMS Banking transactions offered by the bank, a customer can be authorized to carry out either non-financial transactions, or both and financial and non-financial transactions. SMS Banking solutions offer customers a range of functionality, classified by Push and Pull services as outlined below.

Typical Push Services would include:

- Periodic account balance reporting (say at the end of month);
- Reporting of salary and other credits to the bank account;
- Successful or unsuccessful execution of a standing order;
- Successful payment of a cheque issued on the account;
- Insufficient funds;
- Large value withdrawals on an account;
- Large value withdrawals on the ATM or on a debit card;
- Large value payment on a credit card or out of country activity on a credit card.
- One-time password and authentication

Typical Pull Services would include:

- Account balance inquiry;
- Mini statement request;
- Electronic bill payment;
- Transfers between customer's own accounts, like moving money from a savings account to a current account to fund a cheque;
- Stop payment instruction on a cheque;
- Requesting for an ATM card or credit card to be suspended;

- De-activating a credit or debit card when it is lost or the PIN is known to be compromised;
- Foreign currency exchange rates inquiry;
- Fixed deposit interest rate inquiry.

CONCERNS AND SKEPTICISM ABOUT SMS BANKING

Many banks would have some concerns when the prospects of introducing SMS Banking are discussed. Most of these concerns could revolve around security and operational controls around SMS Banking. However supporters of SMS claim that while SMS Banking is not as secure as other conventional banking channels, like the ATM and Internet Banking, the SMS Banking channel is not intended to be used for very high-risk transactions.

THE CONVENIENCE FACTOR

The convenience of executing simple transactions and sending out information or alerting a customer on the mobile phone is often the overriding factor that dominates over the skeptics who tend to be overly bitten by security concerns.

As a personalized end-user communication instrument, today mobile phones are perhaps the easiest channel on which customers can be reached on the spot, as they carry the mobile phone all the time no matter where they are. Besides, the operation of SMS Banking functionality over phone key instructions makes its use very simple. This is quite different to Internet banking which can offer broader functionality, but has the limitation of use only when the customer has access to a computer and the Internet. Also, urgent warning messages, such as SMS alerts, are received by the customer instantaneously; unlike other channels such as the post, E-mail, Internet, telephone banking, etc. on which a bank's notifications to the customer involves the risk of delayed delivery and response.

The SMS Banking channel also acts as the bank's means of alerting its customers, especially in an emergency situation; e.g. when there is an ATM fraud happening in the region, the bank can push a mass alert (although not subscribed by all customers) or automatically alert on an individual basis when a predefined 'abnormal' transaction happens on a customer's account using the ATM or credit card. This capability mitigates the risk of fraud going unnoticed for a long time and increases customer confidence in the bank's information systems.

COMPENSATING CONTROLS FOR LACK OF ENCRYPTION

The lack of encryption on SMS messages is an area of concern that is often discussed. This concern sometimes arises within the group of the bank's technology personnel, due their familiarity and past experience with encryption on the ATM and other payment channels. The lack of encryption is inherent to the SMS Banking channel and several banks that use it have overcome their fears by introducing compensating controls and limiting the scope of the SMS Banking application to where it offers an advantage over other channels.

Suppliers of SMS Banking software solutions have found reliable means by which the security concerns can be addressed. Typically the methods employed are by pre-registration and using security tokens where the transaction risk is perceived to be high. Sometimes ATM type PINs are also employed but the usage of PINs in SMS Banking makes the customer's task more cumbersome.

TECHNOLOGIES EMPLOYED FOR SMS BANKING

Most SMS Banking solutions are add-on products and work with the bank's existing host systems deployed in its computer and communications environment. As most banks have multiple backend hosts, the more advanced SMS Banking systems are built to be able to work in a multi-host banking environment; and to have open interfaces which allow for messaging between existing banking host systems using industry or *de-facto* standards.

Well developed and mature SMS Banking software solutions normally provide a robust control environment and a flexible and scalable operating environment. These solutions are able to connect seamlessly to multiple operators in the country of operation. Depending on the volume of messages that are require to be pushed, means to connect to the SMS could be different, such as using simple modems or connecting over leased line using low level communication protocols. Advanced SMS Banking solutions also cater to providing failover mechanisms and least-cost routing options.

THE POSSIBLE FUTURE FOR MOBILE BANKING

Payment on approval by SMS

This feature allows for joint accounts or business account to have a pre-determined limit to prompt for either supervisor or joint account holder approval. A payment request is made from the account to another pre-nominated account; a message is then send to either the supervisor or joint account holder to also approve the payment.

Two-stage confirmed payment

This payment process is similar to a letter of credit, when the end user sends a payment instruction for goods or services, the amount of the payment will be transferred to a specific account. The beneficiary will be notified that the amount is guaranteed. Once the goods or services are delivered the end user/payee will be able to accept or reject the goods/services and make payment accordingly by approving or denying the payment process.

Mobile payment in retail outlets

Using nothing but their own mobile handset, consumers will be able to make purchased at a wide variety of retail outlets. Let's use the supermarket as a common example: the consumer needs to make a purchase from a supermarket, he/she goes to the cashier and sends a payment request along with his/her password and the specific POS machine number. The system will then send back a Digital Money Sequence Number (DMSN) to the buyer. When asking to pay for the goods, the cashier will use his/her special banking card, and when the buyer is asked for a password all they need to do is enter the DMSN. As long as the transaction is within the daily limit of the account the transaction will take place instantly.

Challenges for a Mobile Banking Solution

Key challenges in developing a sophisticated mobile banking application are:

Interoperability

There is a lack of common technology standards for mobile banking. Many protocols are being used for mobile banking – HTML, WAP, SOAP, XML to name a few. It would be a wise idea for the vendor to develop a mobile banking application that can connect multiple banks. It would require either the application to support multiple protocols or use of a common and widely acceptable set of protocols for data exchange.

There are a large number of different mobile phone devices and it is a big challenge for banks to offer mobile banking solution on any type of device. Some of these devices support J2ME and others support WAP browser or only SMS.

Overcoming interoperability issues however have been localized, with countries like India using portals like R-World to enable the limitations of low end java based phones, while focus on areas such as South Africa have defaulted to the USSD as a basis of communication achievable with any phone.

The desire for interoperability is largely dependent on the banks themselves, where java enabled applications are of better security, easier to use and offer development of more complex transactions similar to that of internet banking while SMS can provide the basics but becomes a hassle to operate with more difficult transactions.

Security

Security of financial transaction, being executed from some remote location and transmission of financial information over the air, are the most complicated challenges that need to be addressed jointly by mobile application developers, wireless network service providers and the bank's IT department.

The following aspects need to be addressed to offer a secure infrastructure for financial transaction over wireless network:

1. Physical security of the hand-held device. If the bank is offering smart-card based security, the physical security of the device is more important.
2. Security of the thick-client application running on the device. In case the device is stolen, the hacker should require ID/Password to access the application.
3. Authentication of the device with service provider before initiating a transaction. This would ensure that unauthorized devices are not connected to perform financial transactions.
4. User ID / Password authentication of bank's customer.
5. Encryption of the data being transmitted over the air.
6. Encryption of the data that will be stored in device for later / off-line analysis by the customer.

Scalability and Reliability

Another challenge for the banks is to scale-up the mobile banking infrastructure to handle exponential growth of the customer base. With mobile banking, the customer may be sitting in any part of the world (a true anytime, anywhere banking) and hence banks need to ensure that the systems are up and running in a true 24 x 7 fashion. As customers will find mobile banking more and more useful, their expectations from the solution will increase. Banks unable to meet the performance and reliability expectations may lose customer confidence.

Application distribution

Due to the nature of the connectivity between bank and its customers, it would be impractical to expect customers to regularly visit banks or connect to a website for regular upgrade of their mobile banking application. It will be expected that the mobile application itself check the upgrades and updates and download necessary patches. However, there could be many issues to implement this approach such as upgrade/synchronization of other dependent components.

Personalization

It would be expected from the mobile application to support personalization such as:

1. Preferred language
2. Date / time format
3. Amount format
4. Default transactions
5. Standard beneficiary list
6. Alerts

These are a few of the most probable challenges that a banking organisation or company will face while newly introducing the mobile banking system into its business processes. However, a bank should see past all the difficulties and drawbacks in the mobile banking system as every aspect of today's world has some negative quality incorporated in it as every coin as two sides and so on.

The main point that such a bank should focus on is the benefit such a system has in the future and how such a system will help the bank to further increase its customer base and increase its business in the future to come of the bank.

For the time being these challenges, and many more which may arise and pose a threat to the adoption of mobile banking and its success, is not to be considered as a real drawback because for every problem or hindrance which may occur in mobile banking, there is a solution and such solutions are being devised, formulated and solved by professionals and experts who do what they do best and that is consult and find the most logical solution for that problem.

For Example, an information security company NSS MSC Sdn Bhd has devised a suitable solution for mobile banking fraud. The main headache, which was caused by this fraud, for the banks were that the instructions regarding what has to be done by them which was told by the account holder, via mobile banking services, would fall into the wrong hands and lead to illegal transactions or, even worse, identity theft.

For this reason, NSS MSC had devised a way to encrypt the message sent by the account holder to the bank. Only the account holders' bank could read the encrypted message and the bank could carry on its duties as instructed by the account holder without the worry or hassle of fraud or information falling into the wrong hands.

Therefore, in future all problems and dead ends of mobile banking will be taken care off which will pave the way for the ascension of mobile banking services throughout all parts of the world.

CASE STUDIES

1. LG Telecom, South Korea

In terms of the evolution of services being offered on mobile applications, South Korea is showing the way.

The big push came when LG Telecom Ltd., the smallest of Korea's three mobile service providers teamed up with the Kookmin bank to launch the 'Bank on' service. Under this scheme mobile users were able to use smart chips embedded in cell phones for accessing all of the transaction and inquiry based services. The chip-based service automated the authentication of users when they accessed their bank's financial services to make the whole process much faster and convenient. The icing on the cake came with the ability of these chip enabled cell phones to be used simultaneously as cash cards. By October 2004 there were already about 100,000 infrared readers adapted to take payment directly from mobile phone handsets in Korea. Users can now use their cell phones to pay for everything, from restaurant bills, travel tickets, merchandise and even haircuts.

2. Reliance Infocomm, India

When Reliance Infocomm, India rolled out its CDMA network, (at the time the mobile market in India was still in its infancy, and data services were almost never heard off) it made sure that all handsets supported Java. The Reliance application platform, also known as R-World brought Java compatibility even to the lower end phones.

Reliance used a novel way to overcome the memory limitations of lower-end mobile phones, which hampered deploying of multiple standalone J2ME based clients. Instead of storing applications statically on their cell phones, users access a single menu based application called R-World, which connects them to the Reliance servers. Using the menu based user interface, mobile users select the application, which they want to run and download them over-the-air to their cell phones. These applications are then executed locally on the mobiles.

From mid-2004 Reliance tied up with two of the popular private sector banks, HDFC and ICICI, to provide a host of their inquiry and transaction based mobile banking services through its R-World environment.

CONCLUSION

With the rapid development of transport and communication, people and services are coming together as if they were just around the corner. If this is the case for many services, then why should the banking industry lag behind?

Internet banking, phone banking, E-banking and now mobile banking all enable the bank to be better connected with the customer and *vice versa.* A customer who is provided with a variety of additional services feels appreciated and is more likely to be loyal to that bank, which is always a good sign for a bank.

In the end mobile banking not only helps a bank to reduce costs but also helps it to retain its valuable customers. And as far as customers are concerned, this facility enables the customer to bank anywhere, at anytime and in any condition, definitely a boon if a customer is stuck in the middle of nowhere and requires banking services as soon as possible.

Thus mobile banking helps both, the customer as well as the bank, to lighten the burden of today's world and to save time, money and energy which is greatly required and appreciated. In a competitive world where everyone is waiting to out do the other, a helping hand, in whatever forms and from whatever source, is definitely god sent and should not go unrecognized.

■ ■ ■

11

RETAIL BANKING IN INDIA–EMERGING ISSUES AND FUTURE OUTLOOK

ABSTRACT

Banks in India, irrespective of ownership, have been performing creditably well, viewed on the basis of performance indices. Growth in resources, credit deployment, profitability, productivity, fall in non-performing assets, rising regulatory capital, etc. are generally considered as strong statements of prosperity for banks. Banks have been taking up aggregative measures for mobilizing the term deposits and also the installation and operations of automatic teller machines (ATMs). With the change in the level of competition, many new dimensions in the retail banking have emerged. In India, banks generally take a lenient view about the various retail banking service dimensions which if continued would take them to the back seat. The banks need to take up aggressive measures for becoming a reliable and responsive to the various retail banking dimensions.

INTRODUCTION

Financial sector reforms in India, of which banking sector reforms constituted an integral part, stressed liberalization of markets, privatization of ownership and globalization of the economy. Retail banking is the complete spectrum of the consumer's evolving needs and requirements including payment of utility bills like water, electricity, telephone and mobile phone bills, payment of insurance premiums on due dates, remittance of funds, demating of shares, bonds, debentures and mutual funds, payment of credit card bills, filling of income tax returns and payment of income tax, bancassurance (selling of insurance products).

Retail credit, notwithstanding the cautionary approach advocated by RBI, is bound to increase further. Banks need to realize that in their enthusiasm to distribute retail credit on a very massive scale, the cardinal principles of lending are not followed. In the present market scenario, the key to success for any bank lies in aggravating and emphasizing on the various retail marketing activities.

RATIONALE OF THE STUDY

The banks in India, since the last one decade or so, have started taking up seriously the need and importance of retail banking. It is on this account that banks in all the sectors have come up with the facilities like automatic teller machines, etc. which is evident from the following data and information.

Despite the above various steps, banks need to be more aggressive about retail banking as the changing consumers' needs, innovative financial products, mergers/acquisitions, deregulation, information technology up gradation and a variety of delivery channels are reshape the financial services industry. To remain competitive in the financial services landscape, banks are required to expand their product lines, add new delivery channels, develop more effective marketing systems and techniques, and enhance service quality levels.

As the importance of retail banking is increasing day by day and also because there is emerging a fierce competition amongst the various sectors in the banking industry to grab the maximum retail banking business, it was considered worthwhile to undertake a research study about these various aspects.

Objectives

1. To know about the share and number of ATMs of various banks in India.
2. To highlight the amounts and shares of time deposits of various banks in India.
3. To measure the level of efficiency of retail banking in India.

RESEARCH METHODOLOGY

The study is based both on primary as well as secondary data. Secondary data has been obtained from various newspapers and journals. For primary data, 150 customers of various banks were interviewed with the help of a structured interview schedule having relevant questions. These customers were selected on the basis of convenience sampling but care was taken that adequate number of respondents from all the banking sectors (public, private and foreign).

DATA ANALYSIS AND INTERPRETATIONS

The analysis and the interpretations of the data obtained for the study has been discussed below.

Automated Teller Machines

From the following chart, it is evident that automated teller machines (ATMs) have emerged as a major tool for banking across major metros as well as smaller cities. And all bank groups have had significant amount of ATMs across the country. With payment services companies offering debit card facilities to the ATM card, the acceptability and usage of ATM cards have gone up. But not many nationalized banks and old private sector banks have put up ATMs outside their branch premises. Foreign banks and new private banks have put up many off-site ATMs at more convenient locations to customers. This is because; cost of setting up off-site ATM is higher than on-site ATMs.

Figures in %

Plastic Money ATMS AND BANK GROUP-WISE SHARE(as at end mar 2006)

50
40
30
20
10
0

Onsite ATMs
offsite ATMs
Total ATMs

State Bank groups
Nationalised Banks
Old Private Banks
New Private Banks
Foreign Banks

Source: The Economic Times, Chandigarh, 18 December 06, pp 12.

Shared ATMs

The table given below depicts that cash withdrawals are possible from shared ATMs because banks hook up to a common network. Most of the banks have tie-ups with other banks or are members of a common network, which permits inter-banks ATM transactions. However access charges can vary depending on the tie-ups.

ATM NETWORKS

From the information given below it is evident that most of the banks are members of multilateral shared ATM networks like Cash net (which includes Visa and MasterCard), National Financial Switch (NFS), Cirrus or BANCS. One bank can be part of more than one network, but all ATMs of a bank may not be on the same network. So a Visa debit card of HDFC Bank can be used at Visa ATM of ICICI Bank and vice versa. However, a Visa card of HDFC Bank cannot be used at a non-Visa ATM of ICICI Bank.

PARTNER BANKS

Partners in Power (Banks which are member of multilateral shared ATM network)

Partners in Power (Banks which are member of multilateral shared ATM network)	
NETWORK	MEMBER BANKS
Visa	Citibank ,HDFC, ICICI, Standard Chartered, HSBC, IDBI, State Bank of India, UTI, Kotak Mohindra, Bank Of Baroda, Centurion Bank of Punjab.
MasterCard	Citibank, HDFC, ICICI, Standard Chartered, ABN Amro, SBI. Centurion Bank of Punjab
Cirrus	HDFC, ICICI, ABN Amro, /State Bank of India, Centurion Bank of Punjab
NFS	ICICI, IDBI, Bank of Baroda, Andhra Bank, Corporation Bank

(**Note:** This list is not exhaustive)

Source: The Economic Times, 27 Dec, 2006, pp 13.

Charges: From the following table it is also evident that charges for using ATMs of partner banks are less than the Non-Partner banks.

Time Deposits

Banks in India have also started taking up serious steps to enhance the time deposits of the various durations. The following diagrams present the figures of the time deposits of various banks.

CHARGES PER TRANSACTION FOR USING DEBIT CARD ON DOMESTIC ATMS OF PARTNER AND NON-PARTNER BANKS.				
Card-Issuing Bank	Partner Banks		Non-Partner Banks under common network	
	Cash withdrawal	Balance Enquiry	Cash Withdrawal	Balance Enquiry
HDFC	20	10	55	15
ICICI	20	10	60	25
Standard Chartered*	-	-	50	20
ABN Amro	Free**	5	50	20
HSBC	-	-	55	15
SBI	25	12	50	12
IDBI	-	-	65	30
UTI	30	10	50	15

Note: All Charges exclude 12.24% service tax
Source: The Economic Times, 27December 2006, pp13.
* First four transactions per month are free.
**Subject to maximum cash withdrawal cash withdrawal per account per month.

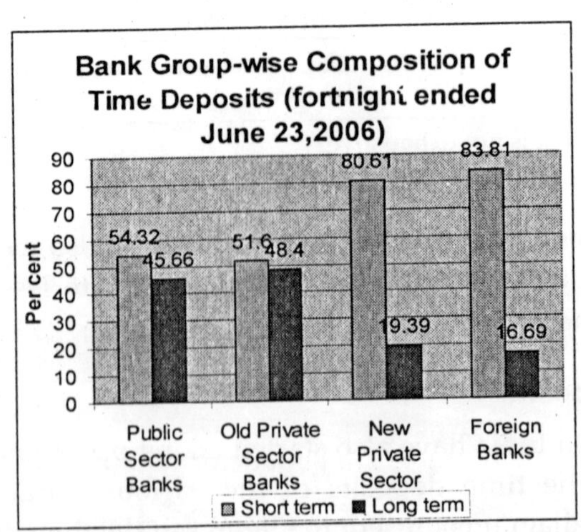

Source: Retailing Banking-Opportunities and Challenges, "The Journal of Indian Institute of Banking & Finance", Oct-Dec 2006, pp6-39.

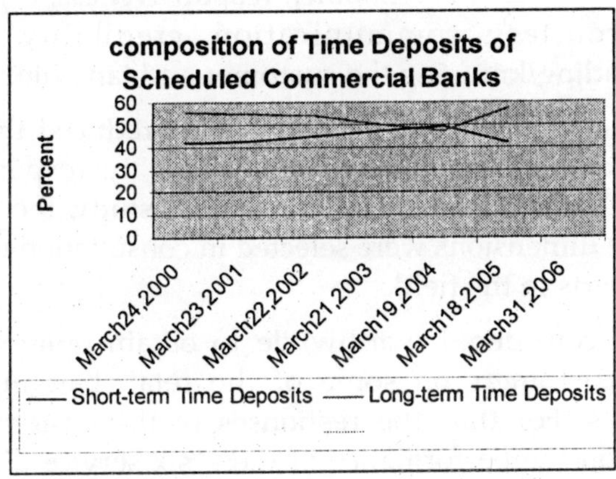

Source: Retailing Banking- Opportunities and Challenges, "The Journal of Indian Institute of Banking & Finance", Oct-Dec 2006, pp 6-39.

Despite the above various steps, banks need to be more aggressive about retail banking as the changing consumers' needs, innovative financial products, mergers/acquisitions, deregulation, information technology up gradation and a variety of delivery channels are reshape the financial services industry. To remain competitive in the financial services landscape, banks are required to expand their product lines, add new delivery channels, develop more effective marketing systems and techniques, and enhance service quality levels.

Efficiency of Retail Banking on Service Dimensions

As the importance of retail banking is increasing day by day, therefore, there has emerged a fierce competition amongst the various sectors in the banking industry to grab the maximum retail banking business.

Various researchers have defined the various determinants of service for retail banking. According to, Parasuram, Zeithmal and Berry (1990)[1] identified ten determinant of service quality

1. Parasuram , Zeithmal and Berry (1990)
 – "Delivering Quality Service
 – Balancing customer perception and expectations", The Free Press, New York, 1990.

that relates to service: reliability, responsiveness, competence, access, courtesy, communication, credibility, security, understanding/knowing the customer and tangible.

Terrence and Gordon[1], subsequently reduced the various services to five, namely tangibles, reliability, responsiveness, assurance and empathy. For the present study, the following six service dimensions were selected in consultation with some of the experts in the field.

It was considered worthwhile to obtain opinions of the banking customers on some of the retail banking service dimensions. For this, the responses of the customers were obtained on the performance of these six service dimensions of banks. In order to know about the efficiency of Indian banks on these six service dimensions, the respondents were asked to weigh the various service dimensions on a score slab 1-5.1 for the least efficiency and 5 for maximum. The responses obtained have been shown in table I.

From the above table it is evident out of the various retail banking service dimensions, maximum level of satisfaction of the banking customers is with regard to the dimension, 'Tangibility'. Hence, this aspect gets the first rank.

Further, on the aspect 'Assurance', the customers are generally satisfied and hence it gets second rank. On the aspects 'Responsiveness' and 'Price', the banking consumers are satisfied only to some extent. The consumers feel highly dissatisfied with regard to the dimensions 'Empathy' and 'Reliability'.

The banks in order to be competitive with their counterparts need to take a note of the above findings as it is not only the opening up of the ATMs or getting large time deposits but also the various factors.

---

1. Terrence Levesque and Gordon H G Mcdougall, "Determination of customer satisfaction in retail banking", *The International Journal of Bank Marketing*, Bradford, 1996, Vol 16, Issue 7, pp. 12-20.

Table I: Level of Efficiency on Various Service Dimensions.

Service dimensions	Scores No. of Respondents					*Total Overall Rank Scores	
	5 (a)	4 (b)	3 (c)	2 (d)	1 (e)		
Tangibility	69	23	11	14	33	531	1
Reliability	43	11	15	22	59	407	6
Responsiveness	40	32	12	8	58	438	3
Assurance	52	23	11	21	43	470	2
Empathy	23	28	32	26	41	416	5
Price	36	24	15	29	46	425	4

Score = "5a + 4b+3c+2d+1e.
Source: Primary data.

CONCLUSION

In the present market scenario, the key to success for any bank lies in aggravating and emphasizing on the various retail marketing activities, therefore various banks in India, since the last one decade or so, have started taking up seriously the need and importance of retail banking. It is on this account that banks in all the sectors have come up with the facilities like automatic teller machines, etc. To remain competitive in the financial services landscape, banks are required to expand their product lines, add new delivery channels, develop more effective marketing systems and techniques, and enhance service quality levels. Automated teller machines (ATMs) have emerged as a major tool for banking across major metros as well as smaller cities. All bank groups have had significant amount of ATMs across the country. Cash withdrawals are possible from shared ATMs because banks hook up to a common network. Most of the banks have tie-ups with other banks or are members of a common network, which permits inter-banks ATM transactions Banks have also started taking up serious steps to enhance the time deposits of the various durations. Banks need to be more aggressive about retail banking on account of the changing consumers' needs, innovative financial products, mergers/acquisitions, deregulation, information technology up gradation and a variety of delivery channels. To remain competitive in the financial services landscape, banks are required to expand their product lines, add new delivery channels, develop more effective marketing systems and techniques, and enhance service quality levels. Out of the various retail banking service dimensions, maximum level of satisfaction of the banking customers is with regard to the dimension, 'Tangibility'. On the aspect 'Assurance', the customers are generally satisfied. On the aspects 'Responsiveness' and 'Price', the banking consumers are satisfied only to some extent. The consumers feel highly dissatisfied with regard to the dimensions 'Empathy' and 'Reliability'. The banks, in order to be competitive with their counterparts, need to take a note of the same.

BIBLIOGRAPHY

Joseph, D.A., "The Future of Retail Banking", Palgrave Macmillan, New York, 2004.

Mohan, Rakesh, "Transforming Indian Banking In Search of a Better Tomorrow", *Reserve Bank of India Bulletin*, January 2003.

Rao, Suba C., Hari Nath, U. and Muniswami, V.V., "Marketing Activities in the Service Sector–A Review", *Indian Journal of Marketing*, Volume 20 No. 7, March 1990.

Reddy, C.R. and Ramana, K.V., "Marketing Approach in Banking", *Indian Journal of Marketing*, Volume 22 No.1-3, March 1994.

Verma, DPS and Hema Israney–"Market Orientation in commercial Banks –A study of Selected Banks in Delhi", Vision, July–December 2001, pp. 7-14.

Yavas, Ugur, Donald. J. Shemwell & Zeynep Bilgin, "Service Quality in the banking sector in an emerging economy: a consumer survey", *International Journal of Bank Marketing*, June 97, pp 217-223.

■ ■ ■

INDEX

A

Account information 3-4, 16, 97, 99, 104, 222, 238
Adhivarahan, V. 205
Akter, Md. Shahriar 205
Andhra Pradesh 44, 47-78
Anti Virus Software 41
Arora, Kalpana 205, 217
Asymmetric cryptography 114
ATM network 254, 258
Authentication mechanism 6
Automated Cheque Clearance 86
  Teller Machine 3, 8, 53, 77, 99, 122, 126, 128, 187
Avasthi, G.P.M. 205, 217
Awasthi, S.K. 151, 170
Axis Technology 63

B

Background investigation 89
Bajaj, K.K. 217
Bakshi, S. 217
Balance inquiry 222, 240, 241
Banerjee, S. 209, 217
Banking business 120, 122, 192
  dimensions 252
  environment 3
  industry 1, 4
  supervision 106
Barman, R. B. 150, 169
Bhasin, T.M. 217
Bill Payment 222, 224
Biometric applications 53
  ATMs 53
  authentication 54
  security 89
  solutions 54
  systems 60
  techniques 63
  technology 52-53, 65
  sales 83
Business Risk 110

C

Chachadi, A.H. 206
Changing environment 204
Checking accounts 10
Cheque Truncation 126, 132, 138-39
Chowdhary, K.C. 151, 170
Clearing House Jurisdiction 152
Communication technology 179
Compliance Risk 18
Computer networks 27
  technology 3
Consumer Education 110
Contemporary banking 98
Cooperative bank 78

Core Banking 210
Cost Benefit Analysis 152
Counter cheques 12
Credit card 4, 6, 50
 risk 18
Crime phenomenon 38
Criminal Tracing System 55
Customer Relationship 188
Cyber Appellate Tribunal 29, 33
 Crime 25, 46
 law 37
 space 38

D

Das, S.C. 206
Debit card 12, 44
Deshpande, N.V. 150, 169
Dharadhar, U A 151, 170
Dhillon, J.S. 206
Digital communication 2
 Economy 7
 Minilab 131
 Signatures 114

E

E Mail – Banking 7
Eapen, P.G. 206
E-banking 7, 97, 216
 customers 103
 services 175, 190
 strategy 134
E-channels 191
E-cheques 164
E-delivery channels 186
Electronic banking 4, 98, 133
 Central Banking 133
 commerce 74
 Data Interchange 9
 E-banking 99
 funds transfer 9
 transactions 213
E-trust Services 110

F

Facial scan technology 63
Financial Institutions 63, 88
 system 138
Fingerprint scanning 89
 Biometrics 63
 Software 76
Foreign court 39
 exchange risk 19
Fund Transfer 224

G

Gandhi, R. 151, 170
Ganesh, S. 185, 206, 217
Garg, I.K. 206, 217
Geetha, D. 206
Global communication 119
Gupta, R P. 217

H

Hardware device 26
High security 86
Human activity 37

I

Imaging technology 139
Inactive account 13
Indian banking 175, 208, 216
 law 35
Information systems 244

technology 37-38, 40, 107, 151, 197, 208
Informational Websites 5
Internal regulations 103
Internet banking 1, 5, 98, 104, 126
banking platforms 17
Banking Risks 17
Banking System 102
Kiosk 131
transactions 20

J

Jalan, B. 217
Jaski, B. 206
Joseph, D.A. 260

K

Key management 73
Kini, Ashok 150, 170
Knowledge Management 199
Kulkarni, R. V. 217

L

Law enforcement 38
Legacy systems 2
Legal Risk 110
Liquidity risk 19
Loyal customers 21

M

Macroeconomic policy 98
Magnetic strip cards 62
Malhotra, P. 206
Management system 20
Marketing activities 253
Methodology 151
Microsoft Money 15
Mittal, S.R. 206
Mobile Banking 6, 126, 128, 219, 228, 230, 245
Mohan, R. 206, 217
Money laundering risk 19
Movie Ticket Kiosk 132
Multi-national banks 2

N

Nair, S.N. 206, 218
National Cyber Crime 46
Notary fees 13

O

Online application 89
Banking 2, 6, 14, 25
loan 4
Operational Risk 109
Organizational structure 5

P

Pai, D.T. 207
Pathrose, P.P. 207
Paul, Justin 207
Payment confirmation 41
Personal computers 1, 3
identification number (PIN) 3
Phatak, D.B. 150, 170
Physical cheques 156
crimes 51
Pillanna Garden 44
Pipreya, B.K. 207

Potential customers 5
Pravir Vora 151, 170
Print technology 78
Private sector banks 2

R

Ram, C. N. 151, 170
Rangarajan, C. 207, 218
Rao, N.V. 207
Rao, P.K. 207
Rao, Suba C. 260
Ray, G., Muhanna, 207
Reddy, C.R. 260
Regional banks 4
Reputation Risk 18, 109
Research Methodology 210
Retail banking 251-53, 257-260
Risk Management 16, 20, 22, 106, 109

S

Security challenges 97
  control 20, 89
  risk 18, 20
Shapiro, C. 207
Shastri, R.V. 207
Singh, Herman 40
Singh, S. 207
Srinivasan, M. R. 150, 169
Srivastava, D.K. 207
Stop payment 14
Strategic risk 17
Sumitomo Mitsui 46

T

Telecommunication networks 1, 97
Teller fee 14
Thumb impression 79
Traditional banking areas 22
  clearing 154
Transaction Risk 17
  speed 15
Transactional systems 6
  websites 5-6
Trivedi, A. K. 207
Trusted organization 111

U

UK Cyber Crime 46
Uppal, R.K. 184, 207

V

Value Added Network 9
Verma, D. 185, 207
Virtual Banks 4-5
Vittal. N. 206
Voice biometrics 79

W

Warehousing Agency 143, 154, 158
World Wide Web 1-2, 124

Y

Yaron Bolondi 46
Yavas, Ugur 260

■ ■ ■